AIRPORT PLANNING

Airport planning – Primary Source Edition

Charles Froesch, Walther Prokosch

AIRPORT PLANNING

By

CHARLES FROESCH, *I.A.S., S.A.E.*

Chief Engineer, Eastern Air Lines, Inc.

and

WALTHER PROKOSCH, *A.I.A.*

Architect, Engineering Department, Eastern Air Lines, Inc.

New York: JOHN WILEY & SONS, Inc.

London: CHAPMAN & HALL, Limited

FOREWORD

Aviation is removing the barriers of distance and time which in the past partly isolated many lands from the rest of the world There is pressing need for clear thinking, imagination, vision, and courage to evaluate correctly the long-term consequences of dynamic aircraft development and application The airport planner must be creative and realistic in designing practical, useful, and economical landing facilities for aircraft in order to promote the welfare of society as a whole. To achieve the best engineering compromise, he must appraise all factors which govern aviation as a means of transportation and must try to weigh what were once imponderables He must direct his efforts toward planning facilities which will be useful units of an integrated whole, forming a broad pattern of civic usefulness and national defense. The economic position of any community or nation that fails to envisage the horizons of aviation and provide adequate aircraft landing facilities will be affected adversely

The authors of this book have clearly and concisely analyzed airport problems from a functional viewpoint. They have endeavored to show how the relationship of the airplane and its airport affects the planning and design of the port They have emphasized the need for flexibility of execution in view of the state of aircraft design. They have stressed the importance of utility without sacrificing appearance, so conducive to civic pride

I commend *Airport Planning* to those who desire to acquire knowledge derived from many years of experience in the design and construction of aircraft and in airline and airport engineering It is written in simple language and is devoid of unnecessary technicalities, yet it imparts comprehensive information and factual data

PREFACE

In 1943 the authors compiled a pamphlet in answer to questions raised by communities served by Eastern Air Lines, as well as by others contemplating airport projects, which received a ready response   The demand for a more complete and detailed coverage of the subject prompted the writing of this book   Consultations with airport engineers and other interested persons confirmed the fact that a modern treatise on the fundamentals governing airport planning and design was lacking, and in view of the rapid expansion of aviation and the tremendous impetus given to the airplane during the last few years, there is need for such a book

The purposes of presenting this book are

1. To indicate the proper relationship of landing facilities to communities or regions they are to serve
2. To analyze the characteristics of aircraft which affect the planning and design of landing facilities
3. To strike a correct balance among the various elements of landing facilities

In this book, the authors have elected to appraise functional factors involved in the creation of new facilities, as well as modernization of existing ones, rather than to explore specific detail design which can be found in existing textbooks, published papers, and articles

This book has been written for those interested in the planning of an airport and contains concise and up-to-date information as a guide for the practical development of their ideas.   It should be borne in mind that aviation is a dynamic science requiring great flexibility of mind to yield fluid solutions of the landing facilities problem, solutions capable of ready and reasonable modification until greater stability has been obtained   It behooves the airport planner and engineer always to remember that any aircraft is just another vehicle of transportation, and, therefore, the fundamental laws governing all transportation apply to it as well

The highway engineer can apply his knowledge of road building to airport runway construction and, likewise, the architect can design suitable building accommodations   But these alone are not sufficient   Each must have a clear conception of the relationship of the aircraft to its landing facilities in order to create efficient and lasting accommodations.

Acknowledgment of sources of information is made throughout the book   The authors are particularly indebted to the persons who checked sections of this book dealing with specialized subjects or who have furnished material used in the book.   Among them are the Civil Aeronautics

Administration, L. E Andrews, Portland Cement Association; Wellwood Beall, Boeing Aircraft Company, Cardox Corporation, M. W. Cochran, Giffels & Vallet, Inc.; F E Davis, Eastern Air Lines, Inc , Douglas Aircraft Company, W. K Ebel, the Glenn L Martin Company; John F. Gill, Eastern Air Lines, Inc., B E Gray, the Asphalt Institute, G. R. Kiewitt, Roof Structures, Inc., M. V Lyle, Wichita Chamber of Commerce; C Earl Morrow, Regional Plan Association, the Port of New York Authority, U S Bureau of Public Roads; H Y Satterlee, Edo Aircraft Corporation, Anton Tedesko, Roberts & Schaefer, Captain C. H. Schildhauer, U S N R , and Major Alford J Williams, Gulf Oil Corporation, also, Kay Hoffman, Annette Jeter, and Josephine Landers, Eastern Air Lines, Inc

Specific acknowledgment is due George Roerig, Assistant to Vice-President in Charge of Operations, and Beverly Griffith, Director of Public Relations, of Eastern Air Lines, Inc , for their constructive criticism and review of the manuscript.

CHARLES FROESCH
WALTHER PROKOSCH

NEW YORK, N Y.
April 1, 1946

CONTENTS

1

THE AIRPORT AND THE COMMUNITY

A dynamic approach is required for the planning of airports What are the factors which distinguish this planning from the planning of more static structures? First, the basic product offered by the aircraft industry is in a continuous process of change and development Second, air transport is the youngest member of the transportation family and, as such, is rapidly outgrowing its clothes Next, the newness of the problem offers little in the way of sound precedent for planning Finally, airport planning is a four-dimensional problem

By comparing the airplanes which have been standard for airline operation for over 10 years with types ready to be inducted into commercial service or with airplanes of 100-passenger capacity and over which are now in the advanced development stage, it becomes apparent that varying door heights, turning radii, landing and take-off characteristics all have a fundamental influence on airport design

As the volume of air transportation grows and new navigational aids appear which allow for safer and speedier rates of landings and take-offs, the technique of planning has to be readjusted constantly to make provisions for such advances With growth come new concepts of passenger handling, flying instruction, personal aircraft servicing all requiring new solutions It is not growth alone which dictates an unusual alertness as a requisite for the airport designer, it is the rapid rate of growth which demands the most enlightened thinking so that obsolescence may be retarded as much as possible

In planning a hospital or a school or a railroad station, visits to a reference library or to outstanding examples of the type or correspondence with outstanding specialists in the field will result in much helpful advice In designing airports existing examples and existing opinion must be carefully sifted, the valuable

retained and the mistakes discarded, and the best features compounded with latest techniques of aircraft operation Each new airport must represent an *advance* in planning, there is no such thing as "copying" an airport design.

To the well-known dimensions of space must be added the one of time, time infects all phases of airport planning A city decides that it will require an airport of a specific capacity How may that capacity be accommodated? Above the proposed runway layout is projected a pattern of moving aircraft—some landing, some taking off, some awaiting the signal to start their descent. None of them can stop, all must continue along predetermined paths The entire pattern is constantly changing The number of aircraft which each runway may dispatch or allow to land within a given period must be determined This air traffic pattern must then be correlated with the runway pattern The design of the aprons and buildings must then be correlated with the runway capacity The dimensions of runways should be designated by their length, width, thickness, and *their capacity per hour*

In the planning for communities or regions where a number of landing facilities will be created, the element of time is still present There the planning of the entire development must allow for the proper correlation of the several air traffic patterns over each of the airports with the general pattern which airplanes must follow to reach each of the individual ones

Historical Influence of Transport on Communities

The history of a city's growth will usually parallel the history of its means of transportation In the early life of our nation the only practical means of transport was by water, therefore, the development of the country was coastal The principal cities of the

1870

FIGURE 1.   GROWTH OF RAILROAD NETWORK IN THE UNITED STATES

day were Boston, Providence, New York, Philadelphia, and Baltimore—all possessing excellent deep-water ports. The only inland cities of any prominence were on navigable rivers, like Hartford or Albany. Roads were few and poorly built; journeys between cities were precarious, time consuming, and uncomfortable. The first step forward in knitting together this loosely held chain was the building of turnpikes or toll roads. Thus, being strongly established by virtue of their original location in regard to water transport, the position of these cities was further strengthened by their being linked together with a chain of somewhat improved roads.

The next significant step was the building of the Erie Canal. This canal opened up the Great Lakes region and made New York the terminus of all this interior commerce. The possession by this city of a port for ocean-going as well as interior trade gave it an advantage over any other coastal city, and this initial advantage has been a prime factor in its growth ever since.

The pattern for the railroad network, which was the next phase of transport development, was dictated by three factors: first, to join the already established cities with each other; second, to link smaller communities with larger ones; and third, to open up areas which could not be tapped by other means. The first factor served to strengthen still further the pre-eminence of cities already established. The second established a pattern of interdependence—cultural and commercial—between larger cities and their satellite communities. The third had much to do with the growth of interior cities, such as Kansas City and St. Louis. The railroad made the development of Pittsburgh possible; waterways could not cross the mountain barriers of the Alleghenies but rails did. Waterways could not span the continent but rails did; and so the entire West was made accessible for development. Just as the crossing of two roads, from earliest times, has been the start of many a village, so the crossing of two railroads has been a highly strategic factor in the development of cities.

The automobile, bus, and truck have brought about profound changes in the development of communities and regions. The motor vehicle has knit together our

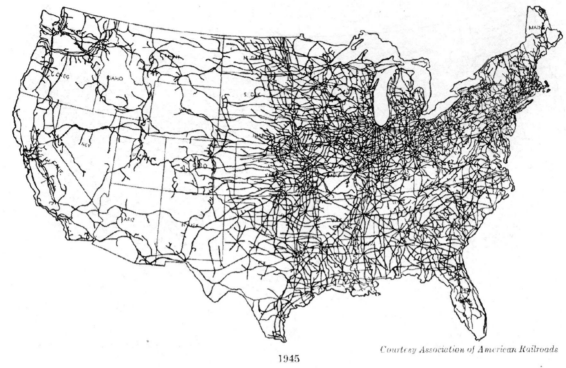

1945

Courtesy Association of American Railroads

FIGURE 1. GROWTH OF RAILROAD NETWORK IN THE UNITED STATES

centers of population more firmly. It has continued the trend first begun by the railroad of opening up inaccessible regions. An interesting new phase in the development of cities has been brought about by the motor vehicle—the process of decentralization. Whereas the railroad tended to concentrate more and more effort in as small an area as possible, the motor vehicle has had just the opposite effect. Thus the population of the Borough of Manhattan of New York has been declining steadily for over three decades. And in newer cities, such as Los Angeles, the motor vehicle has given rise to an entirely different city pattern—population spread out over a tremendous area. Just how far decentralization of cities will go before reaching a balance point is a matter of conjecture, but it is causing many city administrations serious concern.

Another interesting result of the development of motor vehicles and good roads for them to travel on is the number of communities which find existence possible with no other means of transport. More than 54,000 communities are without railroad service, and are dependent solely on motor vehicles.

New City Patterns Created by Air Transport *

What effect will the airplane have on the development of communities? A few prognostications may be made with certainty. In studying the past, it will be found that each new mode of transport has served to strengthen further the position which an established city held. Air transport may be expected to cause this trend to continue. In fact, the first phase of development of this new mode of travel has been concerned with creating a national network linking our principal cities. The next step, paralleling railroad and roadway growth, and in the process of development now, is to link smaller communities with the larger ones. A third manner in which air transport will develop along the lines of railroad development is in the opening up of regions inaccessible by other means; this phase will be carried far beyond that possible by any previous method because of the unique ability of the airplane to overcome any natural barrier.

* The phrase "air transport" includes *all* means of traffic by air, just as "motor vehicle transport" includes automobiles, buses, and trucks, private as well as commercial.

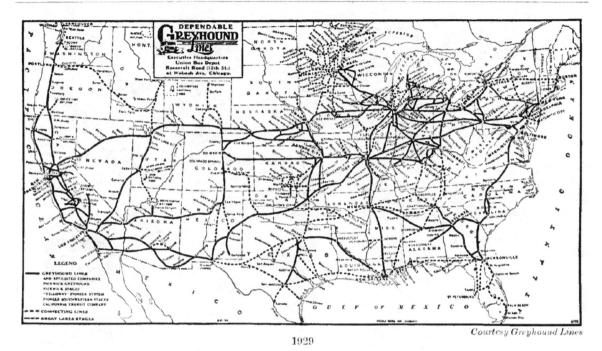

1929   *Courtesy Greyhound Lines*

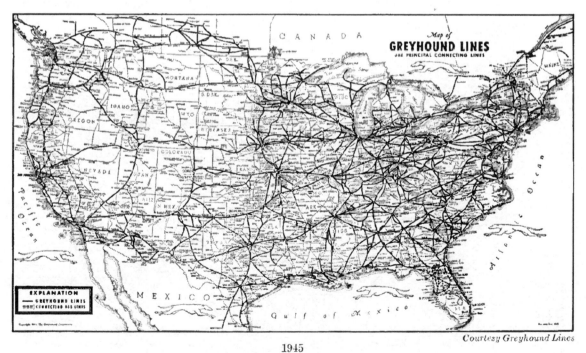

1945   *Courtesy Greyhound Lines*

FIGURE 2. GROWTH OF BUS NETWORK IN THE UNITED STATES

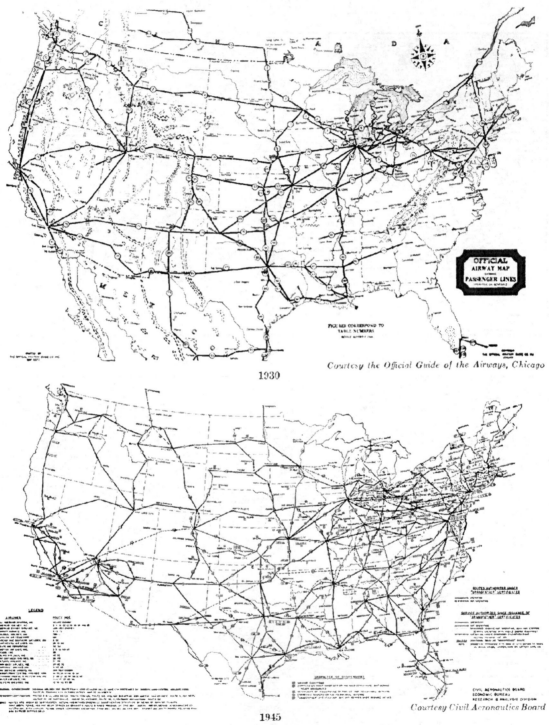

1930

Courtesy the Official Guide of the Airways, Chicago

1945

Courtesy Civil Aeronautics Board

FIGURE 3. GROWTH OF SCHEDULED AIRLINE NETWORK IN THE UNITED STATES

5

Just as the crossing of two roads or railroads has had an important influence on the growth of communities in the past, so will extra benefits accrue to towns situated on the crossing of two air lanes

As to decentralization, it is logical to expect the airplane to further the process already begun by the motor vehicle But to what extent cannot be foretold with any more certainty than for the motor vehicle The radius of decentralization about a larger city will be increased beyond that caused by the motor vehicle, since travel distances are measured by time rather than by mileage The final extent of this development will be a compounding of the number of well-situated and well-planned landing facilities plus the number of air lanes available for different types of air traffic plus aircraft types and their operating characteristics

The speed of the airplane will certainly change travel habits and, therefore the configuration of our cities Areas for recreation which were formerly inaccessible or available only to those of plentiful means, will be opened up for many people who have a limited time for vacationing The habits and habitats of commuters will change as transportation by air becomes more widely available It may not be fanciful to suggest that some future suburbs will be 100 or more miles from the center of a metropolis

When industry begins to make full use of the speed offered by air transport, its methods of doing business and, therefore, its physical plant will change Larger commercial organizations having plant facilities throughout the country or world are planning now to purchase and maintain their own fleets of aircraft They will require airports Thus their factories will be combined with air facilities Smaller companies which engage in trades that may be benefited by speed of delivery of their product will tend to be located near commercial or industrial airports Factories will in time grow up around such airports just as the railroad yard or the water port has influenced industry in its choice of location in the past It will be a different type of industry from the one that depends upon the railroad, an industry which produces a product of higher value per unit of volume or weight

One significant statement that may be made regarding the influence the airplane will exert upon the growth or change of communities in the future is that air transport should be regarded not as an agency which will relegate existing means to the shadows of obscurity, but rather as an agency which will supplement existing means in type and extent according to its unique characteristics To have a national network of transportation which is economically sound and efficient, each form of transport must be employed where its particular characteristics will be utilized to the greatest extent Thus motor vehicles will find their greatest usefulness over short hauls, or longer hauls of lighter-weight commodities, waterways will be utilized for the transport of heavy-bulk commodities where time is of little consequence, railroads will find their greatest utilization in the transport of large volumes of heavy goods over longer distances, and the airplane will attain maximum usefulness where the saving of time is of the utmost importance, and for regions where no other means may be satisfactorily and economically employed

It cannot be anticipated that the advent of air service to a community will change its character or degree of prosperity overnight, too many other factors besides transportation affect the life of a town But it can be stated unequivocally that a community or region possessing good airport facilities will have a competitive advantage over its neighbor not so favorably situated

An "Air City"

The elimination of natural obstacles from the consideration of the airplane pilot in getting from point A to point Z may have a profound effect on the location and development of our future cities One might imagine an inaccessible region rich in natural resources which can only now be made habitable because of this new form of transport Such a condition would present an opportunity for the planning of a true "air city " Since the areas of any city plan may be generally considered as being composed of three basic areas—residential, commercial, and industrial—such a city might be planned to have three types of airports Topographical features, prevailing winds, orientation, and other factors have determined the location of the various areas Airports for recreation are made a part of the residential areas A commercial airport is then located conveniently close to both business and living Airports for cargo have been placed in relation to the most advantageous location of industry These various areas and the airports are then linked together with a network of express highways Feeding these highways and linking them to the working and living quarters are secondary roads

Note first that the basic tenets of city planning need not be changed Planning is still begun with consideration as to where the human being will be able to live most healthily and happily, where he may shop most conveniently, where industry will be best located Then a system of arteries and veins is planted in the body of this new creation so that its lifeblood—the population—may travel freely from one portion to another One does not start with choosing three airport sites and then try to group the other facilities around them. Rather, a new element has been added to the program; new considerations require original solutions.

The final plan may look totally different from those to which one has been accustomed. Airports will, in this example, replace the railroad and waterfront terminals as focal points of the traffic pattern. The larger areas occupied by the airports, together with the clear approaches which they require, will give rise to new planning patterns. The bunching of urban activities will be less intense. The entire plan will be more decentralized, will have a more open appearance. If the approach is based on an understanding of the new problems provoked by a new element as well as the basic issues involved, an interesting, workable, integrated plan will have been developed.

Today the airplane is not an agency for mass transportation. No "air city" will reach full maturity until this stage of development is attained. But present-day thinking and planning should be predicated on the fact that the day will arrive, and that when it does all preparations for this stage should be in order.

New Standards for City Planners

In 1910 "visionary" motorcar manufacturers were predicting vast quantities of automobiles, of low price range, covering the face of our nation. Their predictions have become true—almost alarmingly true. Yet how many communities of that date contemplated such a fundamental change in city planning, made provisions for segregating types of traffic by various types of roadways, or solved parking problems coping with decentralization? And how many plans were actually adopted by cities and conscientiously carried out? Not until comparatively recent times does one find planners designing and building a "motorcar city," incorporating segregation of vehicles and pedestrians, and other features which are now acknowledged requisites.

The disfigurements which the motorcar, plus lack of planning, has visited upon the American scene are well known. The beauties of landscape which are opened up for us by the motorcar and the opportunities for fuller living are equally well known. It has taken a long time to come to the realization that the motor vehicle is not incompatible with a well-planned society. The airplane probably will effect changes in our individual and national lives even more rapidly than the motor vehicle. Planning, in this case, must be based upon anticipation rather than patching up.

The urgent necessity exists for everyone concerned with city planning to acquire the greatest possible fund of knowledge concerning all phases of transportation by air. Air traffic patterns, airway and airport traffic control, airports, their relationship to cities and regions—these and many other elements must be studied and must become new tools in the city planner's kit.

The sociological relationship of air transport and airports to communities should be thoroughly explored. Too often in the past the effects which new mechanical devices might have upon people have not been thoroughly understood until it has become too late to correct serious mistakes.

Effect of Sound Terminal Development on the Community

To function successfully every means of transport must be provided with proper terminal facilities. Transport in general may be divided into two broad categories, commercial and personal. Railroads fall into the first classification only and, therefore, require only one type of terminal. Motor vehicles, watercraft, and aircraft are represented in both classes and require terminals, commercial as well as personal.

Although it is generally recognized that great economies of operation could be effected by the replanning and rebuilding of railroad and waterway terminals, little effort in this direction may be expected because of the tremendous investment in existing facilities, unless undertaken by municipal or quasi municipal agencies (such as local port authorities). These terminals were, in many cases, built before the equipment had reached full mechanical development. The result of an early surge toward premature standardization has saddled these industries with many inadequate terminal facilities. The same thing must not happen in the design and building of airports. Air transport of every form is starting with a comparatively clean slate in the building of its terminals, thus making the challenge even more compelling to plan with maximum foresight and flexibility.

Another lesson which may be learned from past experience is that few terminals have been built with adequate planning as to their relationship to community development. Terminal plans of the future must start with the community, and be planned to take their proper place within the framework of community life.

No airport terminal should be built solely as a monument to the city which intends to erect it. The successful operation of an airport is a business venture, and must represent a sound financial investment. Furthermore, the rate of obsolescence which must occur in building for any agency still in the stages of development indicates a new conception in the financing and amortization of airport terminal buildings. It would

be well to plan and finance these buildings on a life
expectancy, without major alteration, of no more than
twenty years They should be of the simplest construction; of the most functional and direct architectural conception And they should be planned to take
their place as an intimate, useful, and aesthetic part
of community life.

Regional Airport Planning

Airport planning should invariably be done on a regional rather than a local basis Every airport development involves a relatively large capital investment
If local communities were to try to outdo each other
in building bigger and better local airports, the com-
petition would be ruinous Air traffic patterns are constantly increasing in complexity as the volume of air
traffic increases To choose airport sites without regard to adjoining landing facilities would simply not
work Where one airport would serve a region for the
present, more ports might be required as air traffic increases By planning regionally, these needs will be
anticipated, future sites earmarked, and zoning ordinances effected to safeguard the future air needs of
the region   ,

In addition to the more conventional types of airports, regional planning must also include landing
strips These would be placed alongside a network of
superhighways, they should occur every 40 to 50 miles
Every fourth or fifth one should have proper means
for servicing planes as well as motor vehicles, depending upon density of air traffic

The effect which helicopters, gliders, glider pick-up,
mail and express pick-up, assisted take-offs, and similar developments will have on the planning of required
landing facilities must be kept in mind They are discussed more fully in subsequent chapters

Agencies Concerned with Airport Planning

Three distinct agencies should have an interest in
the planning of every airport The Civil Aeronautics
Administration (CAA) of the U S Department of
Commerce has a national perspective in its planning
of airports and airways It maintains an urban planning section which may be freely consulted The
country is divided into seven regions, each of which is
staffed with technicians whose services are available to
any group which is planning airport facilities In addition, the CAA has set up standards for airport classifications and the planning of runway layouts It has
published numerous pamphlets concerned with various
phases of airport planning and equipment The CAA
has also set up a system of lighted airways for night
flying and a radio range network for instrument fly-

ing It maintains weather information services and
often handles airway traffic control

Many states have aviation commissions Their function generally, is to coordinate and supplement the
work of the CAA in their particular state by providing
a more comprehensive and detailed state-wide plan of
airport facilities Their concern is to see that every
local effort is properly integrated with the state-wide
pattern, and that local agencies requiring help—financial as well as planning—may receive it Some states
have made great strides in planning for the future development of their natural, vacation, and other resources
by demonstrating how future airport building will open
up these resources and make them accessible to the air
traveller

The actual detailed work of planning and building
the airport proper must be done by the local aviation
group Legislation should be passed by all states enabling cities, counties, or regions to establish airport
authorities These should be endowed with sufficient
powers to allow them to plan, build, and manage airports Power to issue bonds and condemn property
should be granted The details of financing airport
building, the extent of federal or state aid in this respect, if any, are matters which must be arrived at in
each individual case

Zoning ordinances protecting the areas surrounding
airports against future obstructions should be passed
Without this protection the entire investment could be
jeopardized by the building of a few smokestacks
Since more and more instrument flying will be done, it
will become increasingly important to have airports
whose approaches are entirely free from obstructions

After the airport has been planned and built, the
local airport authority should remain in power to handle the administration of the airport Furthermore,
every such agency should periodically re-examine its
past planning efforts, evaluate them in the light of new
developments, and be prepared to remodel existing facilities or build new ones as the need arises

Regional Surveys

The first order of business of an airport authority
should be a comprehensive stock-taking and analysis
of the economic resources and physical characteristics
of the region which it represents The help of local
planning commissions, chambers of commerce, and similar public and quasi-public bodies should be enlisted
in gathering data Specific analyses should be made
of population densities, character, and trends, land
uses, geographic or topographic characteristics, traffic
studies—rail, motor vehicle, boat—short haul and long

FIGURE 4. POPULATION DENSITY MAP—NEW YORK REGION

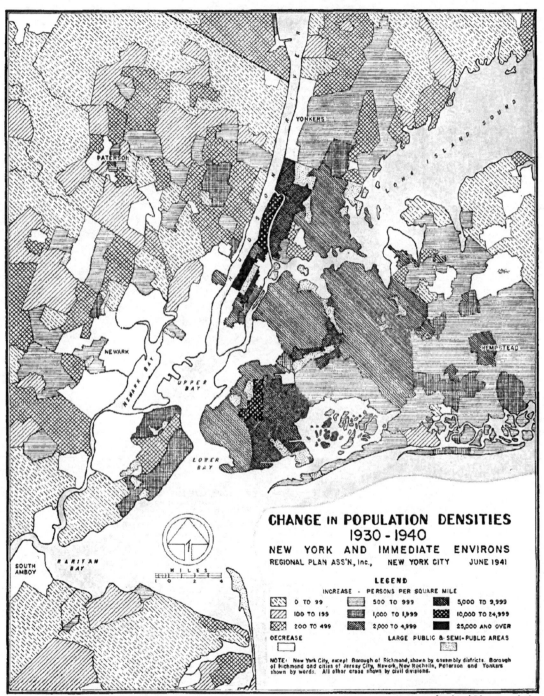

FIGURE 5. POPULATION TRENDS MAP—NEW YORK REGION

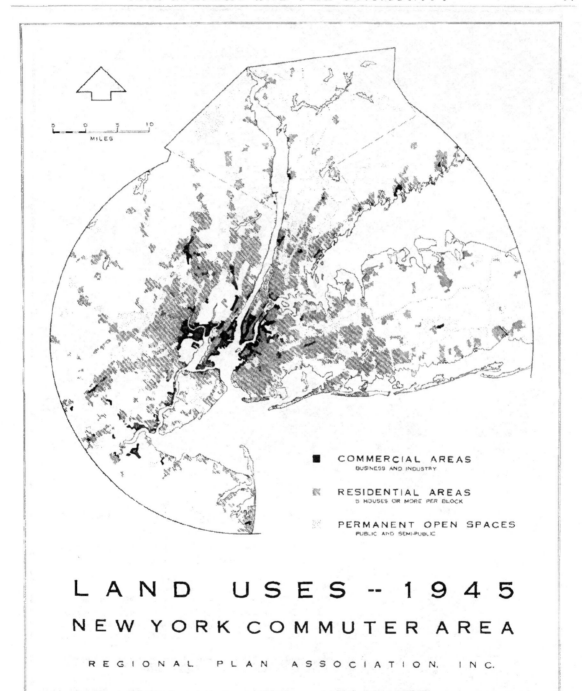

LAND USES -- 1945
NEW YORK COMMUTER AREA
REGIONAL PLAN ASSOCIATION. INC.

Courtesy Regional Plan Association

Figure 6

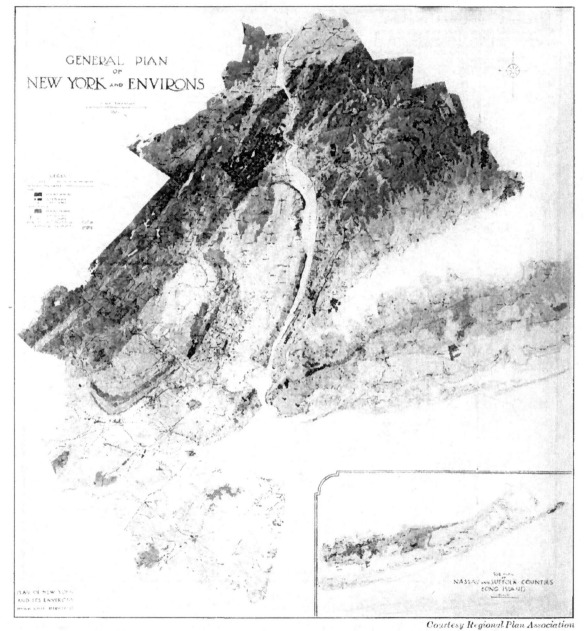

FIGURE 7. GEOGRAPHIC CHARACTERISTICS—NEW YORK REGION

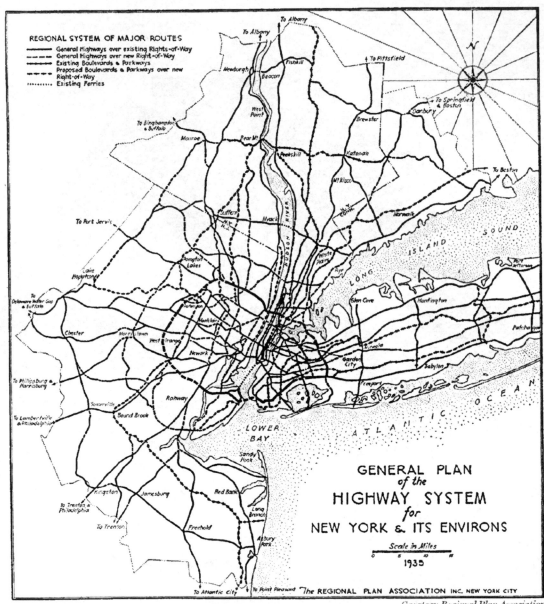

FIGURE 8. PRINCIPAL TRAFFIC ARTERIES—NEW YORK REGION

haul; existing and proposed principal arteries of traf-fic; existing and proposed terminal facilities other than air.

In order to clarify the work of the airport authority outlined in this part of the book, a number of air views, maps, and diagrams of one area are reproduced show-

ing successive steps in regional planning. (A me-tropolis was selected since it best illustrated all the complex phases of regional airport planning.) Fig-ures 4, 5, 6, and 7 show studies of population density, population trends, land uses, geographic characteris-tics of the New York region. Figures 8 and 9 show

THE PORT OF NEW YORK AUTHORITY

RAILROAD TERMINAL MAP

OF

NEW YORK HARBOR

FIGURE 9   *Courtesy Port of New York Authority*

principal traffic arteries and existing railroad terminals

Forecasts must be prepared of the ultimate volumes of air traffic anticipated in each of the principal categories of flying—personal, non-scheduled commercial, and scheduled commercial Each of these should be broken down further into classification by short range, intermediate range, long range, and international. Approximate dates should be established upon which increments of the ultimate volumes will occur as a fundamental of progressive stage planning

Preliminary Planning

If the region is a heavily populated one requiring a series of air terminals it should be broken down into area classifications (with the help of the land use map) such as "industrial," "residential,' "civic" Such a breakdown may disclose that the region possesses a number of predominantly residential areas By reference to the population trends map it would be determined whether these areas had been gaining or losing population By reference to the population density map and by spot checks to show home ownership, monthly home rentals of $100, and over, and ownership of two or more cars would indicate which of the areas might warrant the building of private flying fields Similar analyses throughout the region would determine which of the areas could support an airport, and the general type of airport it should have These analyses would then be checked against the forecasts of anticipated air traffic volumes

When each area has assigned to it the number and type of airports it should have, these data should be analyzed in relation to the geographic characteristics, principal traffic arteries, and existing terminals of the area and the region The first of these would show what land areas might be available for building, the second would show what means of access might be employed in reaching the airport, the third would be of particular importance in integrating air transport with other forms of transport.

The result of this effort might be a preliminary plan for a proposed series of airports This stage should not be considered in any sense a definite plan but only the first gropings for a solution

The next step in planning should be a study, in conjunction with the CAA, of possible arrangements of airways, air traffic lanes, and airport clearances to determine whether airplanes of the types which would use the respective fields would, in fact, be able to use them expeditiously and safely To assure this, each airport of lesser capacity should be surrounded with a given clear area, one of major capacity may need a

10-mile zoned radius * Thus any overlapping of airport air traffic patterns will be disclosed, and, as a result, two smaller airports may have to be consolidated, with allowance for mixed types of air traffic

By means of colored pieces of string and map pins, each color representing one type of traffic, ways and means should be plotted for getting each type of air traffic from the principal directional lanes outside the area into each corresponding airport or airports The results of this study may disclose a number of impossible situations in the original plan, revisions must be made until all traffic flows smoothly through the air.

Access to Airports

When this phase of the planning is satisfactorily solved, the studies of integration with existing and proposed transport means must be resumed Few things will have a more important bearing on the final success of each individual airport than proper means of access and proper integration with existing facilities This phase of the problem has received so little attention in the past that in some cases the travel time on the ground is as much as 100 per cent of the travel time in the air! Means of access should be compatible with the type and ultimate volume of traffic which each type of airport would generate. Thus an airpark or small airport should be connected with the area it serves by means of modern highway, a cargo airport by means of a truck highway and a railroad spur, a large commercial airport by means of arterial highways together with, possibly, rapid transit facilities An airport can no longer be thought of as an isolated meadow situated on the outskirts of town The activities of an airport extend into the very heart of the area it serves The airport proper and its means of access should be planned as one project

Community Airport Planning

For the smaller region whose needs may be served by one airport, the method of attack should be the same as for the larger region The classification of the region into area types plus all of the other aforementioned studies will indicate what type of airport will best fulfill its needs The studies will show what general and specific location will best allow the activities of the airport to be linked with those of the community They will show how access may best be provided for the new project and at the same time be integrated with existing traffic flow

The studies of air traffic patterns will, of course, be thoroughly explored Their main purpose will be to link the flying activities about the airfield with exist-

* Cf Part 5

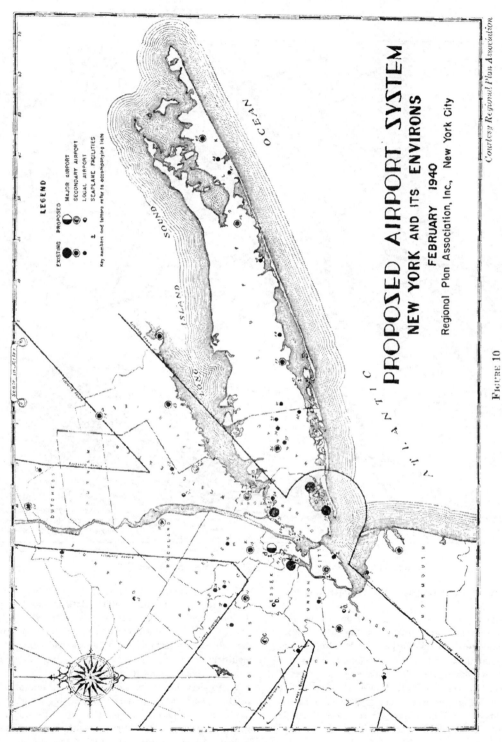

FIGURE 10

(*Note:* The authors have added to the original drawing a circle representing Idlewild Airport.)

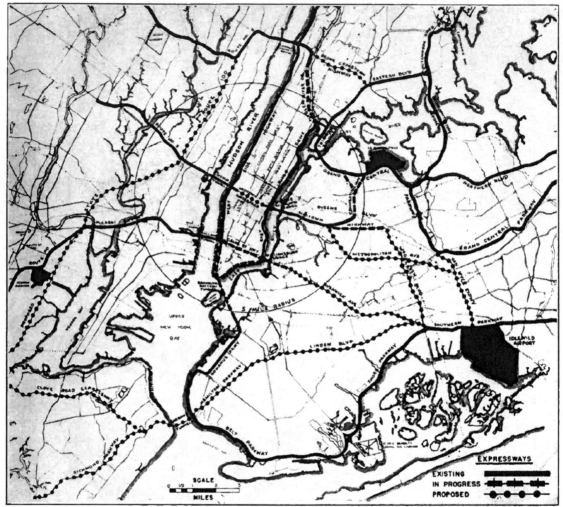

Courtesy Eastern Air Lines, Inc.

FIGURE 11. ACCESS TO AIRPORTS BY HIGHWAY—NEW YORK REGION

ing airways which may pass over or near the community.

If the studies indicate that no commercial air traffic may be expected or required in the near future, planning may proceed on the basis of building a personal-flying airport or airpark. Or again, it may be disclosed that commercial air traffic may be expected within, say, five years. In that case the plan would still be one for building a small airport, but so arranged that it could accommodate commercial traffic with modifications when the necessity became apparent.

Thus the further importance of planning comprehensively and with all available data at hand may be demonstrated. Only some of the effort will become apparent in immediate construction; the major benefits will accrue when the necessity for changes and modifications occur. It is then that sound initial planning will demonstrate its full value.

There may be communities which do not have the funds to embark on airport construction, or whose air needs have not yet reached the building stage. In spite of such a situation, the assembling of factual data and the basic planning should be undertaken. This

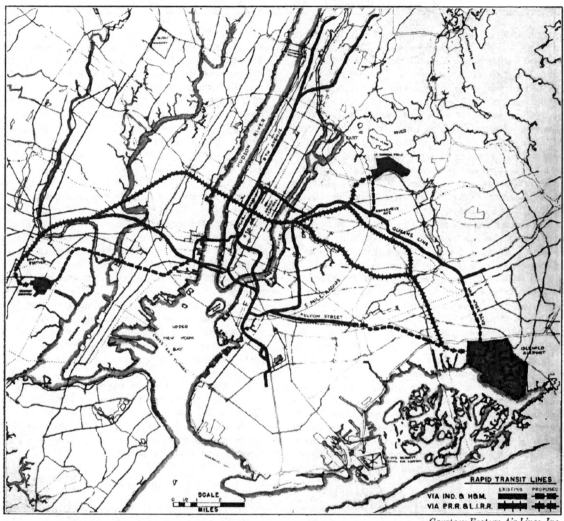

FIGURE 12.   ACCESS TO AIRPORTS BY RAPID TRANSIT—NEW YORK REGION

done, a community will be able to earmark future sites for airport development; it will be able to zone to protect its as yet unborn venture; it will be able to build its roadways and utilities with its future airport needs clearly in mind. These needs will then be met with sites which are both available and useful when the time for building arrives.

Integration, Site Selection, Anticipation

Community or regional airport planning resolves itself into three basic considerations. The importance of the first, integration with existing terminal facili-

ties (of all types) and with the community, is demonstrated when one regards the effect of other types of terminal development on city development. Many suburban communities have grown and flourished around one railroad station. Large segments of a city have grown and real estate values have been maintained by sound terminal development. Industry has, in many cases, grown around freight terminals or freight yards. Thus growth and development may be expected surrounding new airport terminals, and such development should be orderly and planned. The connotation of the phrase "on the other side of the railroad tracks" should not and need never be applied to airports The National Resources Planning Board in its *Transportation and National Policy* states the following "Great improvements in service to the public, better utilization of land and air rights in large urban centers, and the removal of many existing blighted areas would result from the substantial reconstruction of terminal facilities *The objective would be, of course, to fit into the most desirable pattern of urban development a series of coordinated terminals serving all types of transport and open on equal terms to all carriers serving the area "* This is admittedly an ideal, but the best efforts in airport planning should keep such an ideal in mind

The second consideration, site selection, must have as its basis the choosing of the best possible location to serve a designated need The importance of means of access to such a site cannot be overemphasized If the site is properly chosen as to use, and its traffic may be properly integrated with that of the area it will serve, the initial stage of planning may be considered well done Speedy and adequate access to airports is the key to maximum utilization of the airplane—for the personal flyer as well as the airline passenger

The third consideration, anticipation of future needs, is a by-product of sound planning Its importance is as great or greater than the initial planning Too many cases already exist, even in our present embryonic airport network, of facilities which have already become worthless for lack of foresight in the initial planning stages The serious study of future needs together with a continuing interest in the latest development in airport planning practice will pay large dividends

The Master Plan

The interrelated researches and efforts of the planning group should be embodied in a master plan This plan will be based upon the various economic and physical surveys made, upon the studies of airway traffic patterns and of access by air and ground, upon the forecasts of air traffic volumes It will set forth the number, size, type, and location of landing facili-

* Authors' italics

ties ultimately required It will show proposed methods of dovetailing these facilities with existing terminal facilities—rail, water, vehicular, air The plan will present the requirements which will have to be met in the building of roadways, rails, rapid transit, and utilities It will disclose the financial and economic aspects of the entire development—estimated costs of construction and operation, estimated income It will demonstrate the manner in which the entire phase of air transportation will be integrated with the daily life of the region under study

The master plan will show how the growing needs of air transportation may be met in orderly, coordinated stages Based upon forecasts of traffic volume for each of the major categories of flying, it will show how these volumes may be met when they occur Whether these figures are actually attained on the date specified will be of less importance than that the master plan shall contain provisions for meeting them as required

Since the successful accommodation of traffic—by whatever means—is of fundamental concern to the well-being of every community and region, the intelligent creation of and execution of a master plan of airports must become a basic part of every overall city and regional plan

The final goal of every airport authority shall be the creation of an airport building program which will fulfill its function to the community in which it is to be placed, to the region which it will serve, and to the entire national and global network of transportation of which it will become a part

Bibliography

Transportation and National Policy, by the National Resources Planning Board, U S Government Printing Office, Washington, D C, May, 1942

Report on Urban Planning Conference, Evergreen House, Johns Hopkins Press, 1944

Publications issued by the Regional Plan Association of New York

Publications issued by the Urban Planning Division, Civil Aeronautics Administration

'10-Year Planning for Private-Flight Ports,' by Julian Whittlesey, *Architectural Record,* April, 1945

2

PRESENT AND FUTURE AIRCRAFT

Just as air power plays a most important military role in combat as well as in transporting military personnel and equipment, so is air travel profoundly affecting the national and, particularly, the international transportation pattern by virtually shrinking the world. It has been said that we are entering a realistic air age which will revolutionize transportation and, to a large degree, render obsolete some forms of our existing ground transportation facilities. This is a viewpoint not shared by the authors. Rather, the advantages offered by the inherent speed of the airplane must be analyzed and applied in their proper place in order to obtain a well-balanced and economically integrated overall transportation system to fit the requirements of national and global economy.

It is necessary to stretch the imagination and look far beyond what was thought realizable a few years ago, yet in doing so it is essential to remain within the bounds of common sense and reach logical conclusions based on a compounding of facts with creative thinking.

Air transportation as an instrument of commerce and pleasure is now established beyond question, but its expansion and rate of growth will depend upon the technical development of the airplane itself, the available facilities for its use, and the degree of acceptance by the traveler based on safety, convenience, and utility.

Relation of Aircraft to Landing Facilities

The relation of the airplane to the airport can be compared to that of the steamer or motorboat to its dock. A motorboat can be moored to a superliner dock, but a superliner cannot slip into a motorboat dock. The same holds true for the airplane. A proper understanding of present-day aircraft, their various types and sizes, and what improvements can reasonably be expected in the future for each category, is a necessary prerequisite to any intelligent discussion of the planning and the designing of airports to accommodate them.

It is, therefore, essential to know the general and performance characteristics of aircraft which are to use any particular class of airport in order to gain an understanding of the landing and ground facilities required for their handling and servicing.

The best solution may fall short of the ultimate goal, no matter how rationally this problem is studied, because aircraft design has yet to reach stability. A parallel situation may be found in the development of our highway system to accommodate motor vehicles. But if plans are properly conceived, economical corrections should be feasible later without scrapping what has already been built.

Phases of Aviation Development

An era of tremendous aviation expansion lies ahead. This is the direct result of accelerated technical and operational developments during the past few years for military purposes. These developments have profound implications and will speed up the universal acceptance of the airplane as a personal and common carrier. In this respect, it is believed that three successive periods of development lie ahead. They might be outlined as follows:

(1) A *transition* phase of changing from wartime mobilization to normalcy. The duration of this period will depend upon the ability of designers and manufacturers to apply the technical lessons learned during the war to new commercial designs. This transition may take two to three years, during which time military aircraft designs reconverted for civil use will be available. Any new production during this phase will be from the same basic designs with minor improvements dictated by past usage. This statement applies to the light aircraft class as well as to the transport aircraft category. The small types of personal aircraft popular before the war were built in large quan-

tities for observation purposes, such models are, therefore, available. Many improvements were made on these small aircraft to increase their utility, lower their cost of operation and maintenance. Many additional changes can be made to their basic design to raise their performance and thus render them still more attractive as personal aircraft.

Similarly, the airlines will gradually dispose of their 14-passenger Lockheed Lodestar and 21-passenger Douglas DC-3 equipment because of age and replace it temporarily with modified versions of the original DC-3, such as the C-47 and C-53 and the newer 21-passenger Douglas C-117A Army transport, the 44- to 60-passenger conversion of the C-54 Skymaster, known as the Douglas DC-4, and its faster version of 50-passenger capacity, known as the DC-6, also modifications of the Lockheed C-69, to be known commercially as the L-49 Constellation. These military personnel and cargo transport airplanes have better performance and can readily be modified for airline operation since they were originally conceived as air transports which were converted to meet the tactical requirements of the military services.

(2) An *intermediate* period of readjustment and expansion to meet the increasing demands of the private flyer and the requirements of the airlines. This period may last 4 to 6 years, depending primarily upon the ability of the aircraft manufacturer to produce more modern aircraft designed to promote maximum safety, dependability, ease of control, economy of operation, and attractive appearance to meet the demands of the private flyer. Price will be an important factor, and just as the popular-priced motorcar dominates the road, so will the low price airplane dominate the sky.

It will also be during this period that the airlines will begin to operate transport airplanes built to engineering specifications, such as the ATA-A1 and -B1 * drawn from past airline operating experience, in an effort to furnish the air traveler with improved service at lower cost.

(3) A *development* era of efficient large-scale transport operation of large and small aircraft which will firmly establish the air transport industry in the class of mass transportation.

It is conceivable that during this period the number of private aircraft may substantially exceed the number of watercraft now in use.

The above outline of aviation development may well encompass the next ten to twenty years. Human nature always has, in the past, followed definite fundamental laws of thought and progress. The rate of improvement has been generally the same. It has accelerated according to the speed of transportation medium in existence at that time, but such improvements have always been effected by benefits gained from the improved service or the convenience provided. The airplane has basic limitations which will restrict its degree of usefulness. The same thought applies to rotary wing and lighter-than-air craft.

TABLE I

CLASSIFICATION OF POSSIBLE FLYING ACTIVITIES

(A) *Personal*

   (1) Local, commutation, taxi
   (2) Cross country
   (3) Aircraft sales
   (4) School
   (5) Glider
   (6) Autogiro
   (7) Helicopter

(B) *Non-scheduled Commercial*

   (1) Aircraft and engine manufacturing flight testing
   (2) Executive personnel travel and sales representation
   (3) Fixed base operation
   (4) Advance flight training school
   (5) Non-scheduled cargo
   (6) Aerial police
   (7) Forest patrol
   (8) Crop dusting
   (9) Life saving
   (10) Photography and mapping
   (11) Scientific research
   (12) Miscellaneous surveys

(C) *Scheduled Commercial*

   (1) Local schedule
     (a) On line
     (b) Feeder
   (2) Limited-stops operation
   (3) Intercontinental
   (4) Transoceanic
   (5) Air cargo
     (a) Intracontinental
     (b) Intercontinental
     (c) Transoceanic

(D) *Military Operations*

   (1) Flight training
     (a) Primary
     (b) Basic
     (c) Transition
   (2) Tactical
     (a) Observation and photography
     (b) Fighter
     (c) Light bombing
     (d) Heavy bombing
     (e) Patrol
     (f) Medical
     (g) Transport
       (a) Personnel
       (b) Cargo

* *ATA-A1 and B1 Aircraft Specifications*, prepared by the ATA Committee on Aircraft Requirements and issued by the Air Transport Association of America, Inc., Washington D. C.

Classification of Flying Activities

Flying is the most flexible means of transport yet developed It knows no physical barriers, and before discussing the types of aircraft which will ply the airways we should first know what kind of flying will be done.

Table I is a classification of the kind of flying activities which can be carried out by heavier-than-air as well as lighter-than-air craft There are four major classes of flying personal, non-scheduled commercial, scheduled commercial, and military

Categories of Aircraft

Although the characteristics of some airplanes permit them to be used for all kinds of flying, each of the four major classes of air activities requires airplanes which can best meet the specific needs of each of the divisions listed For the purpose of this presentation we shall divide all civil aircraft into four categories

1 Aircraft used for school work and local flying
2 Personal aircraft for cross-country and industrial flying
3 Transport aircraft for scheduled air carrier operation
4 Special aircraft, such as autogiros, helicopters, gliders, and airships

Light Aircraft

First of all, it must be realized that privately owned aircraft will unquestionably constitute an increasing percentage of the total number of airplanes in operation and, therefore, will to a large degree influence the design of a great many airports which will be constructed to accommodate them exclusively

Light aircraft are excellent for the flight training of beginners and have sufficient range and performance to combine worth-while utility with low initial as well as operating costs When suitable landing and take-off facilities are available, they may well be used for commuting and taxi purposes from outlying suburban areas to business centers

Representative airplanes in this category are the Piper Cubs, the one-place Piper Skycycle, the various models of Aeronca known as the Champion, the Chief, the Arrow, and the Chum, the Ercoupe, the Skyfarer of General Aircraft, the Luscombe, the Culver Cadet, the Swift of Globe Aircraft; the Taylorcraft; the Stinson Voyager, and many others

The Piper Cub is a two-place, high wing cabin monoplane of rugged construction, possessing excellent visibility due to its high wing It is built in two models —a Standard Trainer powered with a 65-horsepower

engine and a Super Cruiser equipped with a 100-horsepower engine

The Cub Trainer is licensed for a gross weight of 1 220 pounds, with a range of 200 miles, and lands at 38 miles per hour Its normal take-off distance is approximately 500 feet, and the landing distance from a 50-foot altitude is about 1,000 feet It normally descends, power off, at the rate of 420 feet per minute at an angle of 5 degrees In landing approach it can turn at a radius of 200 feet with a 45-degree angle of bank, and at a speed of 55 miles per hour Its general appearance and overall dimensions are shown in Fig 1 The photograph is of the Cub L-4, also called the Grasshopper, used by the military services for light observation work It is a modification of the Cub Trainer

The Super Cruiser is slightly larger and is licensed for a gross weight of 1,550 pounds It cruises at over 95 miles per hour and has a cruising range of 375 to 400 miles It lands at 45 miles per hour

The Ercoupe, built by Engineering and Research Corporation, is a two-place, low-wing cabin monoplane equipped with a fixed tricycle landing gear and powered with a 65-horsepower engine The structure of the Ercoupe is all metal, as is all covering except the outer wing panels which are fabric covered It is certified by the Civil Aeronautics Administration as "characteristically incapable of spinning " The rudder pedals have been eliminated, and only the control wheel is used to operate the airplane The ailerons, rudders, and nose wheel are mechanically coordinated by the rotation of the control wheel only. Its general appearance and overall dimensions are shown in Fig 2 It is certificated for a gross weight of 1,260 pounds The distance required for take-off is approximately 350 feet, and its rate of climb for the first minute after take-off is 700 feet per minute Its landing run has been checked to be as low as 220 feet, and its turning radius on the ground is less than 15 feet Insofar as rate of descent is concerned its landing gear is designed for a maximum of 15 feet per second vertical velocity, which permits it to descend at steep angles

The Taylorcraft, manufactured by Taylorcraft Aviation Corporation, is a lightweight airplane of four-passenger capacity Figure 3 shows its general appearance and overall dimensions It is of the braced high-wing type and is equipped with a fixed landing gear with faired wheel covers Wing slots and flaps give this airplane exceptionally stable flight characteristics and low landing speed Powered with a 125-horsepower air-cooled engine, it cruises at over 110 miles per hour

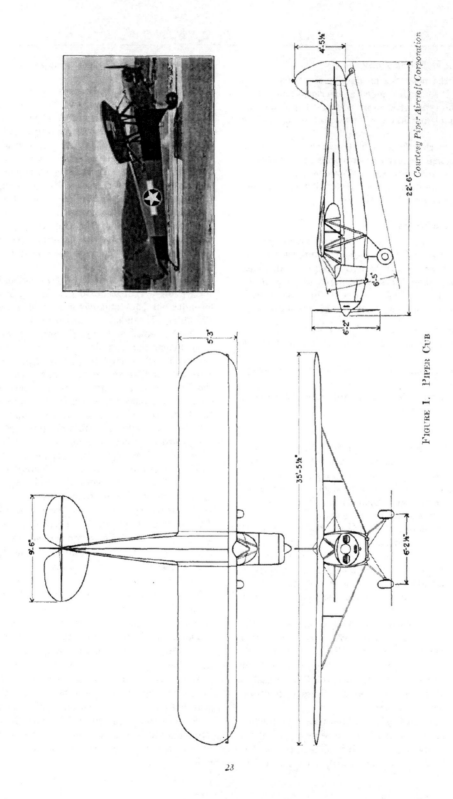

FIGURE 1. PIPER CUB

Courtesy Piper Aircraft Corporation

23

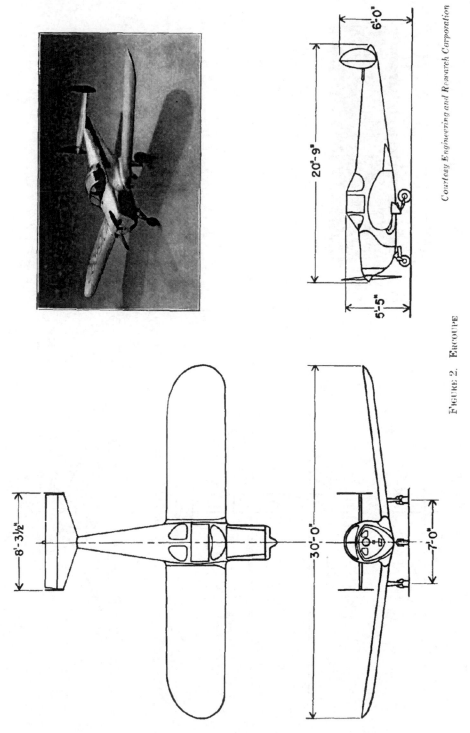

Courtesy Engineering and Research Corporation

FIGURE 2. ERCOUPE

24

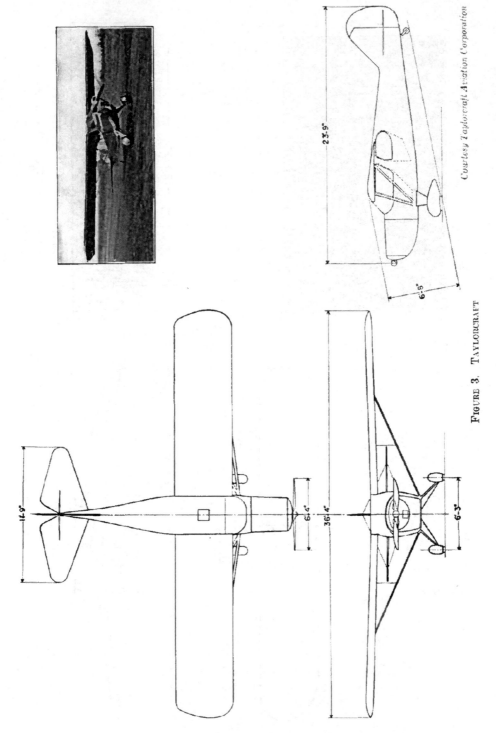

FIGURE 3. TAYLORCRAFT

25

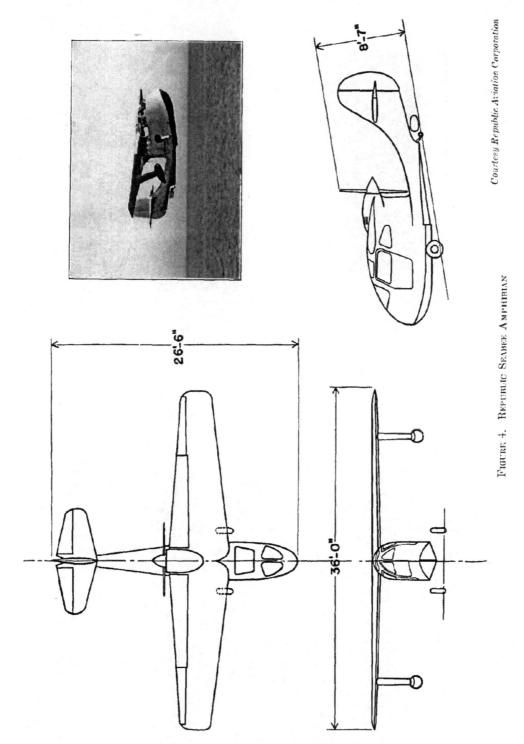

8'-7"

26'-6"

36'-0"

Courtesy Republic Aviation Corporation

FIGURE 4. REPUBLIC SEABEE AMPHIBIAN

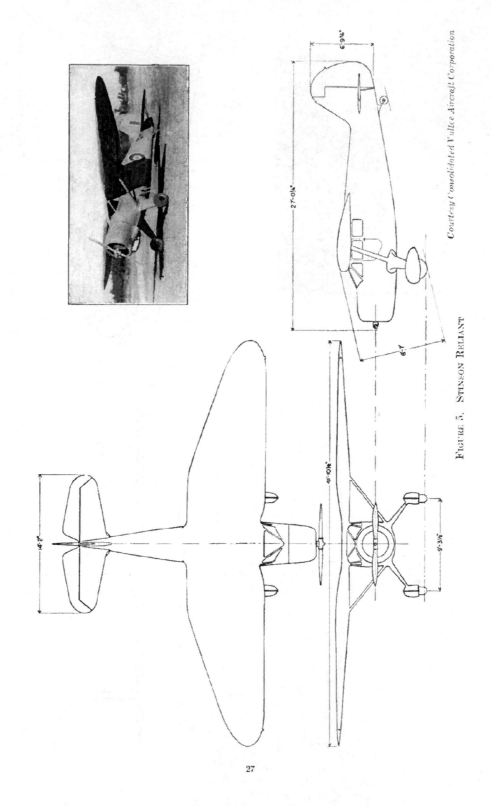

Courtesy Consolidated Vultee Aircraft Corporation

FIGURE 5. STINSON RELIANT

27

Personal Aircraft for Cross-Country and Industrial Flying

Aircraft for private cross-country flying and industrial uses can be typically represented by the new Republic Seabee Amphibian, the Stinson Reliant, the Beech single-engine and twin-engine airplanes, the Grumman twin-engine amphibians, and others in the same category.

The new Republic Seabee Amphibian represents the first effort to offer a low-cost, small four-place aircraft able to alight and take off either from water or land. While it excellently meets the needs and desires of the private flyer, its payload and range can advantageously be used by the sales executive, and its versatility fills the requirements of many industrial applications. Its general appearance and dimensions are shown in Fig. 4. In its present stage of development it is a high-wing monoplane of cantilever design and stressed skin construction. The movable control surfaces only are fabric covered. It is powered with a 175-horsepower engine driving a pusher propeller. The landing gear is fully retractable and electrically operated. The location of the engine and propeller at the rear of the wing and rear portion of the cabin permits exceptional visibility for all cabin occupants. It cruises at 105 miles per hour, takes off as a landplane in 700 feet, and as a seaplane in 1,000 feet. It has a rate of climb of 750 feet per minute and can land in less than 500 feet. Its total weight empty is 1,775 pounds and its gross weight is 2,600 pounds.

Although the Stinson Reliant may not continue in production in its present form, there are so many of them flying that it cannot be ignored. It is a single-engine, four-place, high-wing cabin monoplane, equipped with a conventional landing gear and powered with 210- to 300-horsepower engines. Its cabin interior resembles that of the modern motorcar. It is constructed of steel tubing, fabric covered. Its excellent design and robustness have contributed to its popularity with the sportsman pilot and executive as well. It cruises at 130 to 135 miles per hour. Its general appearance and overall dimensions are shown in Fig. 5. It is certificated for a gross weight of 4,000 pounds; powered with a 285-horsepower Lycoming engine, its take-off distance is 800 feet, and the total distance required to clear a 50-foot obstacle is 1,475 feet. Its landing run is approximately 600 feet. Its normal turning radius in making a landing approach is approximately 500 feet. Its turning radius on the ground for ramp spacing purposes is 41 feet. The excellent stability characteristics and extreme ruggedness of its structures have made this airplane suitable also for airline instrument training, as well as for private flying.

The Beech Beechcrafts D17R and D17S, typically illustrated by Fig. 6, are four- to five-place single-engine cabin biplanes powered with a 450-horsepower engine. Designed for high performance, they combine speed and luxury for the advanced sportsman pilot or business executive. They are licensed each for a gross weight of 4,250 pounds, cruise at 200 miles per hour, and land at 50 miles per hour. They have a cruising range, with reserve, of 670 miles, with five persons and baggage.

The twin-engine Beechcraft Model 18S is a six- to ten-place, all-metal, low-wing cabin monoplane, de-

Courtesy Beech Aircraft Corporation

FIGURE 6.   BEECHCRAFT D17S

signed to meet the requirements of industrial firms with widespread properties and agencies as well as the need of de luxe private ownership with maximum safety. It can cruise well over 200 miles per hour. It is powered with two 450-horsepower engines and equipped with a conventional landing gear. The main wheels are fully retractable. Its general appearance and overall dimensions are shown in Fig. 7. It is certificated for a gross weight of 7,850 pounds. Its take-off run is 525 feet, and its landing run 640 feet. The low power loading of this airplane makes it a popular choice for operation in and out of small fields.

Transport Aircraft

In the transport aircraft category, size is principally related to the type of service to be performed, the smaller airplanes being used for local schedules and the large ones for long-range operation. This is dictated by the facts that traffic volume does not as a rule justify the operation of large airplanes to render a service calling for low mileage between stops, that frequency of schedule is often more important than size in local operation, and, also, that flying long distances between stops requires large aircraft, which can be designed with greater structural weight saving than small aircraft.

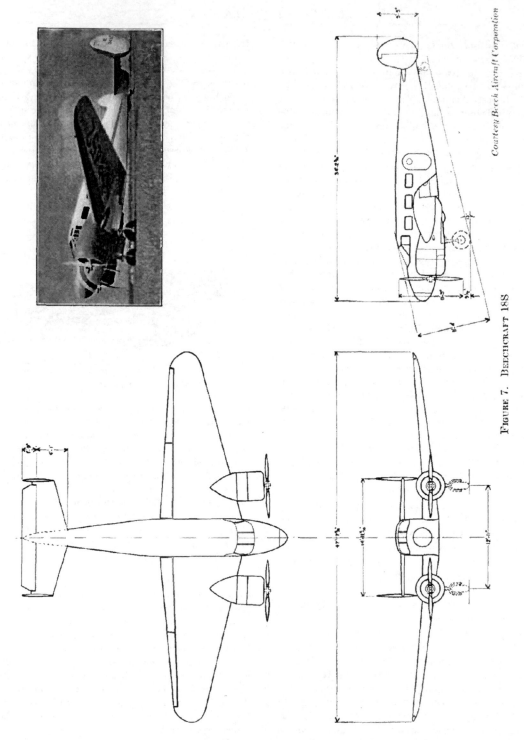

Courtesy Beech Aircraft Corporation

Figure 7. Beechcraft 18S

29

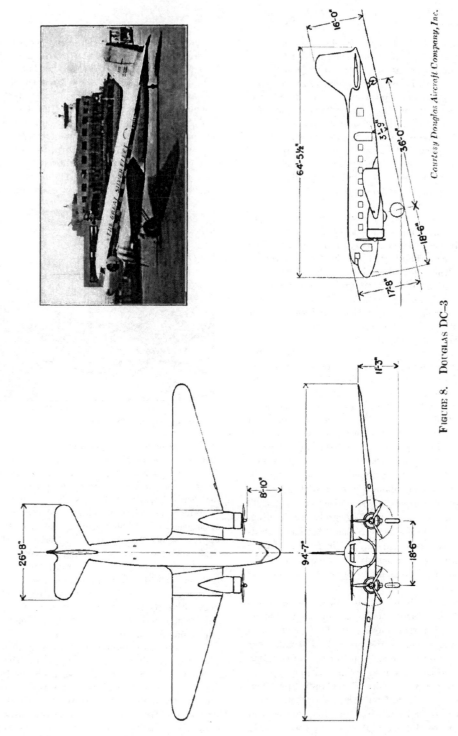

FIGURE 8. DOUGLAS DC-3

30

It is believed that if airports for scheduled air transport operation are planned or modernized to accommodate transport aircraft of today and those now contemplated for operation in several years, such airports should be adequate for a good many years to come if provisions are made in the airport master plan for suitable handling of a larger number of schedules. Future improvements in aircraft design should not cause such airports to become obsolete if properly planned in the beginning. The trend of such improvements appears to lie in greater cruising speed and size rather than in radical changes in landing and take-off performance.

Both these characteristics are well controlled by regulation. Of greater importance to both the airline operator and airport planner is Part 61 of the *U. S. Civil Air Regulations* promulgated by the Civil Aeronautics Board. The regulations in this Part 61 specify a definite relationship between the allowable take-off gross weight and the airport runway length, depending upon the airplane characteristics and the altitude of the airport. This is discussed at greater length in Part 6 of this book, "Airfield Planning."

Local schedule operation requirements will to a large degree be met during the next two years with improved versions of the 21-passenger Douglas DC–3. This airplane has done yeoman service on the airlines for the past ten years, and was known as the truck horse of the Army during the war. Many thousands of them were built, and their maintenance has become so well standardized that they are very reliable and dependable. Its general appearance and overall dimensions are shown in Fig. 8. It is a twin-engine, low-wing, all-metal cabin land monoplane, powered with 1,100- or 1,200-horsepower engines, and is licensed at 25,200 pounds for take-off and 24,400 pounds for landing. This airplane will probably be replaced for local schedule operation by a type of somewhat larger size, with a tricycle landing gear to permit a shorter landing distance and other improvements to better the take-off and climb performance.

Among the new designs to meet these requirements may be cited the Martin Model 202 of 32- to 40-passenger capacity, illustrated by Fig. 9. This airplane will have a cruising speed of the order of 250 miles per hour at 60 per cent of the rated power of its two 2,100-horsepower engines. Its gross weight will be approximately 36,000 pounds. Its take-off and landing performances will meet the U. S. Civil Air Regulations, as defined in Parts 04 and 61, with 3,500-foot runways at sea level, thus combining high-speed performance in and out of comparatively small fields.

Another airplane of this type, possessing similar characteristics, is the 36- to 40-passenger Consolidated Vultee Aircraft Corporation Model 240.

To fulfill the growing need for a smaller transport airplane for operation where traffic density cannot economically support airplanes of the DC–3 size, Lockheed Aircraft Corporation has designed and developed a 14-passenger transport airplane, illustrated by Fig. 10 and known as Model 75 or Saturn, following the policy of Lockheed Aircraft in naming its commercial aircraft after stars. Departing from transport aircraft practice during the past fifteen years, this airplane is

Courtesy Glenn L. Martin Company

FIGURE 9. THE MARTIN 202 TRANSPORT

of the high-wing type, permitting low passenger cabin entrance door height from the ground without sacrificing propeller ground clearance. It is of all-metal construction, and is equipped with a retractable landing gear. Much thought was given to details in order to reduce cost of maintenance and service time. The gross weight is 13,500 pounds and the empty weight approximately 9,800 pounds, including crew and baggage, fuel and oil reserve, and passenger equipment. It has a cruising speed of approximately 190 miles per hour at 5,000 feet altitude. It takes off fully loaded after a ground run of 1,055 feet at sea level. The airport length required at sea level to meet the U. S. Civil Air Regulations, Transport Category Requirements, is approximately 3,700 feet.

Limited-stops schedule operational requirements can be met by the 44-passenger four-engine Douglas DC–4 which may be available also as a 56- to 60-passenger dayplane. Also contemplated for this type of service was the twin-engine Curtiss-Wright of 36- to 37-passenger capacity. These two airplanes were originally designed to airline specifications but were not commercially produced because of the requirements of

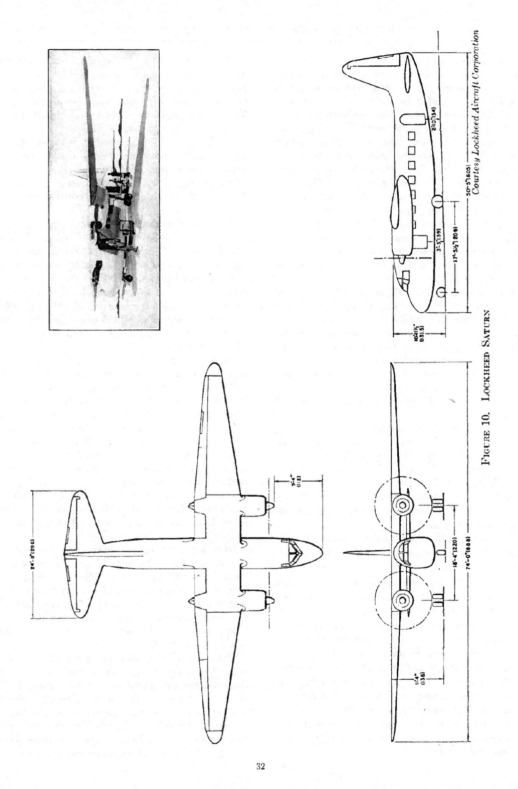

FIGURE 10. LOCKHEED SATURN

32

personnel transport and military cargo airplanes during the war. Extensive military operation has dictated service changes which have been embodied in the revised commercial versions mentioned above to improve their characteristics and performance

The Douglas DC–4 is an all-metal, low-wing cabin landplane with cabin arrangements for 44 passengers and up to 60 passengers for high-density operation. It is equipped with a fully retractable tricycle-type landing gear. It is powered with four 1,450 horsepower engines. Its gross weights are 73,000 pounds for take-off and 63,500 pounds for landing, the difference between landing and take-off weight being available for flight fuel, which gives this airplane flexibility of operation for varying distances between stops. Its general appearance and overall dimensions are illustrated in Fig 11

The Curtiss-Wright CW–20E, an all-metal, low-wing cabin landplane, as shown in Fig 12, will not be built in quantity. Therefore its illustration and characteristics listed in Table II (page 42) are purely academic. But its prototype, the Army C–46 was built in large quantities, and some of these aircraft will undoubtedly be used domestically for a few years in cargo operation. It is powered with two 2,100-horsepower engines instead of 2,500-horsepower engines proposed for the CW–20E.

For long non-stop-flight schedules there are three airplanes now available—the Lockheed Constellation, known as the L–49, the new Douglas DC–6, and the Boeing Stratocruiser, known as Model 377. There is also the Douglas DC–7, commercial version of the Army C–74 cargo airplane, the 400-mph Republic Rainbow, and the Lockheed Constitution with its spacious double-deck cabin

The first three of these airplanes cruise at more than 300 miles per hour and have an economical range greater than 2,500 miles. Yet this range does not preclude their use in domestic operation as economical range is a function of the difference between landing and take-off weights, maximum payload being the difference between landing weight and operational empty weight, which consists of empty weight plus crew weight, supplies, and necessary fuel and oil reserve

The Lockheed Model L–649 Constellation is a low-wing, all-metal cabin landplane, powered with four 2,200- to 2,500-horsepower engines. It has a cabin of 48- to 52-passenger capacity convertible to 22 to 24 berths at night or 60- to 64-passenger capacity for day operations only. Both cabin versions are pressurized for high-altitude flying

It is licensed for a take-off weight of 92,000 pounds and a landing weight of 78,000 pounds. This airplane is the improved commercial version of the Army C–69 of which many were converted for airline operation. The general appearance and overall dimensions of the Constellation are shown in Fig 13

The Douglas DC–6 is basically a larger DC–4, having virtually the same design characteristics with greater speed and substantially more range. Its cabin, seating 52 by day and having accommodations for 26 berths as a sleeper, is pressurized for high-altitude operation

The Boeing Stratocruiser, as shown in Fig 14, is the commercial adaptation of the C–97 of the U S Army Air Forces. It is a cantilever-midwing, all-metal monoplane. Its pressurized double-deck fuselage provides accommodations for 90 passengers besides a substantial amount of cargo. Equipped with four 3,500-horsepower engines it can cruise at well over 300 miles an hour. Commercial specifications call for a take-off gross weight of 135,000 pounds and a landing weight of 121,700 pounds

To provide greater luxury, longer range, or larger capacity, several larger airplanes can be expected to make their appearance during the next few years. One of these airplanes is the Douglas DC–7. It is a long-range high-capacity landplane for passenger and cargo transport. It will provide accommodations for 113 passengers in a pressurized cabin to permit high-altitude, long-distance, high-speed operations. It will be powered with four 3,000-horsepower engines. Its weight empty is expected to be close to 95,000 pounds. It is being built for a landing weight of 127,500 pounds and a take-off weight of 162 000 pounds or 81 tons. Its general appearance and overall dimensions are shown in Fig 15

Of still greater capacity is the new Lockheed Constitution now being developed. It is a midwing four-engine transport having a double-deck fuselage capable of accommodating upward of 130 passengers. It is expected that its take-off weight will exceed 90 tons and its landing weight 80 tons. As to dimensions, its span is approximately 190 feet, its length 156 feet, and its overall height 50 feet

There is also the 204-passenger capacity and 2,900 cubic feet cargo capacity transport airplane project contemplated by Consolidated Vultee Aircraft Corporation and known as the Convair Model 37. Such payload with a suitable transoceanic range calls for a gross weight of the order of 130 to 160 tons. Its cruising speed is expected to be more than 300 miles per hour. It is powered with six 5,000-horsepower engines, has a

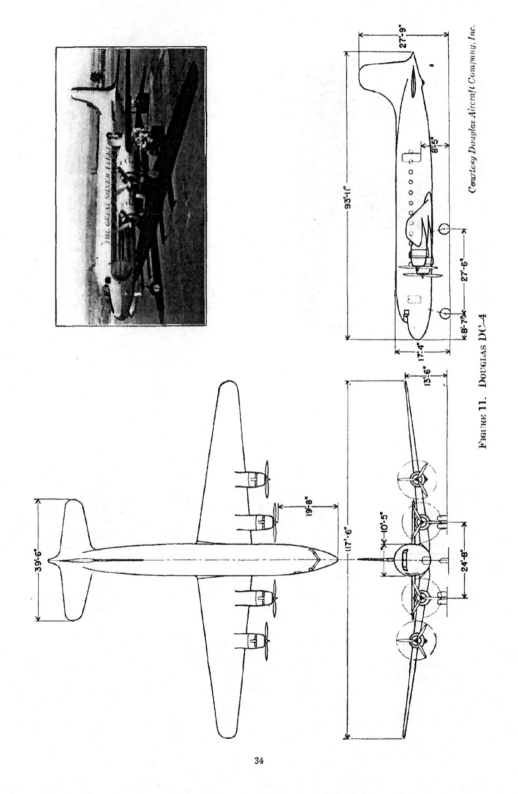

Courtesy Douglas Aircraft Company, Inc.

FIGURE 11. DOUGLAS DC–4

34

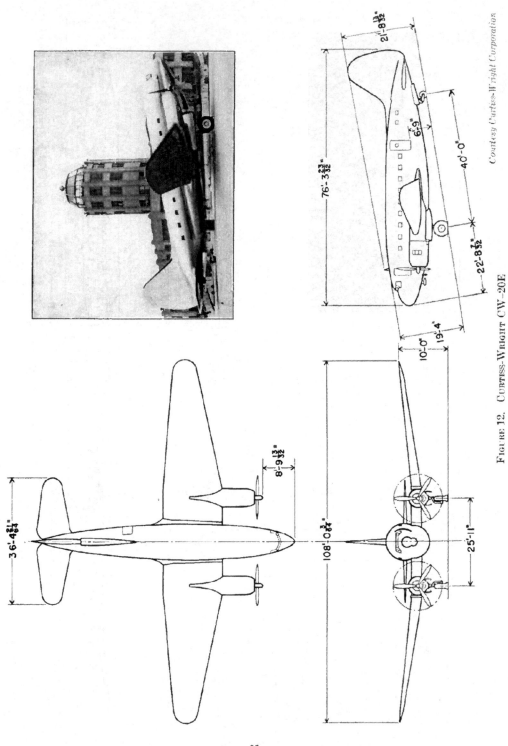

Courtesy Curtiss-Wright Corporation

FIGURE 12. CURTISS-WRIGHT CW-20E

35

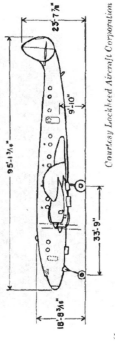

23'-7⅞"

95'-1⅜"

9'-0"

33'-9"

18'-8⅜"

Courtesy Lockheed Aircraft Corporation

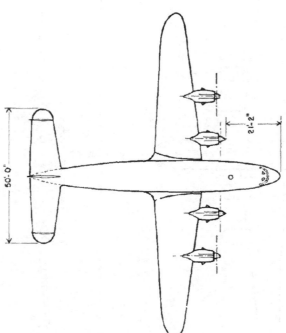

50'-0"

21'-2"

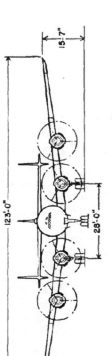

15'-7"

123'-0"

28'-0"

FIGURE 13. LOCKHEED CONSTELLATION

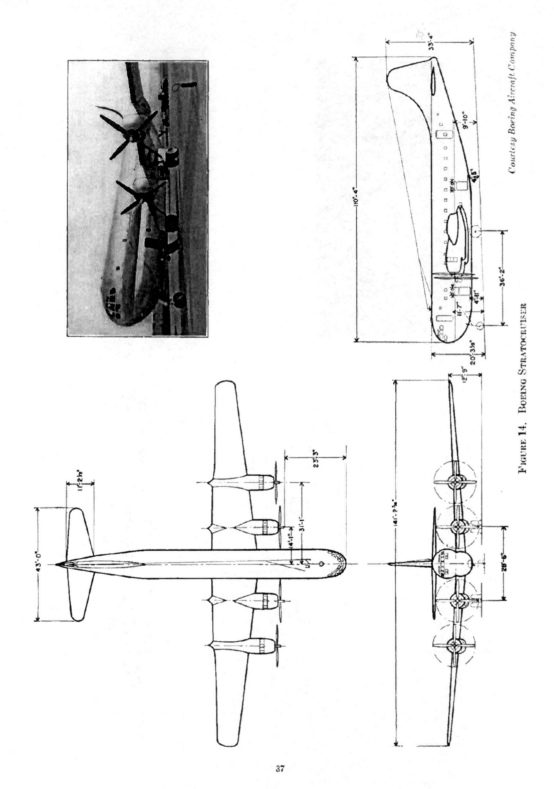

Courtesy Boeing Aircraft Company

Figure 14. Boeing Stratocruiser

37

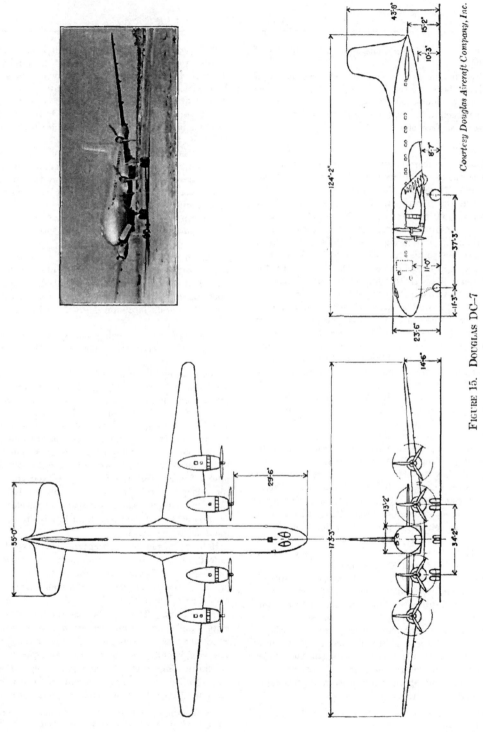

Courtesy Douglas Aircraft Company, Inc.

Figure 15. Douglas DC-7

38

fuel capacity of 21,000 gallons, and an oil capacity of 850 gallons

Mention should also be made of the possible use of large flying boats of the Martin Mars type and even larger ones for long-distance overwater flying, particularly where conditions at the termini points permit all-year operation free of ice.

Special Aircraft

Interest in commercial air cargo has been developing rapidly as the result of large military cargo movements by the Air Transport Command of the Army Air Forces and the Naval Air Transport Service of the U S Navy to all parts of the world Much discussion and experimentation have centered around the promotion of domestic and foreign air cargo, and the extent of the possible volume of business to be obtained in the future depends on its cost to the shipper and the benefits derived by the consumer from air shipments

It is obvious that in a competitive world air cargo will begin with the transport of goods and merchandise having a high intrinsic value per pound or per cubic foot Having captured this market and developed equipment permitting lower operating costs and rates, it can broaden its volume base to a point where it will compete with ground means of express transportation *

Raw materials of low value, such as coal and lumber, or heavy parts, such as steel castings and farm machinery, will continue to move by rail freight except, perhaps, in case of emergency needs

Calculations, combined with some speculation, indicate that flying wings, perhaps of the order of 300,000 pounds or more, to obtain at least 7-foot headroom clearance in the cargo loading area, would permit total operating costs sufficiently low to attract a very large volume of cargo The elimination of the fuselage as a load-carrying element is primarily a question of aircraft size, that is, the wing must be sufficiently large so that its thickness can serve as cargo compartment and permit ease of loading and unloading

The use of cargo gliders towed by cargo airplanes or what might virtually be termed "aerial locomotives" also offer possibilities for low operating costs per ton mile, particularly when operated in conjunction with pick-up devices to eliminate landings and take-offs to pick up gliders between termini points of a given route It can be said that the principal problem to be solved before cargo glider operation becomes practical is the development of air train operational technique for all weather conditions

The possibility of using large dirigibles for long-range overwater flying should not be totally disregarded Lighter-than-air craft of very large size have been conceived having lower operating costs than a fleet of airplanes of similar payload capacity An intensely practical study of the application of the airship has been made by Lt. Commander Neil MacCoull, U S N R, † which shows the utility value of the dirigible as a cargo carrier where maximum speed is of secondary importance and non-stop distances to be negotiated are great This analysis shows that the airship can be made to deliver four times as much cargo as the airplane per gallon of fuel consumed

Airships do not need airfields and can be handled from landing and take-off areas consisting of a large, level plot of ground, although their operation can be combined with that of aircraft used for industrial flying or cargo transport They should not be mixed with private flying activities or scheduled air transport traffic, as the former needs only small fields and the latter needs large-zoned areas, to be discussed in Part 6

Semi-rigid airships will probably be used for sight-seeing and advertising, as before, and for coastal patrol

Helicopters are still in the stage of development. They require considerably greater skill to fly than airplanes and, in the present state of the art, have definite limitations in size and speed The ability to land and take off from any clear plot of ground, as well as to hover above the ground at any height desired and move forward or backward at will, has endowed the helicopter with a utility which has gained considerable public favor But the difficulty of coordinating its controls is at present a bar to its popularization Furthermore, a great deal of thought and development is yet needed to bring its cost down to meet the means of the average private flyer.

Helicopters require no airport. They meet low-altitude flying requirements admirably, and their speed deficiency is offset by accessibility to traffic hubs to permit direct travel from point of traffic origin to ultimate destination without the use of any other means of transportation They can become the link between remote traffic generating centers and airline airports which are now connected by highways or rapid transit The Greyhound Bus Lines have contemplated such a system in connection with their ground operations and have applied to the Civil Aeronautics Board for permission to operate transport helicopters, as shown by

* "A Motor Carrier's View " by Michael H Froehch, *Flying*, July, 1944, AC-10

† "Transoceanic Air Cargo " by Lt Commander Neil Mac-Coull, U S N R , *S A E Journal*, October, 1944

the model illustrated in Fig. 16, in local air service for many thousands of route miles.

Figure 17 shows three different models of Sikorsky helicopters flying in formation. To the left is the R–4B, the first model to be built in quantity for the U. S. Army Air Forces; in the center is the R–5; and to the right, in the background, is the smaller R–6. Each seats two persons. The R–4B is powered with a

FIGURE 16. HELICOPTER AIR BUS

180-horsepower engine, and the R–5 with a 450-horsepower engine.

The extent to which the helicopter will be used as a private flying machine or as an aerial taxi is difficult to predict. Equipped with multiple rotors, it has been proposed for feeder operation and, as such, may find limited application because its relatively low speed is

FIGURE 17. SIKORSKY HELICOPTERS

offset by its ability to land nearer the ultimate destination of its passengers.

In view of the great engineering activity on helicopters, planning agencies should not eliminate them from considerations in their long-range planning, as witnessed by the PV-3 ten-passenger Piasecki transport helicopter designed for the U. S. Navy and Coast Guard by the P-V Engineering Forum to carry out

sea rescue and transport personnel, illustrated by Fig. 18.

Many of the engineering developments fostered by the war will contribute toward material improvement of future aircraft.

The tactical requirements of bombing missions have demanded the use of higher wing loadings, that is, the weight per square foot of wing area, and higher speeds. These requirements have been reflected in the creation of more efficient auxiliary lifting devices, wing flaps, and the like to keep landing speeds within human limitations, and airport runway length within reason. These improvements will find their place in larger and faster transport airplanes having great range with high payloads.

Wing loadings have increased 300 per cent in the last twenty years, during which time commercial air

FIGURE 18. PIASECKI TRANSPORT HELICOPTER

transportation has become an organized business. Yet power loadings are only 10 per cent lower than they were twenty years ago, thus reflecting a vast aerodynamic progress. The real limitation will remain the airport runway length dictated either by the rate of climb with one engine inoperative or by economic reasons. However, the application of assisted take-off means, either by auxiliary jet propulsion or mechanical means, may substantially increase the efficiency of aircraft without necessitating larger landing and take-off areas, particularly for long-range operation using heavily loaded airplanes.

Jet propulsion, although highly inefficient at low altitude, may, in combination with the conventional propeller driven by a gas turbine, provide an answer by combining excellent low-altitude performance with very high speeds at high altitude This offers great possibilities

The use of reversible pitch propellers will substantially reduce the landing run, save brakes, and increase operating safety

The application of controllable pitch propellers to light aircraft will greatly increase their take-off performance and economy

Wider use of modern materials will undoubtedly lower production costs which will automatically open wider markets

Engineering studies have shown that no technical obstacles limit the size of airplanes but that landplanes appear to be more efficient up to 250,000 to 300 000 pounds, with flying boats having the advantage at higher gross weights

This difference is indicated by a recent design analysis on a 480,000-pound gross weight flying boat powered with six engines totaling 28,880 horsepower. Such a flying boat would have a 250-foot wing span and an overall length of 175 feet Its wing loading would be 42 pounds per square foot, and power loading 16 6 pounds per horsepower The product of the wing and power loading would be 697 and, assuming a factor of 15 for such aircraft, its sea lane length would be but 10,455 feet

Effect of Aircraft Characteristics on Airport Size

Table II is a tabulation of aircraft characteristics which are of primary interest to the planner and designer of commercial airports Weights and wheel loads give an indication of the type of runway and apron needed to handle medium and large transport aircraft satisfactorily Turning diameters can be used to determine the size of aprons required to meet peak traffic periods Fuel and oil capacity have been added as bulk storage and refueling problems have become of great magnitude with large fleets and large airplanes

These are specifications which affect the layout and arrangement of ground airport facilities The most important airplane characteristics, however, are those of take-off and landing distances to meet the transport category rules of the U S Civil Air Regulations, known as 04 75T and 61 712, which became applicable to existing models and have to be met by all aircraft after December 1, 1947 Airplanes previously certificated, such as the DC-3, do not, obviously, come under these new regulations, which limit the stalling speed to 80 miles per hour for landing and require that operating runway length permit take-off *and* landing if the pilot so elects, immediately after reaching critical controlling speed in case of power plant failure after take-off

The Civil Aeronautics Board has recently revised these Civil Air Regulations by eliminating the fixed 80 miles per hour limit on stalling speed in favor of more realistic limitations imposed by other requirements such as climb performance and airport size. These new regulations become mandatory for new transport airplane designs to be flown for the first time after January 1, 1948

The airworthiness and operational requirements under which prewar transport airplanes were certificated were that they should be able to take off in not more than 1,000 feet, show good flying characteristics, demonstrate a rate of climb with one engine inoperative, and have a landing speed not greater than 65 miles per hour This phase of the regulations as affecting airport size is discussed at greater length in Part 6, "Airfield Planning," but as a guide for runway length evaluation Table III lists the take-off and landing distances of the transport airplanes used in the preparation of Table II

In a publication entitled *Airport Design,** issued by the Civil Aeronautics Administration of the U S Department of Commerce, a simple yardstick is given for determining runway length for the safe operation of any airplane It is based on the fact that airplane performance is related to wing loading, that is, the weight carried per square foot of wing area, and power loading, which is the weight carried by the total horsepower of the engine or engines used There are other important factors which also affect performance, such as pilot technique, which is affected by many variables, and particularly, the human element, the size of the airplane which effects "cushioning" on landing, the coefficient of tire tread friction to runway and landing area, as well as the character of such area surfaces, air temperature, and altitude

Leaving aside any possible variations in coefficient of lift obtained by the different types of auxiliary lifting devices, such as flaps and the like, the higher the wing loading, the higher the landing speed, and, vice versa, the lower the power loading for a given wing loading, the shorter the take-off distance

Table IV lists the gross weight, the landing speed, the product of the wing and power loading, and this product multiplied by 15 to derive an approximate safe runway length for each of the airplanes discussed in this chapter

Although this method of evaluating the relationship between a given airport and airplane is not absolutely applicable to all cases, particularly four-engine air-

* *Airport Design,* Civil Aeronautics Administration, U S Department of Commerce Washington, D C, 1944

TABLE II
AIRCRAFT SPECIFICATIONS OF PRIMARY IMPORTANCE FOR AIRPORT DESIGN *

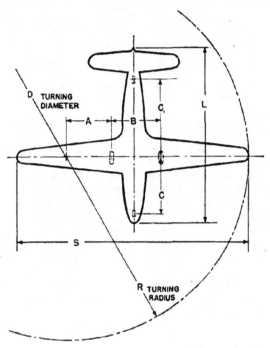

	Douglas DC-3	Martin 202	Curtiss-Wright CW-20E	Douglas DC-4	Lockheed Constellation	Boeing Strato-cruiser	Douglas DC-7
Span (S)	94' 7"	92' 9"	108' 1"	117' 6"	123'	141' 2\frac{3}{4}"	173' 3"
Length (L)	64' 5\frac{1}{2}"	71' 11"	76' 4"	93' 11"	95' 1\frac{1}{2}"	110' 4"	124' 2"
Take-off gross weight	25,200 lb	36,000 lb	50,200 lb	73,000 lb	92,000 lb	135,000 lb	162,000 lb
Landing weight	24,100 lb	34,300 lb	46,400 lb	63,500 lb	78,000 lb	121,700 lb	127,500 lb
Maximum static load on main wheels (right or left side)	11,575 lb	19,650 lb	23,000 lb	39,500 lb	43,000 lb	61,000 lb	76,800 lb
Maximum static load on nose or tail wheel	2,150 lb	3,900 lb	3,800 lb	11,700 lb	11,000 lb	13,500 lb	19,250 lb
Landing gear tread (B)	18' 6"	25'	25' 11"	24' 8"	28'	28' 6"	34' 2"
Landing gear wheelbase (C or C_1)	36'	22'	40'	27' 6"	33' 9"	36' 2"	37' 3"
Tire footprint area, sq in., per main wheel	237 MW	340 MW	336 MW	330 MW	300 MW	328 MW	452 MW
Loading per sq in. per tire area, MW	49 lb	51 lb	69 lb	64 lb	72 lb	93 lb	85 lb
Turning center to inner main wheels (A)	0 †	0 †	0 †	15' 2"	14' 4"	0 †	30'
Minimum turning radius (R)	57'	59'	72' 6"	86' 3"	90'	85'	131'
Clearance diameter for complete turn (D)	114'	118'	145'	172' 6"	180'	170'	262'
Fuel capacity, gal	822	650	1,056	2,875	4,800	7,055	11,000
Oil capacity, gal	66	34	46	88	184	280	340
Cabin door sill height from ground	3' 9"	7' 6"	6' 9"	8' 5"	9' 10"	9' 10"	10' 3"

* Weights, clearances, and capacities are variable according to aircraft loading and design changes to improve operating conditions. Figures shown can be taken as averages.

† The minimum turning radius of airplanes with full swivel tail wheels has been assumed to be that of the tire radius, thus permitting the wheel to make one complete revolution for a full airplane turn to prevent tire tread shearing loads.

TABLE III

	Douglas DC-3	Martin 202	Curtiss-Wright CW-20E	Douglas DC-4	Lockheed Constellation	Boeing Stratocruiser	Douglas DC-7
Take-off ground run	960'	1,200'	1,800'	2,000'	1,600'	. . . . .	. . . . .
Distance to reach 50' altitude	1,700'	2,000'	2,700'	3,400'	3,000'	. . . . .	. . . . .
Landing distance from 50' altitude	1,100'	2,100'	2,400'	2,700'	2,500'	. . . . .	. . . . .
Required CAA runway length, S.L.	3,500'	3,700'	5,200'	5,200'	5,300'	6,400'	9,500'

Note: These distances are approximate and for maximum permissible weights, sea level, and standard air conditions.

craft, it represents a workable method which can be applied by the airport planner in determining what constitutes a reasonable amount of land acreage, including provisions for subsequent expansion. A comparison is made of safe runway lengths calculated by the CAA formula, shown in Table IV, and figures derived from actual tests or accurate aerodynamic calculations, as shown in Table III. The differences should provide ample margin for runway surface conditions and errors in operating technique.

It can be noted in Table IV that the general belief that aircraft size and weight require proportionally larger landing facilities is erroneous. For instance,

TABLE IV

	(1) Gross or Landing Weight	(2) Landing Speed	(3) Wing Loading Power Loading	(4) * Safe Runway Length (3) × 15	(5) Safe Runway Length (3) × 12
Piper, Standard Trainer	1,220	38	136	2,040	
Piper, Super Cruiser	1,550	45	157	2,750	
Aeronca Arrow	1,450	48	170	2,550	
Ercoupe	1,260	48	170	2,550	
Thunderbolt Amphibian	2,600	53	226	3,390	
Stinson Reliant	4,000	48	209	3,140	
Beechcraft D17R	4,250	50	142	2,200	
Beechcraft 18S	7,850	61	166	2,400	
Lockheed Saturn	13,500	80	329	4,800	
Douglas DC-3	25,200	68½	268	4,020	
Curtiss-Wright CW-20E	50,200	80	339	5,085	
Douglas DC-4	73,000	80	455	6,830	5,820
Lockheed Constellation	92,000	80	515	7,720	6,180
Boeing Stratocruiser	130,000	80	682	10,020	8,190
Douglas DC-7	162,000	80	871	13,080	10,452

* It appears that the factor 15 is too high when applied to four-engine aircraft. The use of 12 as a factor gives a better approximation of safe runway length requirement for such aircraft, as shown in column 5.

while the Beechcraft 18S is six times the weight of the Piper Cub, its safe runway length requirement is but 17½ per cent more than that required for the Piper Cub. Similar comparison cannot readily be made with the larger aircraft because of the difference in permissible operating range. However, if the take-off

weight of the 4 four-engine transport aircraft listed is reduced to meet operating requirements for a maximum of 1,500 to 2,000 miles range, sufficient for domestic and continental operation, it will be found that they also can be safely operated from airports having a maximum runway length of 6,000 feet at sea level. It is only when maximum range is required, such as for transoceanic operation, that airport runway length needs to be greater. Thus it would appear that 8,000-foot runway length should be ample for major terminals and 10,000-foot runway length for terminals that serve as international airports.

Summary

In concluding this chapter on present and future aircraft, it is reasonable to expect that the performance of today's personal aircraft can be taken as standard for the determination of landing area sizes and facilities needed to handle them for the present as well as the future. The use of wing flaps, better cockpit visibility, and controllable pitch propellers will improve their performance, thus automatically increasing safety of flight, maneuverability, and landing approach for a given airport size. Also their size, that is, 2-, 4-, and 6- to 8-place capacity, will not materially change.

The two most popular sizes will remain as before, the small two-place aircraft for local flying, selling between $1,000 and $2,000, and the four-place cabin aircraft for touring, selling between $2,000 and $5,000, depending on performance desired and cabin appointments. Many of the aircraft in this class will be amphibians, that is, flying boats with retractable landing gear. Almost all of them will be powered with one engine.

The application of light aircraft for taxi work to supplement the taxicab where moderate distances must be traveled in the shortest possible time is a practical possibility.

Insofar as transport aircraft are concerned, impiovements in performance can be looked for primarily in speed without substantially changing take-off and landing characteristics definitely fixed by present U S Civil Air Regulations These regulations may be further liberalized to improve the economy of long-range aircraft which will mean longer runways for international airports This must be taken into consideration in the planning of superairports However, many technological improvements may offset this tendency to increase runway length and tend to reduce airport dimensions rather than increase them beyond the figures quoted in this chapter.

3

AIRWAY AND AIRPORT TRAFFIC CONTROL

Importance and Functions of Air Traffic Control

The fundamental reasons for any kind of traffic control are, first, to safeguard life and property by avoiding collisions and, second, to expedite the movement of such traffic in an orderly manner and prevent congestion and delay

The problems of handling ground vehicular traffic are relatively simple when compared to those applying to the control of aircraft flying in an invisibly charted medium It is a simple matter to stop a line of motor vehicles on a street or a highway to let others pass or cross their path In case of trouble, the vehicle affected drives to the side of the road without seriously retarding the flow of remaining traffic or changing its direction Furthermore, the same control methods and procedure apply in good and bad weather alike

Two basic characteristics of the airplane prevent the adaptation of these ways and means to the control of air traffic The airplane can fly in any direction and must keep on flying to stay aloft Thus a new direction to control is introduced, and traffic must always be kept in motion An airplane cannot stop in the air to let another pass, and when anything goes wrong it must land within a gliding range dictated by the altitude at which the trouble occurred The only possible exceptions are the lighter-than-air craft and the rotary wing aircraft which can hover as long as engine power is available It has been indicated in Part 2 that it is unlikely that rotary wing aircraft, either helicopter or autogiro, will form a very large proportion of future air traffic because of basic speed limitations However, if this aircraft is developed to a point where it can become popular, its large usage will add new traffic problems, particularly in metropolitan areas when it will be mixed with personal and transport airplanes landing at the same airports

Lighter-than-air craft are costly and must be large to be efficient Their commercial use in the past has been limited to advertising and, in a small way, to long-range transport operation

It has been estimated that the 25,000 odd prewar airplanes which used the domestic airways made about a million and a half take-offs and landings per year With several hundred thousand airplanes in operation and the predicted expansion in landing facilities, it is conceivable that landings and take-offs may reach fifty million yearly, and even more, in the comparatively near future

Aircraft and airports are material things which can be quickly designed and built, but their orderly, efficient, and economic utilization will depend on the conception and establishment of an airway and airport traffic control system to handle mass movements of all types of aircraft safely and expeditiously

Flight from point to point involves four basic actions First, the aircraft must take off from an airport and later land at an airport Second, it must be maintained in the proper attitude while in the air Third, it must be navigated from point to point and, fourth, it must be kept from colliding with other aircraft in flight as well as natural or man-made obstructions in the flight path. It is with the first and the last two that air traffic control is primarily concerned

The primary functions of air traffic control are

1 To regulate the movement of aircraft in flight along the airways by keeping each aircraft properly spaced along the airway it is following, with adequate lateral and vertical separation to avoid accident by collision, particularly when visibility is poor. This is known as *airway traffic control*

2 To direct aircraft desiring to take off or land from a given airport and guide them from and back to the airways within a predetermined controlling

45

area around such airport, and to do so in an orderly manner and with the least possible delay Also, to control the taxiing of arriving and departing aircraft on the airfield between the apron and the take-off runway This is known as *airport traffic control*

3 To disseminate weather and airway information to aircraft in flight and maintain airway and airport navigation aids in order This is known as *airways communications*

4 To regulate the movement of aircraft not flying the airways to prevent interference with airway traffic This may be defined as *general or non-airway traffic control* It is this type of control which must receive most serious study to arrive at a simple and effective solution if personal flying is to become a commonly accepted means of travel by a large number of people

Airway Traffic Control

Flying through the trackless air space was accomplished in the early days by visual contact with known landmarks This method was supplemented later with lighted beacons and reception of weather conditions at point of destination by two-way radio communication. With the advent of instruments for flying without natural horizon and the development of an instrument flying technique to use them, it became possible to fly safely in poor weather conditions without ground visibility. The necessity then arose for the need for invisible airway markings Such airway marking was accomplished by means of a simple system of radio beams emitting signals to indicate to the pilot, through his radio receiver earphones, the course to be followed The projections of these narrow radio beams form what might be termed an air highway system These beams transmitted by radio range stations mark out the domestic network of airways shown in Fig 1, which illustrates the domestic radio range system of the CAA Twice each minute, a special code signal is emitted, identifying each radio range station Intersecting radio beams, located off course and emanating from other airways, serve to provide "fix points" The radio range stations are usually located near a terminal airport or an intermediate landing field, and, whenever possible, they are so situated that one of the four courses lies along the principal runway of the landing area of the airport, thus facilitating radio approach landings under conditions of low visibility

Accurate position is obtained when passing over the range station Directly above the antennas or towers of the radio range stations there is a "cone of silence " This is a limited area shaped like an inverted cone

Just before the aircraft enters the cone of silence, the volume of the signal in the pilot's earphones increases rapidly As the aircraft enters the cone, the signals fade out abruptly for a few seconds, the length of time depending on the speed of the aircraft and the diameter of the cone at the altitude crossing is made. As the aircraft leaves the opposite side of the cone, the signals surge back with great volume before they begin to fade as the distance from the station increases

Because the cone of silence does not always provide a positive and reliable means of determining the exact position of a radio range station, so-called Z-type markers are installed at almost all radio range stations for this purpose They operate on an ultra-high frequency of 75 megacycles (75,000 kilocycles) and send out a small inverted cone-shaped signal field directly above the range station Owing to the high frequency used, a special receiver must be installed for their reception Upon passing over a Z-type marker, the pilot is furnished a positive check, both visually and aurally, the first by means of a small light on the instrument panel which reaches maximum brilliance directly over the station, and the second by a steady high-pitched signal which likewise reaches maximum intensity over the station Like the cone of silence, the duration of the Z-type marker indication increases with increasing flight altitude

In conjunction with the radio ranges, several other types of radio navigation aids are used along the airways Their main purpose is to assist the pilot of an aircraft in obtaining definite "fixes" of position at points intermediate between the range stations Among the most important of these supplementary aids are the following types of radio markers

Fan-Type Marker These high-frequency markers operating on 75 megacycles are used as position markers on the beams of certain radio ranges Their chief value is in conjunction with range stations serving congested traffic areas, such as New York and Chicago One such marker is usually placed on each beam of the range at some desirable distance from the station, such as 20 to 25 miles, and is used to facilitate traffic control about the station In addition, the markers provide the pilot with a positive check on his distance from the station, and by means of a coded signal, identify the beam

Inner Markers and Outer Markers are also provided at some locations to facilitate instrument approaches The inner marker is located at the boundary of the airfield in line with the runway aligned with the glide path, whereas the outer marker is generally located about 2 miles from the airfield boundary Figure 2 il-

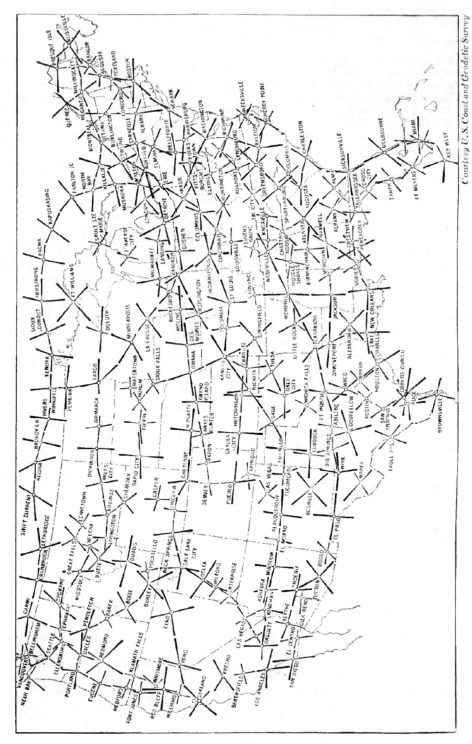

FIGURE 1. RADIO RANGE SYSTEM OF THE CAA

47

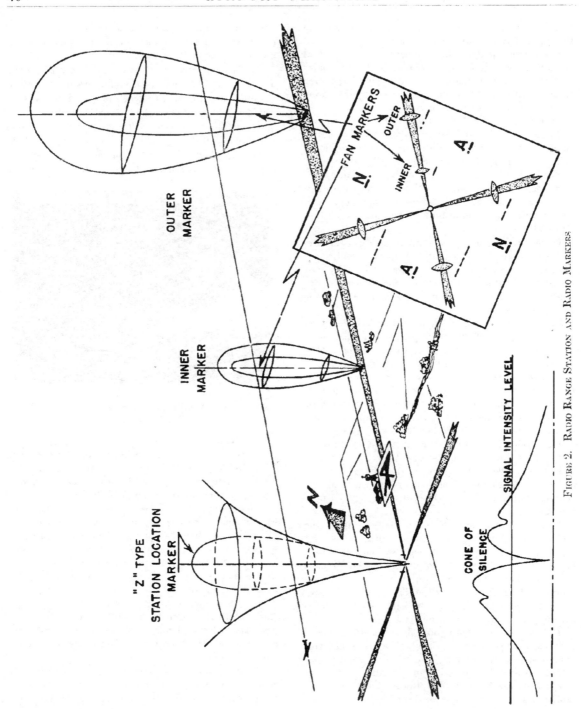

FIGURE 2. RADIO RANGE STATION AND RADIO MARKERS

lustrates diagrammatically a radio range station and the types of radio markers just discussed.

The airway pattern interconnecting all important cities today was gradually developed by linking major centers with direct routes and continually expanding from one city to another until it formed the zigzagging network of airways shown in Fig. 1.

In order to take full advantage of the greater range of larger aircraft, this airway pattern will be supplemented with a system of radio aids to navigation enabling all major cities to be connected by great circle routes having the shortest point-to-point distance, thus permitting faster schedules and lower operating costs. This arrangement will delegate the present airway network for the operation of limited stops and local schedules as before.

To obtain proper air separation, express schedules will fly at high altitudes, that is, 17,000 feet and above, whereas flying on the present airways will be carried below this altitude. Control of this separation can readily be accomplished by radio because of radio wave characteristics.

Radio waves propagate at approximately the speed of light, that is, 186,284 miles per second. Radiowise, a frequency is the number of cycles per second. Thus low frequencies mean long wave lengths and vice versa. The characteristic of long waves is to travel close to the earth. The short waves travel in straighter lines and are less affected by so-called global interferences. As the radio ranges which outline the airway network, shown in Fig. 1, are of the low-frequency type (200 to 400 kilocycles), they provide radio navigation aids for low-altitude flying, and the new VHF radio ranges (120 to 130 megacycles) serve to channelize great circle courses, until such time as the newer electronic developments can be adapted to control all air traffic domestically.

As a matter of fact, the CAA plans to apply the VHF radio range system to the present airways. By replacing the low-frequency range stations with very high-frequency range stations suitably spaced, perhaps 100 miles apart, and duplicating their frequency every fourth station, it would be possible to fly anywhere along the airways with aircraft equipped with a receiver permitting 4-frequency tuning. Long-range and high-altitude aircraft could fly great circle courses between high-powered stations of intermediate frequency spaced approximately 1,000 miles apart.

Offices under the direction of the Airways Control Division of the Civil Aeronautics Authority were established to control and coordinate the movement of airplanes in good and bad weather. Today there are twenty-three areas covering the entire United States,

and each area is in charge of an airway traffic control center which regulates the flow of air traffic along its portion of the civil airways.

The prime purpose of airway traffic control is to create fixed air channels or imaginary roadways. It is obvious that without definitely allocated flight paths it would be virtually impossible to control aircraft movements without collisions. These airways—10 miles wide and 17,000 feet high—permit an orderly flight pattern by allowing regulation of the distance between any two aircraft flying in the same direction along a

Courtesy CAA

FIGURE 3. AUTOMATIC AIRWAY TRAFFIC POSITION RECORDER

given airway as well as the altitude separation between them and those flying in the opposite direction. Thus, by assigning "air spaces" as each airplane progresses on the airway, a semblance to the well-known "block system" of the railroad is obtained.

The control of these airways must be coordinated locally to insure proper flow into each airport and also integrated regionally to prevent airway congestion, as experienced at large centers by what is commonly known as "stacking" during instrument landing conditions and peak traffic hours. By stacking is meant the holding of aircraft above given fixes near an airport, with proper altitude separation, thus forming a stack while the aircraft at the bottom of the stack proceeds to land. Proper and accurate control, however, depends today on information received from aircraft in flight.

The determination of the exact position of an aircraft on the airways by its pilot is a simple matter in good weather, but it depends on good navigation and the correct interpretation of radio signals in instrument flying weather as well as accurately and quickly reporting such position to the airway traffic control center for posting and follow-up.

As to the mechanics of operation of each airway traffic control center and since even the normal flow of air traffic is too complex for one man to follow, each control area is subdivided into sectors, each manned by an air traffic controller who is responsible for all aircraft operating within his sector to assure a smooth and orderly flow of traffic. To control this traffic, he posts on narrow strips of paper progress information on each flight. These strips are slid into strip holders clipped on flight progress boards. The boards are divided into sections, one for each major radio fix along the airways. Thus the controller is able to obtain a clear picture of every airplane flying on his sector.

However, with the rapidly rising volume of air traffic and increased flying speeds, this method is entirely too slow and requires too much work. The Civil Aeronautics Authority has designed and built automatic recording equipment similar to the automatic ticker tape stock quotation recording boards in brokerage offices (Fig. 3).

Airport Traffic Control

The problem of controlling and air-spacing aircraft along the airways is not so serious as the problem of handling incoming and departing aircraft, particularly the incoming. This problem is critical today and will probably remain so during conditions of poor visibility until the time when instrument landings can be accomplished as quickly as landings under unlimited ceiling and visibility.

Approach on instruments today is necessary when visibility and ceiling are below certain minimums, which vary according to the topography of the terrain surrounding the airport. They are, however, minimums until such time as complete instrument landing

systems have been installed at all airports used by scheduled air carriers. But even by using the best instrument landing system it appears that thirty blind landings per hour are the maximum that can be hoped for at this time. With dual parallel runways and a suitable air pattern allowing a similar number of take-offs per hour, a total of sixty aircraft movements can be obtained. This number is only half the capacity of a good dual parallel runway system under unlimited ceiling and visibility conditions. This relatively low efficiency in poor visibility is due primarily to the inability to space flights uniformly on the approach path and the time element required for airplane-to-ground communication should a change in instructions be needed in the event of a missed approach; also, the time required to vacate one level and descend to another while maintaining the basic holding pattern.

To grasp fully the procedure involved and present it in its simplest form, reference is made to Fig. 4, which illustrates a typical instrument approach and landing procedure. After passing over the Z marker of the radio range near the airport, and knowing beforehand the relative location of the airport and the range station, the pilot descends at a given rate and airspeed for a given time. He then makes a "procedure turn" to orientate the aircraft toward the airport on which he is to land, continuing to descend until he again flies over the Z marker of the range, but at a much lower altitude. This altitude is invariably higher than the authorized airport minimum and sometimes higher than the actual ceiling of the overcast, thus requiring further descending on instrument from final crossing of the range station to the authorized minimum ceiling for the airport on which landing is to be made. At that time he should break through the overcast, bringing the airport in plain sight for a normal contact landing. This operation takes a minimum of approxi-

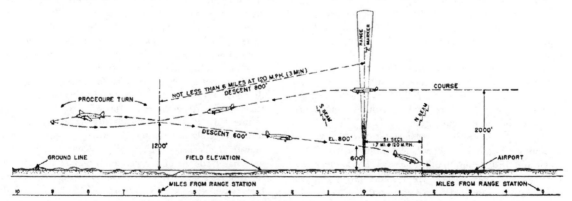

FIGURE 4. INSTRUMENT APPROACH AND LANDING PROCEDURE

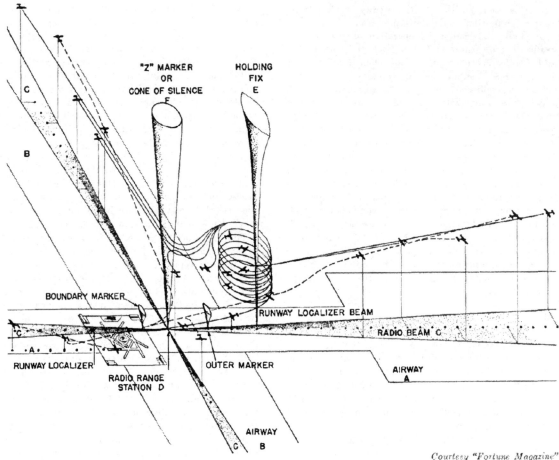

"Z" MARKER
OR
CONE OF SILENCE
F

HOLDING
FIX
E

BOUNDARY MARKER

RUNWAY LOCALIZER BEAM

RADIO BEAM C

RUNWAY LOCALIZER

OUTER MARKER

AIRWAY
A

RADIO RANGE
STATION D

AIRWAY
B

FIGURE 5. INSTRUMENT FLIGHT PROCEDURE

mately 10 to 12 minutes. Thus, whereas it is possible to land an aircraft on a given runway at an airport at the rate of 30 per hour in good weather, poor visibility will reduce this capacity to one-fifth of this figure at best.

It is to lower this procedure time that instrument landing systems were developed. But as the time required by such systems still falls short of good weather operation, some "stacking" will continue to be experienced during peak hour traffic.

Figure 5 shows in diagrammatic perspective the principle of operation of a typical integration of airways and instrument landing system for a given airport, as conceived by the Air Traffic Control Division of the Civil Aeronautics Administration. While flying the airways, aircraft are directed by the radio range beam C emanating from the radio range station D, and they are in constant two-way radio communication with the airport control tower which advises each aircraft as to what altitude it should maintain. Lateral separation of aircraft moving in opposite direction is obtained by flying on the proper side of the beam as dictated by airway traffic rules, and aircraft flying in the same direction are further separated by time. Aircraft coming in the airway A hold their course until they pass the holding fix at E, and then begin to circle as shown. Aircraft coming in on the airway B continue until they pass over the Z marker or cone of silence of the range station D and join the holding fix circle. Every two minutes, the airport control tower directs the aircraft at the bottom of the stack to slide out and begin its final approach to the airport, instructing all other aircraft in the stack to descend to the next lower level and keep circling As each aircraft slides out of the bottom of the stack, it picks up the instrument landing beam and proceeds to land By equipping the control tower with radar equipment, in addition to its two-way radio communication, the airport controller can virtually see each aircraft approaching the field and give emergency directions if necessary

While this landing procedure is going on, departing aircraft follow the radio beam, taking off from another runway After leaving the airport, they take their place on the airways as directed by the air traffic controller through the airport control tower

To forestall air traffic congestion as the volume of personal and schedule flying increases, much greater attention must be devoted to the circulation of aircraft around an airport or system of airports, as the case may be By circulation is meant proper channelization of all air traffic to assure maximum air traffic control efficiency and to utilize properly the capacity of any airport or group of airports in any given region under all kinds of weather conditions Three fundamental factors are involved·

Adequate separation of airports
Proper segregation of air traffic
Uniform airport approach

Adequate Separation of Airports

The spacing of airports or any other landing facilities in any region or metropolitan center depends primarily on the shape of the air traffic pattern for each airport serving the area It has been suggested that, for strictly contact operation, various types of landing facilities be separated as follows.

Class I airport—2-mile radius, that is, 4-mile spacing
Class II airport—2½-mile radius or 5-mile spacing
Class III airport—3-mile radius or 6-mile spacing
Class IV airport and above—4-mile radius or 8-mile spacing

Although these separations may be perfectly satisfactory under contact operating conditions, they fall short of the required air space for simultaneous operation under instrument weather conditions For instance, if it is found that 6- or 7-mile radius is needed for operation in poor visibility at a major airport, all flying must cease at any and all secondary airports within this radius, thus limiting their utility to good weather use.

The proximity of one landing area to another will be determined by the type of aircraft using the airport and the type of operations being conducted For landing aircraft, a straight-in approach should be made from an altitude of not less than 300 feet as an absolute minimum, and preferably from 500 feet At a rate of descent not to exceed 500 feet per minute, it means that the straight-in approach must be made from approximately one minute from the edge of the runway, maximum, and the distance will depend on the gliding speed of the airplane No two airports should be so close together that circling aircraft are closer than half a mile from each other, and possibly farther apart than this The distance away from an airport needed for circling depends on the speed of the aircraft A plane flying at 120 miles per hour will make a 180-degree turn in 1 minute if banked at approximately 15 degrees However, an aircraft flying at 180 miles per hour will make a 180-degree turn in approximately 2 minutes if banked at approximately 15 degrees, and in order to make the turn in 1 minute it would have to be banked at approximately 30 degrees It may be seen, therefore, that in the first case, if the approach was being made downwind, the airplane would have to approach approximately 1¼ miles off the runway to be used and would have to be approximately 3 miles downwind from the end of the runway at the farthest point in turning in to land In the second case, if the bank were kept to 15 degrees, the plane would have to make its approach approximately 3 miles off the center line of the runway and would be approximately 5 miles off the end of the runway at the farthest point during its turn in for a landing In the latter case, two airports so situated that they would be using runways in line with one another would have to be at least 12 miles apart for safe operation

Obviously, little can be done about existing airports which have insufficient separation except to protect their continued usefulness to the largest possible extent, but the ever-present danger is a tendency to develop new facilities too close to existing ones without giving proper consideration to their individual air space requirements for satisfactory operating traffic patterns There is a general agreement that all runways of all airports used for scheduled commercial air transportation and at least one runway of non-scheduled commercial airports shall be used for instrument landing with straight-in approaches This presumption should definitely be made for planning purposes Furthermore, it is safe to anticipate that air traffic patterns must be identical for both contact and instrument operation in order to permit standardization of airport procedures and promote safety of operation.

The majority of airports will probably be of the single- or dual-runway type; and whereas the air traffic pattern will be essentially the same for both types, the diameter of the air traffic pattern or "umbrella" may vary considerably, thus requiring similar variations in separation. Available area, accessibility, local weather, and many other factors will continue to influence the selection of new landing facilities as it has in the past, but their relative location to existing facilities must be thoroughly analyzed if they are to be utilized to the full extent of their projected capacity.

It may thus be found that to locate an airpark 6 miles from a major airport will be satisfactory if the airpark ceases operation under instrument weather conditions. Likewise, if the umbrella for such a major airport is found to cover a 10-mile radius for operation in poor visibility conditions, no other airport can be located within this radius if it also contemplates

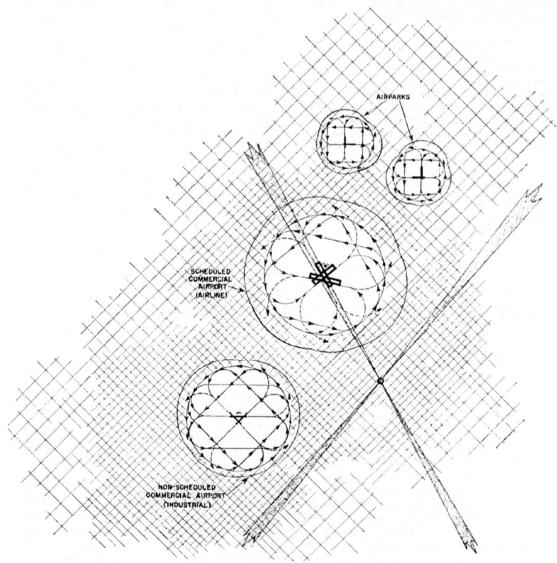

FIGURE 6. REGIONAL AIRPORTS SHOWING CLEARANCES

instrument operation   The spacing between such airports should be equal to the radius of the air umbrella for both plus a reasonable tolerance for errors in operation   Similarly, it may be found that airparks do not need 4-mile separation

Figure 6 illustrates a hypothetical area showing possible air traffic pattern areas and clearances   It emphasizes the importance of thoroughly studying the air traffic pattern for each type of airport to eliminate interference under all wind conditions and obtain maximum utility by proper location and runway orientation

Proper Segregation of Air Traffic

When a large volume of mixed traffic is expected to be controlled, it will be found desirable to assign definite flight areas and altitudes to each type of traffic   For instance, personal airplanes used for local flying and commuting might be excluded from the airways and limited to an altitude of 1,000 feet   Similarly, scheduled air transport aircraft would have to remain above 1,500 feet up to a 4- to 6-mile radius limit on the airways   Helicopters might be restricted to 500 feet within metropolitan areas

Traffic at small fields used primarily in good weather or emergencies can be controlled readily by proper runway outline and a wind direction indicator, which can be either a wind sock mounted atop a hangar or pole or a tee and a red warning flag used in case the field is unsafe for landing   If such landing facilities are to be used at night also, lights will need to be added, with a red and green control signal light

Landing facilities which meet the specifications of Civil Aeronautics Administration Class I and II fields do not require two-way radio facilities, as a receiver for obtaining Weather Bureau information is sufficient   However, although visual control seems satisfactory for the time being, increases in air traffic will eventually demand that radio traffic control apply to all fields and airports

Uniform Airport Approach

Any selected form of air traffic pattern and control must meet the civil air regulations concerning take-off and landing rights of way, circling of airfield, approach procedure in good or instrument weather, and overtaking and passing on the airways, thus definitely affecting such pattern for any given area

The approach control pattern will depend on the location of the airport or airports in relation to the airways serving it and the orientation of the airport runway system   It has been pointed out that multiple airports should be laid to permit simultaneous operation with safe separation.   The first step is to select locations which will prevent confusion in the overall air traffic pattern in good or instrument weather   No traffic pattern should overlap another, and each airport must, of course, have its own instrument landing system   The importance of the overall airway and airport traffic control pattern for any community or region cannot be overemphasized   It must be carefully conceived as well as planned jointly by all agencies concerned with the development of landing facilities and city planning

The control of air traffic, under poor visibility conditions, around an airport is a problem which has not yet been solved   The lack of solution may suggest additional airports to relieve congestion by decentralizing air traffic, either by segregation of different types of air traffic, such as airline traffic and industrial and personal flying in metropolitan centers, or by dividing the total volume of air traffic among several landing facilities   It is admitted that segregation or division is not entirely desirable because it limits the overall utility of aircraft   But the operating characteristics of each type of aircraft require that it be done in the interest of safety, just as motorboat docks are separated from ocean-going liner piers

The Airport Control Tower

The nerve center of an airport is its control tower   The safety of operation and effective capacity of any airport depend to a large degree upon the ability of the personnel manning its control tower   It is obvious that to forestall air traffic congestion as the volume of personal and schedule flying increases—particularly in metropolitan areas—much greater attention must be devoted to the proper circulation of aircraft around an airport, or system of airports, as the case may be

The airport controller directs the movement of aircraft on the ground and in the air within the airport zone, either departing or arriving   To do this effectively, the control tower must be located so as to command an unobstructed view of the airfield, that is, from the parking apron to the farthest point of any runway and its approaches   Visibility of the approach ends of all runways from the control tower, in good weather, cannot be overemphasized   It becomes a problem with runway lengths of the order of 8,000 feet and longer because, even with unlimited ceiling, haze and smoke often restrict visibility to approximately 5,000 feet   One answer is to use a mobile traffic control tower during restricted visibility which can plug in at various stations of the airfield and operate the central control tower transmitters by remote control   This has been done successfully

The walls of the control tower room and, in some cases, its roof are large, unobstructed glass panes, arranged at angles which will cause the minimum glare and reflection. They are colored to minimize eye strain, and those facing the airfield are equipped with window wipers to keep them clean in snow or rain. The control tower is generally located atop the administration building for the sake of convenience, as offices for the local Civil Aeronautics Administration and Weather Bureau are, as a rule, also located in the administration building. It is, in addition, a radio sta-

Courtesy Caldwell-Wright Airport,
Curtiss-Wright Corporation

FIGURE 7. CALDWELL-WRIGHT AIRPORT CONTROL TOWER

tion, both receiving and sending, in order to keep in constant communication with aircraft proposing to take off and land or flying over the airport reporting their position. It issues information to pilots regarding airport conditions, airway traffic, speed and direction of ground winds, barometric pressure, and other important information for the safety of operation.

Figure 7 is an excellent example of an airport control tower as applicable to a Class II or Class III airport.

Figure 8 illustrates a typical layout for a control tower serving a small airport. Note the signal light used to flash either a red or green light to aircraft not

equipped with radio. Figure 9 illustrates an airport control room applicable to an industrial airport.

Figure 10 is a photograph of the interior of the Washington National Airport tower, showing the runway control board on the desk of the controller. Fig-

Courtesy CAA

FIGURE 8. CONTROL TOWER ROOM FOR SMALL AIRPORT

ure 11 illustrates the exterior of this tower from the airfield and shows the revolving beacon atop the tower, anemometer, obstruction lights, and clock on its front face.

Courtesy CAA

FIGURE 9. AIRPORT CONTROL ROOM APPLICABLE TO INDUSTRIAL AIRPORT

Although many landing facilities and small airports today do not have an airport traffic control tower, the authors feel that none should be planned without it. Its need may not be felt at the beginning owing to low air traffic volume, but as flying activity increases, it will be necessary to control and direct such activity to utilize fully the capacity of the airfield.

The layout of a typical control tower design is shown in Fig. 12. Floor space should be at least 150 square feet, size depending on type and capacity of airport. For instance, it is estimated that the floor area of the Idlewild superairport control tower will need to be 8,000 square feet to provide adequate space for control

Courtesy CAA

FIGURE 10. AIRPORT CONTROL TOWER ROOM, WASHINGTON NATIONAL AIRPORT

boards, controller stations, radio equipment, teletype system, and communications. This space does not appear excessive for an airport which is expected ultimately to handle 360 airplane movements per hour and coordinate the air traffic pattern for the Greater New York area.

A modern tower should also be equipped with radio communication for emergency purposes in order to permit it to communicate with its fire and emergency airport truck and local police cars, thus being able to police the entire airport area effectively and quickly.

Improvements in Air Traffic Control

The present methods and procedures followed for the control of airway and airport traffic control in the United States must be radically improved in order to utilize fully the possibilities of the airplane as a common means of transportation. These methods and pro-

cedures have definite limitations which must be overcome in order to speed up air traffic movements and increase the permissible air traffic density within a given air space.

Their fundamental defect is that in poor visibility the airway and airport controller must rely on the pilot of an aircraft in flight for information to determine the position of such aircraft on the airway. This means that air separation, in both altitude and distance, must be several times greater than required in good weather. Furthermore, this information must be imparted by means of two-way radio conversation, which is slow, with the result that posting in the airways control center is always behind time. With aircraft having approximately the same cruising speed, the airport controller is able to form a pattern which,

Courtesy CAA

FIGURE 11. AIRPORT CONTROL TOWER, WASHINGTON NATIONAL AIRPORT

although late, can be fairly accurate. But with the advent of aircraft having a wide range of cruising speeds, this task becomes increasingly complex and definitely limits the number of aircraft which can be controlled at any one time. The capacity of the airway then becomes a function of communications and personnel limitations, both on the ground and in the air, involving the human capacity for work.

To meet the requirements of scheduled air transportation, which may well employ several thousand airplanes compared to the few hundreds flown today, radieal departures in air traffic control, along the airways and within the control area of the airport, must be conceived. Thus far, in instrument flying weather, the pilot has had to work out his own navigation and orientation problems, as well as landing procedures, hav-

mum of approximately 2½ minutes, which means at best a maximum of twenty-four blind landings per hour. During this flight procedure, the airport controller must depend entirely on radio information from the airplane making the approach to place it within the airport control area. This means that only one airplane can be handled at a time, preventing any other movement at the same time.

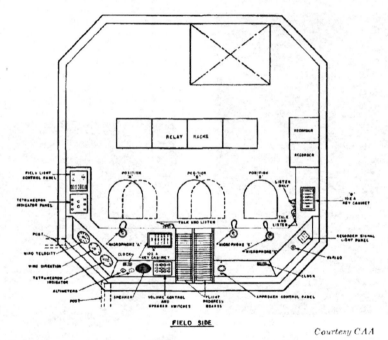

FIELD SIDE

Courtesy CAA

FIGURE 12. TYPICAL AIRPORT CONTROL ROOM PLAN

ing at his disposal the radio range and marker beacons. Recently, landing beams directing him and locating his direction with reference to the landing runway have been satisfactorily tested. This localizer beam, in conjunction with fan markers, gives him his position fairly accurately during an approach so that when he breaks through the overcast or ground fog he finds himself at the beginning of the airport runway ready for a landing. However, the flight procedures involved, that is, passing over the Z marker of the radio range as a preliminary fix, then making a precision turn to pick up the airport localizer beam at the correct altitude, following it to the ground and getting location by passing the outer and inner markers, take time and a great deal of attention which should rightfully be devoted to flying the airplane.

Recent tests have indicated that to go through the above procedure in zero-zero weather requires a mini-

To increase the capacity of an airport in instrument weather, it may be found necessary to reverse the procedure and have the airport control tower direct—or actually fly—the airplane to the ground from the time it enters its control area. It will also be equally essential that the pilot of an approaching aircraft receive, automatically and continuously, all the necessary information, aural and visual, to give him an accurate indication of what is in the air. The airlanes must be open for approach flight and landing to enable the pilot to carry out his own control procedure and instructions from the airport control tower according to the regulations governing the region.

Furthermore, with mass movements, as must be expected to be handled during peak hour airport operation, it will be necessary for the airport controller to have, instantly, accurate knowledge of the location and altitude of all airplanes which are expected to land within the airport at any given time Recent electronic developments such as pulse modulation, will permit this to be accomplished Ground search radar can also have a definite place as an aid and adjunct for aircraft not equipped with pulse electronic equipment For instance, it is conceivable that the present radio range might be replaced with a series of two-way radio beacons which could automatically record the passing of a plane overhead, as well as its altitude, and transmit this information back to the airplane flying over it and to the airport control tower at the same time The information could be recorded at the airport on a master board similar to the control board of a railroad dispatcher office To do this, all that would be needed on the airplane would be an automatic transmitter emitting a given code signal, which would be screened by the recording beacon for transmission to the airport

When the airplane entered the airport control area, this automatic airway check would be taken over by the airport controller, who by means of electronic scanning would register the position of all airplanes in the terminal control and approach areas on radar screens, and direct each by radio voice along a predetermined flight path around the airport air space to the end of the runway As the airplane would circle closer to the airport boundary, losing altitude at the same time, sharp fan markers properly located could serve as visual check for the pilot—to follow the directions of the airport tower controller It would thus be possible for the airport controller to direct several airplanes on the glide path as well as caution any airplane which appeared to be too close to other traffic, and control it accordingly.

By having a visual indication on the electronic screen, actuated by scanning disks, of every airplane within its control area, it becomes an easy matter to guide each plane orally to the end of the runway with greater speed and accuracy than can be possible by having each pilot work out his own flight path By this procedure, it should be possible eventually to bring in airplanes in totally blind weather at the rate of thirty to forty-five per hour This procedure is predicated on the same "approach" speed for every airplane thus handled Thus for mixed traffic it may be that fast airplanes will be brought together and slower-speed ones likewise unless airplane designs progress to a point where all airplanes, large or small, feeders and limiteds, can approach at the same speed

In a paper entitled "Traffic Control Problems for

Future Airports," [*] M G Beard, director of flight engineering for American Airlines, Inc, outlines an automatic system of traffic control possessing the following basic features

(1) A central traffic control system having automatic indication of the position of each plane in the control area as well as individual plane identification

(2) The central control to have all transmitting facilities necessary to set up all tracks for all planes leaving and entering the area and to transmit takeoff and landing runway assignments and frequencies to all planes in the control area This traffic information to be automatically received and indicated in the plane

(3) All planes allowed in the control area to have automatic receiving and indicating equipment and panels to show all necessary data such as traffic lane frequency, landing and takeoff runway, and prescribed altitude, also visual indication of traffic lane to be followed and visual portrayal of landing runway outline Assignments to be made and received by plane before entering the control area

(4) All planes to be equipped with obstruction indication devices scanning 180° ahead and giving continuous indication of this area Scanning of the 180° to the rear may be done intermittently if weight-saving and simplification of apparatus are gained by this reduction

(5) All planes to have necessary radio for the instrument landing system used at the airport, in addition to the panel indication of Item (3)

(6) Absolute altimeter and automatic direction finder should function in conjunction with other radio to provide distance indication and direction from the centrally located traffic control transmitter antenna, thus providing a double check on circling path and landing glide path indicators

(7) Two-way radio communication to be used in emergencies only when a plane loses signal, gets out of line, or is having difficulty

The runway localizer and glide path system of instrument landing supplemented by Ground Approach Control radar, known as GCA should meet the qualifications outlined above and expedite operation in bad weather.

It might be added that to permit simultaneous takeoffs and landings, approach within the airport control air space should be made at a relatively high altitude, say 3,000 feet to 4,000 feet, and take-off altitude limited to one-half that height, thus preventing any possibility of collision

The swift strides in radio technology have upset the fixed conceptions and well-thought-out procedures for radio communication and radio navigation used since the development of instrument weather flying Control equipment is being automatized more and more, permitting the improving and expediting of procedures to meet gradually increasing air traffic control demands. The improvements forcefully accelerated by

[*] "Traffic Control Problems for Future Airports," by M G Beard, *Aeronautical Engineering Review*, July, 1944, The Institute of the Aeronautical Sciences, New York, N Y

the war may even render the present system of air traffic control obsolete in a comparatively short time because the efficiency of airway and airport operation as well as the safety of flight will decrease at a greater rate than air traffic growth unless a vastly improved air traffic control system is instituted A satisfactory solution requires that the method of controlling air separation by time be replaced by space control, and that such space separation between aircraft be accomplished automatically It will mean relieving the airway traffic controller of his present responsibility to maintain separation and permit him to devote his time to the arrangement and planning of aircraft movements However, it will also require that, within the airport approach zone, the speed of landing aircraft be governed to maintain proper space separation if contact rate operation is to prevail during instrument landing conditions

Bibliography

"Engineering the Airways," *Fortune*, November, 1943

"Improving Air Traffic Control," by Glen A Gilbert, *Flying*, January, 1945

"Sight Unseen," by Gerard E Nistal, *Air Tech*, July, 1944

"Air Traffic Control Limitations,' by Glen A Gilbert, *Flying*, November, 1944

"Sky Highways," by David E Postle, *Flying*, July, 1944

The Coming Air Age, by Reginald M Cleveland and Leslie E Neville, Whittlesey House, McGraw-Hill Book Co, New York, 1944

"A System Specification for Air Navigation and Traffic Control Development," by S P Saint, *Society of Automotive Engineers Paper*, 1945

4

AIRPORT TYPES

Need for Airports

History seems to repeat itself. The automobile preceded the network of highways, and the development of the airplane is preceding the development of suitable accommodations to service and house it on the ground. The time has come when a closer relationship must exist between the airplane and its landing facilities because of the capital investment required to build new facilities, both in size and number. Furthermore, these facilities must be conceived for a greater degree of permanence and utility. The community which does not provide landing facilities to meet its requirements—whether they be for personal, industrial, or scheduled air transport—will lose the benefits inherent in flying and forfeit its place among the progressive and forward-looking towns and cities that keep pace with the growth of our national and international economy.

The full measure of the utility of any aircraft cannot be obtained without providing adequate landing and take-off facilities for its operation. These facilities must be geared to the type of service to be rendered if maximum usefulness plus safety is to be realized.

The question of safety is very important if flying is to become a commonly accepted means of travel. Safety will demand the establishment of airports to a much larger degree than now anticipated. The need for more and better airports is great * and must be satisfied to stimulate and promote widespread interest in aviation. They must be of the right kind and located in the proper places to do the most good.

It has been said that an airport is like a telephone. It has little value by itself but becomes increasingly useful as its numbers grow. Taking off and landing always at the same airport is most monotonous and is

* *National Airport Plan, 1945*, Civil Aeronautics Administration, U S Department of Commerce, Washington, D C

not conducive to improving the utility of personal aircraft or to promoting flying, even for pleasure. Many extravagant schemes have been advanced to provide facilities for the private flyer as well as the commercial air traveler. Some have been conceived without a fundamental knowledge of the history of past transportation development, which has been evolutionary rather than revolutionary. Upon ground facilities depend the safe beginning and ending of any flight.

The airplane, as was the case with all motor vehicles which preceded it, will decentralize our daily activities to a degree proportional to its speed. The time traveling to and from housing or parking facilities and the overall cost of transportation plus availability of airports will remain the fundamental factors to affect the extent of its use.

In the early days of aviation, flying fields, as they were known then, were chosen to meet the landing and take-off characteristics of airplanes of that period, and consisted primarily of sod landing areas wherever they could be found and acquired. Later these areas were marked with a circle at their center and crude hangars were built on one side of such fields, preferably adjoining a highway. A wind cone was added to indicate the wind direction to the pilot. Still later, hard surface runways in given directions were developed and a small administration building was added. Thus many such airports just grew to their present configuration without definite plans for lack of knowledge as to what stage of development the airplane would eventually reach, and how it would ultimately be used.

Although the development of the airplane has by no means reached a static stage, its design and operation have advanced to a point where further improvement can be reasonably predicated without revolutionary changes which would necessitate the scrapping of ground facilities planned for its orderly and rational use now. This means that one can classify the types of airport facilities with a fair degree of accuracy ac-

60

cording to flying activity and individual community needs.

Airport Classifications

All the flying activities listed in Table I of Part 2 can be carried out from four principal categories of airports:

1. Airports for the operation of personal aircraft.
2. Airports for industrial uses and fixed base operations (non-scheduled commercial).
3. Airports for scheduled air carriers (which may be used only under controlled conditions by personal aircraft).
4. Airports owned by the federal government for the exclusive use of its military and research establishments.

Table I shows the official classification of airports of the Civil Aeronautics Administration of the U. S. Department of Commerce, according to type of community served, as given in its publication, *Airport Design*.

Tables II, III, IV, and V, also taken from this informative publication, list airport size, planning standards, lighting standards, spacing of runways, and recommended clearances between runways and airport buildings, and also taxiway layouts for each of the five classes of airports shown in Table I.

Class I airport requires a minimum area of 60 to 150 acres, depending upon the airfield layout, its location, and the length of landing strips. Similarly, Class II requires a minimum area of 160 to 250 acres; Class III, 300 to 500 acres; Class IV, 550 to 750 acres; and Class V, 800 acres and over, depending on the configuration of the runway system, buildings, hangar areas, and other accommodations.

In 1944, the average size of all *airports* in the United States was 368 acres. Class I airports averaged 117

TABLE I

RECOMMENDED AIRPORT DESIGN STANDARDS FOR COMMUNITIES, CITIES, AND METROPOLITAN AREAS

Type of Community	Planning Classification	Recommended Landing Strip Lengths, Sea Level Conditions, Clear Approaches *	Type of Aircraft Which Airport May Safely Accommodate
Small communities not on present or proposed scheduled air carrier system, and auxiliary airports in larger metropolitan areas to serve non-scheduled private flying activities.	1	1,800′ to 2,700′	Small private-owner type planes. This includes roughly planes up to a gross weight of 4,000 lb, or having a wing loading (lb/sq ft) times power loading (lb/hp) not exceeding 190.
Larger communities located on present or proposed feeder line airways and those which have considerable aeronautical activity. General population range 5,000 to 25,000.	2	2,700′ to 3,700′	Larger-size private-owner planes and some small-size transport planes. This represents roughly planes in the gross weight classification between 4,000 and 15,000 lb, or having a wing loading (lb/sq ft) times power loading (lb/hp) of 190 to 230.
Important cities on feeder line airway systems and many intermediate points on the main line airways. General population range 25,000 to several hundred thousand.	3	3,700′ to 4,700′	Present-day transport planes. Planes in this classification are represented approximately by those between 10,000 and 50,000 lb gross weight, or by those having a wing loading (lb/sq ft) times power loading (lb/hp) of 230 and over.
Cities in this group represent the major industrial centers of the nation and important junction points or terminals on the airways system.	4 and 5	4,700′ to 5,700′ 5,700′ and over	Largest planes in use and those planned for the immediate future. This approximately represents planes having a gross weight of 74,000 lb and over, or having a wing loading (lb/sq ft) times power loading (lb/hp) of 230 and over.

Note: Paved runways shall be 200′ shorter than landing strips.

* Approaches shall be clear within a glide path of 20 to 1 from the end of the usable area for Class I airports and 30 to 1 for Classes II, III, IV, and V airports, except instrument landing runways for which the ratio shall be 40 to 1. These ratios represent the minimum permissible. In all cases it is highly desirable to clear approaches to runways *on as flat a ratio as is possible* in the interest of safety. A 50 to 1 ratio is a desirable minimum.

TABLE II

Airport Size Planning Standards

Recommended Minimum Standards	Class I	Class II	Class III	Class IV	Class V
Length of landing strips *	1,800' to 2,700'	2,700' to 3,700'	3,700' to 4,700'	4,700' to 5,700'	5,700' and over
Width of usable landing strips	300'	500'	500'	500'	500'
Length of runways	None	2,500' to 3,500'	3,500' to 4,500'	4,500' to 5,500'	5,500' and over
Width of runways	None	150' (night oper.) 100' (day oper. only)	200' (instrument) 150' (night oper.)	200' (instrument) 150' (night oper.)	200' (instrument) 150' (night oper.)
Number of landing strips and runways † determined by percentage of winds, including calms ‡, covered by landing strip and runway alignment	70%	75%	80%	90%	90%
Facilities	Drainage Fencing Marking Wind direction indicator Hangar Basic lighting (optional)	Include Class I facilities and lighting Hangar and shop fueling Weather information Office space Parking	Include Class II facilities and Weather Bureau Two-way radio Visual traffic control instrument Approach system (when required) Administration bldg. Taxiways and aprons	Same as Class III	Same as Class IV

* All the above landing strip and runway lengths are based on sea level conditions; for higher altitudes increases are necessary. (One surfaced runway of dimensions shown above is recommended for each landing strip for airports in Classes II, III, IV, and V.

† Landing strips and runways should be sufficient in number to permit take-offs and landings to be made within $22\frac{1}{2}°$ of the true direction for the percentage shown above of winds 4 miles per hour and over, based on at least a 10-year Weather Bureau wind record where possible.

‡ Calms: Negligible wind conditions of 3 miles per hour and under.

acres each; Class II, 151 acres; Class III, 426 acres; Class IV, 762 acres; and Class V, 1,050 acres.

It will be noted that the CAA airport classification is based primarily on runway length. It is also qualified by the slope of runway approach path: 20 to 1, (that is a slope of 20 feet horizontal distance for every foot of height) for Class I, 30 to 1 for the other classes, with the provision that any runway used for instrument landing under poor visibility conditions should have a 40 to 1 approach glide path. Basically and from a practical viewpoint, there are three types of civil airports—domestic, continental, and global.

It is evident that the size of the community and its needs will determine the kind of landing area it should plan and build. If its requirements are very small,

even a Class I airport may be too spacious, and a simple flight strip will do. If its size warrants local airline service, a small airport of Class II type may be satisfactory. If it requires Class III or IV, such airport will probably need to be supplemented by conveniently located flight strips for personal aircraft only, or even a small airport meeting Class I specifications, if personal aircraft traffic warrants it. The larger industrial cities may develop flying activities requiring one or more airline airports, one or more industrial airports, and numerous "airparks" strategically located close to shopping districts as well as residential areas.

To handle safely the heavy scheduled air traffic expected, it is imperative that the larger communities

TABLE III

AIRPORT LIGHTING STANDARDS

Minimum Recommended Facilities	Class I	Class II	Class III	Class IV	Class V
Airport Beacon *	Include	Include	Include	Include	Include
Boundary lights † (including range lights)	Include	Include	Include	Include	Include
Obstruction lights	Include	Include	Include	Include	Include
Illuminated wind cone	Include	Include	Include	Include	Include
Contact lights (including range lights)		Include	Include	Include	Include
Illuminated wind tee or tetrahedron			Include	Include	Include
Landing area floodlighting ‡			Include	Include	Include
Apron floodlighting			Include	Include	Include
Ceiling projector			Include	Include	Include
Taxi lights				Include	Include
Approach lights §				Include	Include

Note: All lighting facilities provided in any case should conform to the requirements of the Standard Specifications for Airport Lighting Equipment and Materials, issued by the CAA.

* The installation of auxiliary beacons, such as identification code beacons, will depend upon individual requirements in each case.

† Use boundary lights in lieu of contact lights at all-way type field having no all-night operator to select landing directions.

‡ Landing area floodlights are considered necessary in northern climates where blowing snow conditions are encountered.

§ Approach lights should be installed for every instrument runway.

TABLE IV

RECOMMENDED STANDARDS FOR DISTANCE BETWEEN CENTER LINES OF PARALLEL RUNWAYS, AND BETWEEN THE CENTER LINE OF RUNWAYS AND AIRPORT BUILDINGS OR LOADING APRONS AND PLATFORMS AS WELL AS TRANSVERSE AND LONGITUDINAL GRADES FOR LANDING STRIPS AND RUNWAYS

Recommended Standards	Class I	Class II	Class III	Class IV	Class V
Minimum distance between center lines of parallel runways.	None	700'	700'	700'	700'
Minimum distance between center line of runway and airport buildings. Instrument landing runway.		750'	750'	750'	750'
Minimum distance between runway center line and aprons and loading platforms. Instrument landing runway.		500'	500'	500'	500'
Distance between center line of runway and airport buildings. All other runways.	Desirable minimum	500' / 350'	500' / 350'	500' / 350'	500' / 350'
Minimum distance between center line of runway and aprons and loading platforms and parking areas. All other runways.		250'	250'	250'	250'
Maximum landing strip and runway grades. Transverse.	2%	2%	$1\frac{1}{2}\%$	$1\frac{1}{2}\%$	$1\frac{1}{2}\%$
Maximum landing strip and runway grades.* Uniform longitudinal.	2%	$1\frac{1}{2}\%$	$1\frac{1}{2}\%$	1%	1%
Grade breaks longitudinal.† Maximum algebraic difference.	3%	$2\frac{1}{2}\%$	2%	2%	2%

* In the development of initial units the grades should be established to conform with the standards for the ultimate development. In special cases it may be necessary to exceed these maximums for economic reasons.

† Longitudinal intersecting grades on a runway or landing strip should be joined by a vertical curve, if the algebraic difference in grades is 0.40% or more. The vertical curve should be at least 300' long for each 1% change in grade. It is also recommended that the tangent interval between the point of tangency of one curve and the point of curvature of the succeeding curve be not less than 1,000'. If economically practical, grade breaks should be controlled so that the sight line will be unobstructed from any point 10' above the surface of the runway to any other point 10' above the runway.

TABLE V

RECOMMENDED STANDARDS FOR TAXIWAY LAYOUTS, ETC.

Recommended Standards	Class II	Class III	Class IV	Class V
Minimum width of taxiways	50'	50'	50'	50'
Minimum distance between runway center line and parallel taxiway center line	275'	275'	275'	275'
Minimum distance from boundary fence, obstructions, etc., to taxiway center line	100'	150'	150'	200'
Maximum longitudinal grade	3%	$2\frac{1}{2}\%$	$2\frac{1}{2}\%$	$2\frac{1}{2}\%$
Maximum transverse grade	$1\frac{1}{2}\%$	$1\frac{1}{2}\%$	$1\frac{1}{2}\%$	$1\frac{1}{2}\%$
Minimum angle of taxiway intersection with runway ends	60°	60°	60°	60°

Runway grades should not be altered to accommodate taxiway intersections or connections. At large airports where traffic is heavy it may be advisable to construct a warming-up apron and by-pass on taxiways connecting to the ends of runways.

Taxiways should not connect to the ends of runways at an angle of less than 90° to incoming traffic.

completely separate scheduled air traffic from private flying, instructional activities, and industrial operation. It is mandatory that a clear radius dictated by the air traffic pattern for the region be allowed around a commercial airport to permit safe movements of transport aircraft under flight instrument approach and landing conditions.

Logical planning for the smaller communities dictates that additional airports for the segregation of flying activities be contemplated before the time when dual runways are required at any one airport for scheduled commercial operation, that is, when the peak hour traffic exceeds forty aircraft movements per hour.

The CAA airport classification and respective specifications are not to be construed as rigid rules to be followed in the design of airports, but rather as a guide for minimum safety standards for each type listed. They are recommendations derived from many years of experience in the field of airport planning and building and the best thinking of the aviation industry. They form a practical background and yardstick for the airport planner. The CAA is charged by law to exert every care and protection for the safety of the scheduled air traveler and, in this role, has jurisdiction over the approval of airports used by the air carriers engaged in the transportation of mail and passengers. Although its primary concern is to see that the operating specifications of the air carriers and the airports they serve are safe for flight operation, it is also interested in the safety of any landing facilities. Any community can build an airport which does not fully conform to the specifications outlined in the CAA airport classification, but it must meet these minimum requirements if the airport is to be used for commercial air service. The most important point is that each community which wants landing and take-off facilities must build the *proper* kind of airport.

Too much emphasis has been laid, in the past, on facilities for airline operation with the result that other types of landing facilities have had to shift for themselves and grow in a haphazard way. This neglect was due partly to the high cost of owning and operating personal aircraft before the war and the lack of general acceptance of flying for convenience and pleasure. Stringent physical examinations for pilots and restrictive regulations also served to discourage personal flying to a large extent. Their liberalization will vastly encourage personal aviation.

Personal Aircraft Landing Facilities

The word "airport," which has been used heretofore to designate any aircraft landing and take-off area, has, to a large degree, been connected with the more expensive facilities that have characterized scheduled air transportation and thus has become associated in the public mind with civic pride and the investment of substantial sums of money.

The Personal Aircraft Council of the Aircraft Industries Association has proposed a more practical terminology for designating landing facilities for the exclusive use of personal aircraft, calling such facilities "airparks" for landplanes and "air harbors" for seaplanes. The word "airpark" was coined by the Honorable Robert Hinkley, a former Civil Aeronautics Administration official. It excellently describes the type of ground facilities needed by the private flyer. In addition, small emergency fields for intermediate landings are called "flightstops," rather than flightstrips, which refer primarily to military emergency landing facilities.

Airparks

Airparks should be inexpensive, should have one flight strip in the prevailing wind direction, or two at the most, should be shaped in the form of a T, L, V, or X, according to the available land and prevailing wind directions, or topography. Airparks need not be paved, as a well-drained, hard-turfed surface is adequate for the satisfactory landing and taking off of almost any small type of personal aircraft unless traffic volume is great enough to require paving. A landing strip length 1,800 to 2,000 feet by 250 to 300 feet width should provide maximum operating safety.

Airparks should be planned and built to serve the suburban shopper, the tourist, the sales representative or executive coming to town to transact his business, and the commuter. They should include accommodations for servicing and refueling, storage, and completely equipped, though not necessarily expensive, restrooms. They should be designed essentially for

short-distance flying by small aircraft of the order of 25 to 100 miles. Their surrounding area should be zoned to meet Class I airport requirements.

Additional airparks can be built as the community grows or its residential areas spread out without excessive financial burden. An excellent example of progressive planning to provide personal aircraft landing facilities is the Wichita Airpark Plan conceived to serve business, industrial, and residential areas.

Figure 1 is a map of the City of Wichita, Kansas, showing the approximate location of four possible airparks (marked 1, 2, 3, and 4). To the southeast, as in-

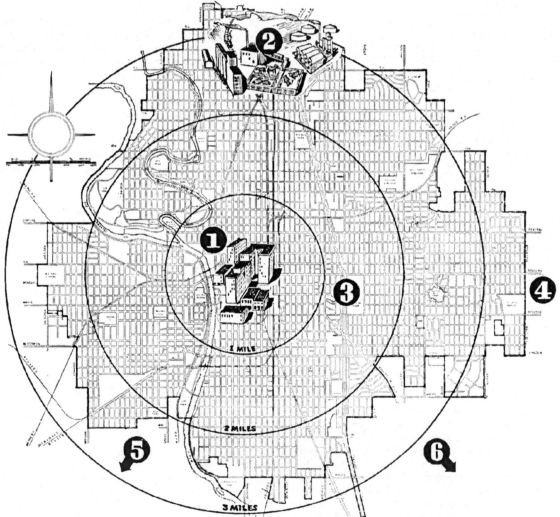

FIGURE 1. WICHITA AIRPARK PLAN

Courtesy Wichita Chamber of Commerce

dicated by the arrowed figure 6, is the Wichita Municipal Airport for scheduled air transport. To the southwest, as shown by the arrowed figure 5, is the auxiliary municipal airport to care for miscellaneous flying activities, such as practice flights and instruction, fixed base operations, and other non-commercial and non-scheduled activities.

the proposals for an airpark in the residential areas (see 3 and 4 on the map) is shown in Fig. 4. Here it is suggested that an unsightly drainage canal be covered with a flightstrip. Suitable servicing and storage facilities would be provided surrounded with shrubbery in keeping with the esthetic character of the neighborhood.

Courtesy Wichita Chamber of Commerce

FIGURE 2. DOWNTOWN AIRPARK

A two-strip airpark, as shown in Fig. 2, to serve the business district and within walking distance of the shopping district would be placed along the river (see 1 on the map). It would have paved runways 1,600 to 1,800 feet long and 100 feet wide or turfed strips 1,800 to 2,000 feet by 300 feet, with a service station, parking garages, and a small administration building.

Figure 3 illustrates an airpark proposed for the industrial district (see 2 on Fig. 1). If sufficient land is available, the landing strips could be up to 2,500 feet long to accommodate the larger types of personal aircraft used for sales and executive activities. One of

Another variation for a suburban airpark is shown in Fig. 5. Proposed by Oliver Parks, President of Parks Air College, St. Louis, Missouri, it covers approximately 100 acres and has two strips arranged X-shape, each 2,000 feet long and 300 feet wide. The plot is 2,600 feet long and 1,500 feet wide. Hangars for several hundred personal aircraft arranged in rows on each side, as illustrated, can be provided. By slightly increasing the surrounding areas and landscaping them, a park-like spaciousness can be obtained to harmonize with the adjacent residential areas.

For congested areas, Oliver Parks proposes an L-shaped airport as illustrated in Fig. 6. It would have two landing strips at 90 degrees separated, of necessity, by a main thoroughfare. Its location, as indicated on the drawing, would preferably be close to the business section of the city and perhaps occupy some of the blighted areas often found between the shop-

pass wide enough for small aircraft to taxi through, going under the thoroughfare. The two ends of the runways that are closest together and are connected by this underpass would have underground hangar facilities directly under the runways, 200 feet wide and at least 800 feet long, so that, all together, it would have

Courtesy Wichita Chamber of Commerce

FIGURE 3. AIRPARK FOR INDUSTRIAL DISTRICT

ping center and the residential districts of large cities. The landing strips would be at least 1,800, and not more than 2,000, feet in length, depending on the street configuration of the city. The width of each strip would be one city block. The first 50 feet around the outside would be planted in shrubbery and grass; the next 25 feet would be paved taxi strip; then 25 feet of grass; then 150 feet of paved landing strip; then 25 feet of grass; 25 feet of taxi strip; and 50 feet of shrubbery and grass on the outside again.

The two landing strips are connected by an under-

a hangar space 1,600 feet by 200 feet, with appropriate taxi aisles and parking space accommodations for approximately 400 airplanes.

It will also be noted that this layout is designed so that if the runways are one block wide and five blocks long, only two streets will be closed on each landing strip and that the remaining streets, if necessary, can be underpassed, just as is often done under a railroad track in our metropolitan areas.

Figure 7 illustrates another proposal for an L-shaped two-runway elevated landing deck for congested areas. It consists of an elevated structure which can be erected over railroad yards. The runways are 1,600 feet long and 200 feet wide. At the end of each runway there is a ramp for the aircraft so that, after landing, they can get out of the way and go down to storage provided by a lower deck of

people congregate to live and participate in civic activities.

Air Harbors

The countless bodies of water in this country and abroad offer a natural solution to the problem of pro-

Courtesy Wichita Chamber of Commerce

FIGURE 4.   AIRPARK FOR RESIDENTIAL AREAS

sufficient area to park 450 small aircraft, with a 70-foot wide taxi aisle in the center. The landing deck is 60 feet above the ground. As a safeguard, there is a woven steel fence around both runways to prevent aircraft from falling off in case of skidding.

Thus, generally meeting CAA Class I airport size specifications, the airpark should be designed for personal flying and located within or adjacent to the corporate limits of the community. It should be beautiful and utilitarian and should serve as a community recreation center. It might be combined with a country club. Realism dictates that it be located where

viding adequate landing facilities for the thousands of communities built on their shores. On the United States map (Fig. 8) the circles represent the location of bodies of water where large flying boats and seaplanes could safely land and take off. There are thousands of other inland lakes and rivers which could accommodate personal seaplanes.

The "Air Harbor," water counterpart of the airpark, is relatively inexpensive to create. Airparks involve the leasing or acquisition of substantial amounts of real estate, whereas air harbors require only the building of low-cost docking floats and beaching ramps.

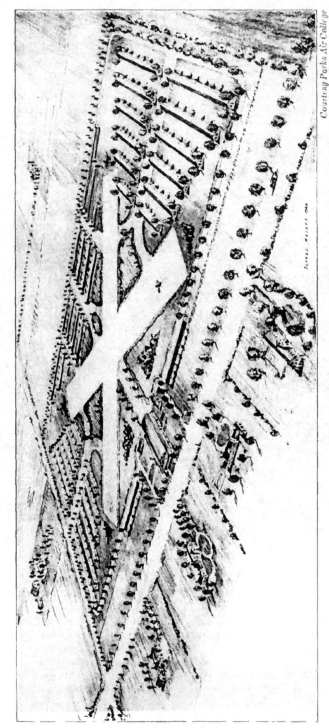

Figure 5. Suburban Airpark

FIGURE 6. DOWNTOWN AIRPARK LAYOUT

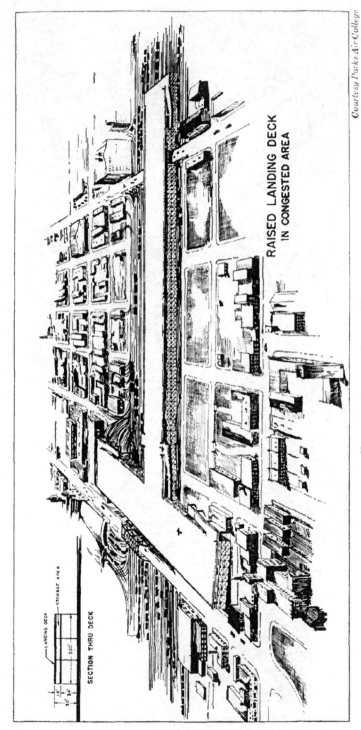

FIGURE 7. ELEVATED LANDING DECK

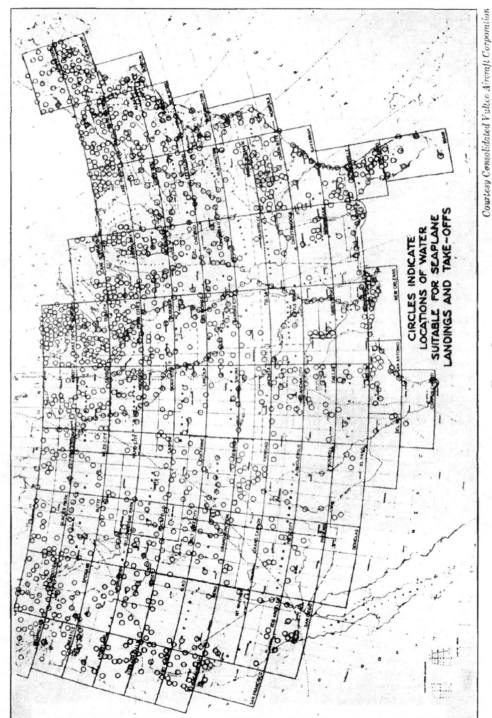

CIRCLES INDICATE
LOCATIONS OF WATER
SUITABLE FOR SEAPLANE
LANDINGS AND TAKE-OFFS

FIGURE 8

and relatively little land. A typical example of the simplest kind of seaplane facilities is shown in Fig. 9. It is a single seaplane float 22 feet long and 10 feet wide, supported by empty steel drums, usually oil bar-

FIGURE 9. SEAPLANE DOCK

rels, and anchored a short distance from shore. Seaplanes can be moored directly to its side and fended off with sections of automobile tires for bumpers. A short gangplank that can be hinged to the float provides the necessary access to it from the shore. Designed by the

FIGURE 10. SMALL SEAPLANE HANGAR

CAA, it provides an inexpensive and efficient landing platform and can be used in multiples and arranged to meet local shore line conditions.

Where waters are deep enough and the shore ground level, such as found on many lakes, seaplanes can be docked even closer to shore as shown in Fig. 10, which illustrates the accommodations of the Adirondack Air Service in northern New York. Some private seaplane owners with homes on the waterfront have combined docking facilities with their residence, as illustrated in Fig. 11.

Where traffic warrants it and docking space is limited, combination floating docks and ramps with turn-

tables make ideal air harbors. Figure 12 illustrates such seaplane handling facilities as used for downtown New York City; they are located on the East River.

Another type of seaplane facility is the low-slope ramp so arranged that the seaplane to be docked properly grounds on the float when taxiing in, yet does not slide back into the water when the engine is shut off.

FIGURE 11. PRIVATE SEAPLANE FACILITIES

Such a ramp, as a rule, is built on piling and is planked with wood. The most important characteristic of inclined ramps is that their slope must not exceed a value of about 1 to 9.*

Still another type of inclined ramp is the marine railway, which consists of tracks set at any angle on

FIGURE 12. WALL STREET SEAPLANE RAMP, NEW YORK CITY

piling. The seaplane or flying boat to be beached is taxied on to a platform car, which picks it up and tows it up the incline by motive power provided by a winch on the shore. The platform of the car is built

* "Marine Air Terminals," by George B. Post, *Aero Digest*, October, 1935.

at such an angle to the axles of the wheels as to give the correct grounding angle (1–9) when the car is in the water. At the top the tracks are at such an angle to the level surface of the ground that the platform is level with the ground. The chief advantage of the

FIGURE 13. SEAPLANE LAUNCHING WITH BOSTON DOLLY

marine railway is that its angle can be very steep and, therefore, it does not have to extend far out into the water when the bank is high. Thus it does not interfere with river traffic, is not so susceptible to ice damage as the long ramp, and is cheaper to build.

Courtesy CAA

FIGURE 14

A Boston Dolly may be used in conjunction with the marine railway as is shown in Fig. 13. This same Boston Dolly may also be used on a ramp.

One or more mooring buoys are always useful to tie seaplane or amphibians to when it is desired to leave them in the water and still keep the docking facilities clear.

Figures 14, 15, and 16 illustrate air harbor facilities suitable for small cities, the facilities of Fig. 15 comprising a series of float units, the facilities of Fig. 16 providing docking and beaching facilities for storage and servicing purposes.

Air harbors for privately owned seaplanes and flying boats can be built adjacent to communities located on quiet bodies of water or protected by coastal bays or inlets. As suggested above, they should and can be inexpensive, devoid of frills, still providing adequate ramp and hangar facilities as well as passenger accommodations. Air harbors can be located close to the

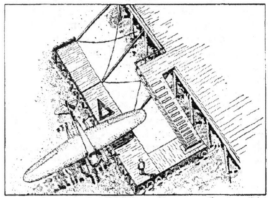

Courtesy CAA

FIGURE 15

heart of both business and residential areas of communities bordering waterfronts. They can be built without the expense of clearing and grading land, which must be done for the airfield portion of airparks and airports, and are generally freer from obstructions. The only drawback in the larger industrial communities

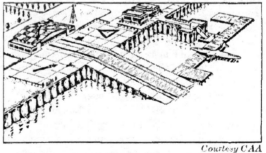

Courtesy CAA

FIGURE 16

and seaports is the danger of striking driftwood or other hard floating objects.

Flightstops

The flightstop is nothing more than a strategically located landing and take-off strip, preferably along a highway and adjacent to a gasoline service station, thus combining motorcar and airplane service to assure maximum and dependable service. It is not an airport or an airpark, but should be considered a part of our national highway system. As such, it should be constructed, serviced, and maintained by highway departments. It is, therefore, conceivable that it should be part of highway right-of-way, that is, public land and adjacent to a public road, thus having the legal status of a highway.* It should meet CAA Class I airport specifications and be preferably as long as the maximum strip length of this classification, that is, 2,700 feet if unpaved or 2,500 feet if paved. It should be designed for aircraft having a gross weight of 6,000 pounds to be able to support most personal aircraft types. Furthermore, it should be properly and easily identified from the air and on the ground.

No arterial motor highway should be built in the future without including adjacent flightstops every 30 to 50 miles for the personal flyer. Flightstops will mean a landing area for practically every town and hamlet located on such superhighways, thus providing those small communities with an additional means of transportation. An excellent start along this line was made in the late 1920's, when Richfield Oil Corporation established a series of small landing fields adjacent to the principal West Coast highways and combined them with its service stations from Canada to Mexico. The depression of the early 1930's and the fact that the personal aircraft was still too expensive in both initial and maintenance costs prevented the commercial success of the scheme at that time.

Non-Scheduled Commercial Airports (Industrial)

Industrial flying, ranging from the various kinds of civilian patrol to airplane flight testing and other miscellaneous industrial flying activities, needs more elaborate facilities and more stringent obstruction zoning than the airpark or Class I airport. Specifications for airports providing safe and satisfactory accommodations for industrial flying should meet CAA airport requirements for Classes II to IV. Longer runways may even be required if they serve an aircraft manufacturer engaged in the production of military aircraft. Although a three- or four-runway system may be adequate for most industrial airports, the larger cities should plan for at least doubling, in the future, the capacity of the original layout to meet normal business growth and increased flying activity. An industrial airport, as its denomination implies, should be located as close as possible to the industrial and business areas of the community.

* *Flight Strips for Civilian Use,* by Colonel Shumway Hanks, American Flight Strips Association, New York, N. Y.

As scheduled air transportation grows and needs larger facilities, it will be found that many of today's "airline airports" can be readily adapted to industrial flying because of their location and capacity. A case in point is the Chicago Municipal Airport, located on the west side of the city close to many large industrial plants. Another example is the Lockheed Air Terminal at Burbank, California, serving aircraft manufacturing and accessories producers and located in an area comprising many industries, such as parts manufacture and motion pictures. A third example is the

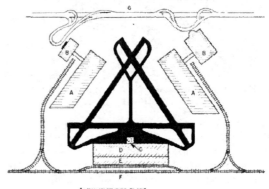

A - MANUFACTURING PLANT
B - PLANT OFFICE
C - CONTROL TOWER
D - HANGARS OR SALESROOMS
E - WAREHOUSES
F - RAILROAD
G - HIGHWAYS

FIGURE 17. TYPICAL INDUSTRIAL AIRPORT LAYOUT

Baltimore Municipal Airport, located close to shipbuilding and refinery activities. There are many similar airports which, although modern in most respects, fall short of what they should be in long-range planning. Because of their particular location, these three airports are cited as examples offering possibilities for use in industrial flying because they will not fully meet scheduled air transport requirements in the future, owing either to inadequate size for desired expansion or zoning obstruction for instrument landing operation on a large scale. They will provide needed facilities for industrial flying, thus serving to increase the business activities of the community besides preventing substantial loss of revenue on the invested funds originally raised to build them.

Where new facilities to accommodate industrial flying will be required, they might take the shape of an airport shown schematically in Fig. 17. It will be noted that ample space is available for hangar, servicing, and overhaul facilities, as well as storage. These accommodations are absolutely necessary if this type of airport can ever be self-supporting. Economy of aircraft operation can be obtained only if runway capacity and shop activity are in proper balance. Both must be busy. Utility should be the keynote.

Scheduled Commercial Airports

Many airports for scheduled air transportation have been built primarily as civic monuments. They are rapidly becoming obsolete owing to the rapid growth of commercial air travel and the inability to visualize as well as interpret the operating requirements of airplanes designed for this type of service, which calls for safety as the primary requisite and dependability as a necessary qualification.

The size and type of airport used by air carriers depend on the kind of service required by the community to be served. This service, in turn, is related to the size of the community and the volume of travel that such a community can generate. It can be stated that such an airport may fall within the CAA airport classification, with the exception of Class 1 which is too small to handle any transport airplane economically.

In an effort to classify airports according to capacity of operation, the Air Transport Association Committee on Airport Developments has prepared the classification shown in Table VI, based on the number of permissible operations per hour and types of aircraft or flying service to be accommodated. This Committee believes that runway lengths of 5,000 feet should be ample for Class C and 6,000 feet for Class D for sea level locations with land acreage provided for extension to 8,000 feet later on if ever found necessary.

It will be noted that the Air Transport Association Committee recommendations are more liberal than those of the CAA for the larger airports. They anticipate the need for longer runways to meet the revised Civil Air Regulations on performance.

Scheduled air traffic may well be developed in the future to the point where all towns of over 5,000 population will have air mail, air cargo, and air passenger service. The extent of such service will depend, in good measure, upon the policy of the federal government regarding air mail service and/or traffic requirements.

TABLE VI

Classification of Airports

CAA Class	Type	Type and Size of Community to Be Served	Type of Aircraft or Flying Service to Be Accommodated
II	Airports for Non-Scheduled Operation	Small communities not on present or proposed scheduled air carrier systems or auxiliary airports in larger metropolitan areas to serve private flying activities.	Basically small aircraft for private flying, non-scheduled and special charter flights, charter service, industrial flights, etc.
III	Non-Scheduled Service or Feeder Line Airports	Larger communities located on present or proposed feeder line airlines, which have considerable aeronautical activity.	Larger size privately owned aircraft and small transport aircraft. Private aircraft, and aircraft of other industries, charter service, localized commercial service, and airline alternate stops.
IV	Local Service Airports	Cities on feeder line airline systems or intermediate points on trunk airline routes.	Present and immediate future transport aircraft. Scheduled and non-scheduled localized commercial flying, regional airline service, and intermediate "local" stops for trunk airline service.
V	Express Service Airports	Cities which are potential major industrial centers of the nation and important junction points or terminals on the airline systems.	Commercial aircraft in use and those planned for the immediate future. For airline service only.
VI	Super Airports	Cities which are major terminals of domestic and/or international airline operation.	Commercial aircraft in use and those planned for the future. For airline service only.

Local Schedule Airports

For local schedule operation, all airports must meet CAA Class II airport requirements. The type of aircraft used for this service will be relatively small, with low landing speeds and short take-off requirements. It will be designed primarily for short flights using airports of limited capacity. However, such service, based on skip-stop schedules for maximum operating efficiency, will require an airport size of virtually Class III type to meet civil air regulations until such time as new types of airplanes embodying the latest technical advances are available to permit the use of safe operation in and out of smaller fields.

Class II airport design is illustrated in Fig. 18. It represents the utmost in simplicity. The runway pattern has been held to minimum requirements and is simply arranged; loading apron is placed so that a minimum of taxiing is required; all the administrative, mail, cargo, passenger, and spectator needs have been lumped together into one simple building. Even here, however, passengers have been segregated from spectators after leaving the ticket window by means of fencing. Both buildings and runways are designed so that alterations may be made in the future should increased traffic warrant it, without jeopardizing the original scheme.

Limited-Stops Schedule Airports

Airports for limited-stops operation will be terminal points for local schedule flights and branch stops on the trunk line. As such, they must be designed to accommodate planes of various sizes and characteristics. They must also be designed to handle expeditiously the transfer of passengers, baggage, and mail from local schedule traffic to trunk line. Such an airport will probably not handle aircraft of the largest contemplated category for long-range operation. Aircraft of the order of the Douglas DC-3, Martin 202 and 303, Douglas DC-4, and DC-6, Lockheed Constellation, and the like, will probably represent the average types handled.

A typical layout for such an airport is shown in Fig. 19. Runways and loading apron have ample capacity, and visibility from the control tower is good over the

TABLE VI *(Continued)*

Airport Capacity in Peak Hour	Loading Apron Capacity in Peak Hour *	Characteristics of Landing Surface	Taxiways †
Indeterminate, depending upon type of aircraft using field.	Small loading area.	Sod, gravel, or possibly paving. 2,500' to 3,500' in length, 100' day, 150' night.	Taxiways optional; 50' wide.
Indeterminate, depending upon type of aircraft using field.	Loading apron for 10 to 15 parking positions.	Paved, 3,500' to 4,500' × 150'; graded and stabilized 500' wide.	Taxiways adequate for uninterrupted traffic; 50' wide.
40 operations per hour.	Loading apron for 10 to 15 parking positions.	Paved, 4,500' to 5,500' × 150', with provision for future runway extensions and widening to 200'; graded and stabilized 500' wide.	Taxiways adequate for uninterrupted traffic; 75' wide.
Up to 120 operations per hour.	Loading apron for 30 to 40 parking positions.	Paved, minimum 6,000' × 200', with provision for future runway extensions to 8,000'; graded and stabilized 500' wide.‡	Taxiways adequate for uninterrupted traffic; 100' wide.
120 or more operations per hour.	Loading apron for 30 or more parking positions, depending upon runway capacity.	Paved, 6,500' to 8,000' × 200', with provision for future extensions to 10,000' of 1 or 2 runways; graded and stabilized 500' wide.‡	Taxiways adequate for uninterrupted traffic; 100' wide.

Note: Above lengths based on sea level elevations. Add 250' for each 1,000' of increased altitude.

* To be built in stages as required by traffic volume.

† All taxiways should have a minimum of 75' radius at all connection points.

‡ International operation or long-range domestic operations may require additional runway lengths over those shown.

entire field of operations. Ample provisions have been made for future expansion to handle increased traffic. Future expansion of runways contemplates a dual runway pattern. An attempt has been made to maintain a proper balance of capacity at all times between air traffic and ground facilities in order to obtain a sound and equitable financial picture.

The possibility should be kept in mind for both Classes II and III airports of tying in community in-

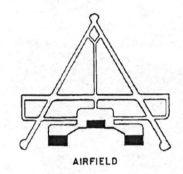

AIRFIELD

LOADING RAMP

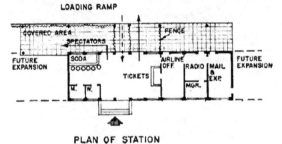

PLAN OF STATION

FIGURE 18

terest in aviation with airport facilities. A comprehensive program might be written including clubrooms, meeting rooms for civic groups, restrooms, and recreational facilities. These facilities, located in a building adjacent to the passenger depot, would tend to bridge the gap between civic interest in aviation and commercial air transport. (See Part 9.)

Express Schedule Airports (Major Terminals)

Express intracontinental, intercontinental, and transoceanic air travel will originate from large airports conforming to Civil Aeronautics Administration Classes IV and V airports and higher. From these airports and superairports will originate non-stop or one-stop coast-to-coast flights, flights to Europe, Asia, and Central, North, and South America. They will also be the terminal points of the main-line traffic handled by limited-stop or Class III airports.

It may be seen readily that such airports will be expected to handle a huge volume of traffic as well as a great diversity of aircraft types. In fact, traffic volume may be such that these airports will handle only passengers, their baggage, and first-class mail, with all other air cargo being handled from "cargo" airports. In many cases, present airport facilities will be well suited to cargo airport operations with a minimum of conversion. This arrangement will allow the municipality to make full use of existing facilities and funds already spent, and still create new first-class facilities for growing air passenger traffic.

The size of these airports will depend to a large extent on their location. If situated inland, Class IV standards will probably be found sufficient for domestic operation; but if designated as ports of entry for foreign air traffic, the size of their runway system will depend on the longest non-stop mileage from point of origin of aircraft to point of destination.

Figures 20a and 20b illustrate typical Class IV airports having a dual parallel runway system with an administration building and passenger station designed so as to permit future expansion. The general layout permits the addition of separate cargo-handling facilities when air cargo volume will warrant them. The runway pattern shown by Fig. 20a is of the triangular type with each set of runways at 60 degrees or according to the prevailing wind directions, whereas Fig. 20b shows a quadrangular pattern with each set of runways at 45 degrees. The principal advantage of the latter, which can also be obtained with any triangular pattern by proper runway separation, is the wide separation between the two vertical parallel runways for instrument operation. The same result can also be gained with the other runways, but at the expense of building space for the available area and increased taxi distances.

An example of this type of airport is the National Airport at Washington, D. C., which is illustrated in Fig. 16, Chapter 6. Its capacity, however, is limited to single runway operation, except in favorable weather, and the airfield area is considered insufficient to modernize it into a dual parallel runway scheme at present.

Superairports

The number of "superairports" will be small because their cost will be prohibitive to any but the largest cities in this country or major ports of entry. In conceiving this type of facility, the airport designer can deviate from standard arrangements to create an arrangement dictated by civic demands and traffic volume, as well as type of traffic. The two principal cri-

FIGURE 19

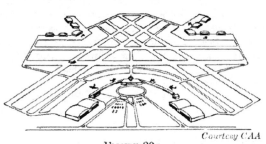

FIGURE 20*a*

Courtesy CAA

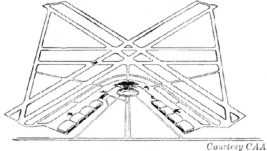

FIGURE 20*b*

Courtesy CAA

teria are most efficient land utilization because of the necessarily large area involved and the exercise of the best possible judgment in balancing airport and airfield capacities to permit anticipated expansion with minimum alterations, which would be extremely expensive if not considered in the original plan. This type of airport should anticipate for its ultimate development landplanes with wing span up to 200 to 250 feet having gross weights of 250,000 to 350,000 pounds gross weight. If the airport is located along the sea-

board, it would be desirable to combine it with a seaplane base for the operation and docking of flying boats of large capacity.

A study of these requirements and their application to a practical layout might result in an arrangement of the kind shown in Fig. 21. Here the designer has centralized the administration building and passenger terminal. He has used a converging and diverging pattern of runways to provide the proper flight separation after take-off and during landing, as well as to reduce taxiing distances to a minimum. Incoming airplanes are also segregated from those taking off, thus permitting the division of traffic control by functions—one controlling take-offs, another controlling landings, and a third directing all ground traffic. It will be noted that simultaneous landings and take-offs can be made by using two runways on each side, with cross winds at not more than a 22½ degree-angle from their direction. Provisions for extension of most runways have been anticipated in the plan if found desirable in the future.

New York City, with its great population and its location as the country's major trading center, has been the first port of the United States in shipping. It is, therefore, natural that it should attempt to become its major air center by adopting a realistic and comprehensive airport program. With this goal in mind, it is now building an airport which will dwarf its LaGuardia Field, so well known to air travelers,

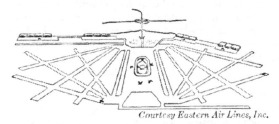

Courtesy Eastern Air Lines, Inc.

FIGURE 21. DOUBLE-RUNWAY SUPERAIRPORT PLAN

and may well be one of the largest airports in the world. In its final stage of construction the new airport * is expected to have a capacity of 360 plane movements per hour based on one movement, that is, a landing or a take-off per minute per runway.

Provisions will be made in the New York airport plan to handle transport helicopters when they make their appearance. Within the city, itself, accommodations for helicopter service might be combined with any existing airparks for private aircraft, or with already established facilities for railroads or buses. Figure 22 shows how Greyhound Lines envisions this type of arrangement to supplement its bus services with helicopter connections by using the roof of the bus terminal as a helicopter port.

It is believed that this airport will not be exceeded in size and cost in the future. It is the opinion of many authorities on airport design and administration that it would be wiser to build additional airports rather than larger ones on the assumption that smaller airports can bring air travel facilities closer to traffic-

* "Fabulous Idlewild," by Oscar Landing, *Air Transport*, December, 1945.

generating centers to save overall travel time and reduce overall operating costs which must either be absorbed by the airlines operating on such airport or by the city for whose benefit the airport is created.

Courtesy Greyhound Lines

FIGURE 22. HELICOPTER—BUS TERMINAL

Another airport of this type is the San Francisco Bay project, covering 3,200 acres. The airport plan includes eight runways 8,500 feet to 10,000 feet long and 250 feet wide. Seaplanes will be accommodated in a basin 1,500 feet wide and sealanes 6,800 feet long, with 38 feet draft.

Still another airport project worthy of mention is the study made by the Chicago Plan Commission for a Lake Front Airport, may be situated directly opposite the

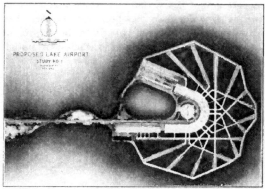

Courtesy Chicago Plan Commission

FIGURE 23. PROPOSED LAKE FRONT AIRPORT PLAN FOR CHICAGO

Chicago Loop District and sufficiently distant from it on Lake Michigan to permit a satisfactory air traffic pattern under instrument weather operation. Figure 23 illustrates this plan, which consists of a converging and diverging runway pattern with a central administration building area, a protected seaplane basin, and provisions for a helicopter field later

Air Cargo

Thus far, aircraft have been designed to carry passengers primarily, with but little thought devoted to the efficient transportation of cargo in large volume

The experiences of the Air Transport Command of the Army Air Forces and the Naval Air Transport Service in flying enormous quantities of all sorts of supplies to the various war theaters have clearly shown that passenger transport aircraft are not entirely suitable for carrying merchandise in bulk Airplanes designed strictly for air cargo transportation, such as the Fairchild Packet, will be used extensively in the near future, and ground facilities must be provided for handling them and their cargo

These airplanes will require the segregation of cargo operation, including loading and unloading as well as storing, from passenger service Warehouses must have proper ventilation as well as temperature control It is probable that for a while cargo and passengers will be handled at the same airport although separation will be provided Later on, it may be found advisable to segregate cargo flying from passenger travel totally and to provide a cargo airport located close to the source of shipments, that is, alongside railroads, docks, or industrial areas

Airport design has so far met the requirements of the airplane, and a point has been reached where the airplane characteristics will have to fit the airport as the airport cannot be enlarged indefinitely if initial cost and operating expenses are to remain within practicability Perhaps we shall see the use of devices to assist take-off, either in the form of ground appurtenances or additional power. The additional power might come from a smaller airplane having very low power loading, temporarily hooked on the heavily loaded transport airplane taking off pig-a-back fashion, or from disposable rockets, so successfully employed on military aircraft to shorten take-off distances It seems that something of this sort would be cheaper than longer runways, which are extremely costly to build, particularly to handle large aircraft, and reflect to a degree increased charges to the airplane operator

No mention need be made here of airports for the exclusive use of the armed forces or government research, as the type of facilities will in each case be guided by their particular needs Location with reference to community activities is often unimportant, and freedom from obstructions surrounding the landing and take-off area is generally the parameter which determines such location

Bibliography

Proceedings, Joint Airport Users Conference, July 21, 25, 1944, National Aeronautic Association of the U S A, Inc, Washington, D C

Proceedings, Joint Aviation Users Conferences, Airports, Third Session, August 20, 21, 1945 National Aeronautic Association of the U S A, Inc, Washington, D C

Seaplane Facility Plans, Civil Aeronautics Administration, U S Department of Commerce, Washington, D C

Airports, by John Walter Wood, Coward-McCann, Inc, New York

5

FUNDAMENTAL AIRPORT REQUIREMENTS

Landing and take-off facilities, whether they are airparks, air harbors, flightstops, or airports, and their ground accommodations, are the pillars which support aviation. They are becoming increasingly important elements in the community plan and, as such, must be carefully integrated with the provisions made for other forms of transportation. It is, therefore, most essential that they be developed along sound, functional, constructive, and long-range thinking.

Airport planning must be visionary, yet rational. Any airport plan must meet the test of common sense and be balanced judiciously to fill the needs, present and future, of the community for which it is designed. Bad judgment will be costly—both in money spent and failure to provide adequate service. Each community has its local pride, and justifiably so, but it must, nevertheless, analyze its individual problem in the light of its present needs and anticipate the future expansion of such needs according to its probable growth in a manner which will not overtax its financial structure. Landing facilities must be considered as civic enterprises for the benefit of the community and region they are planned to serve by providing increased or new transportation means. They must be justified by community needs determined by careful analysis of the economic factors and travel habits of the region and adjacent areas.

A careful study may convince many communities with good means of surface transportation that their desire to be a trunk-line stop on an airline route is not justified by their traffic potential and that the cost of establishing such facilities prohibits their consideration. Yet it may be found that because of the density of their population and the nature of their local activities, the communities could readily support several airparks for personal flying or even a Class II airport for mixed operations, such as crop dusting and charter service.

Historical Background

A brief historical review of landing field specifications may well serve as a prelude to a discussion of fundamental requirements for landing areas. As a consequence of the demobilization of the Army Air Forces after World War I, a large number of landing fields built to meet military aviation requirements were dismantled. The baneful effect of this drastic reduction in the number of landing fields on the development of civil aviation, which was just beginning, was soon realized and a cooperative plan between the United States Army and municipalities desirous of establishing landing facilities was adopted. This plan transitory in nature, provided that the municipalities interested should establish municipal landing fields built according to specifications prepared by the Army Air Service and the municipalities would receive in return steel hangars from the government. The maintenance of the field, when completed, was to be assumed by the municipalities.

Progressive communities quickly adopted the plan and on January 1, 1920, the U S Air Service issued revised landing field specifications, which are here quoted verbatim

In the selection of landing fields at a city, special attention should be given to the following points

1 Location

(*a*) The field should be situated close to transportation facilities, both passenger and freight, and electric power and water supply should be available

(*b*) An effort should be made to select a location in a place where the field is unlikely to be later surrounded by building operations

(*c*) If the city is unable to provide for a field of the ideal size, if possible, a site should be selected which is capable of expansion, to a larger size, when the development of aviation makes such expansion necessary

(*d*) A special effort should be made by cities on the main aerial routes, as the development of transcontinental aviation depends upon the establishment of fields at such points

2 Size

(a) The size of municipal landing fields depends upon so many factors that it is impossible to prescribe exact regulations concerning it, and it is realized that a great many cities will not be able to establish airdromes to meet the requirements of the specifications set forth herein The minimum size recommended by this office at the present time and with the present types of machines, is one that will allow 600 yards "Runway" in any direction from which the wind may be likely to blow

Such a field would permit any type of machine at the present day to be landed by an average pilot, and to be taken off without accident, should there be no failure of the motor To have a field large enough to enable the average pilot to take any and all types of machines away from the field and to keep the machine always in such a position with reference to the field as to be able, in case of failure of the motor, to return to it and to land the plane without accident, it is necessary that there should be a "Runway" of at least 1,000 yards in any direction from which the wind is likely to blow

Fields complying with these specifications are designed to take care of airplanes of all types under all conditions of traffic, weather, etc These specifications are not intended to discourage the establishment of small fields, as the presence of small fields en route are of vital importance, and as such, they will function as emergency fields for airplanes that need a great deal of room to take off and land, and as landing stations for small or slower planes In the establishment of these fields, the general specifications should be followed in regard to shape, character of ground, approaches, obstacles, etc Should there be obstacles around the field, the portion of the field available for use will be shortened by a distance depending upon the height of the obstacle An obstacle 100 feet high will make at least 700 feet of the field unavailable for use The length of the "Runway" available for use should be computed by subtracting seven times the height of the obstacle surrounding the field from the length of the field in the direction in which the "Runway" is being computed

(b) Another factor which enters into the size of fields is the question of the surrounding country Should a field be located in a locality where there are fields available for emergency landings immediately adjacent to the municipal landing fields, the danger of accident due to failure of motor, immediately in the vicinity, will be much lessened and the need of the 1,000 yard "Runway" is not so urgent Should the country surrounding the field, however, be covered with buildings, or be of such a character that it is impossible to land upon it with safety, the best interests of aviation demand that the field should be large enough to enable the pilot to circle the field in any type of machine, keeping always in such a position as to be able to return to the field in case of the failure of the motor

(c) It would thus seem that it is impossible to make a classification of landing fields according to size, which would show their relative suitability for aviation purposes and, accordingly, all classifications heretofore made are withdrawn

(d) In addition, it may be further noted that there are types of machines with which it is possible for the average pilot to land in a field, without chance of accidents, with much less than a 600 yard "Runway" It is also possible, with average luck, for good pilots to land any present type of machine in fields of smaller dimensions than 500 yards

3 Shape

The best shape for a field is that of a square, but an "L" shaped field will suffice, providing each arm provides a satis-

factory length of "Runway" It must be pointed out, however, that an "L" shaped field does not provide all the advantages for a return to the field in case of failure of motor, which are possessed by a square field

4 Character of Ground

The ground should be firm under all weather conditions A light, porous soil with natural drainage is recommended as the most suitable A field with clay soil invariably demands special drainage and is unsatisfactory as a rule during wet weather It is possible, however, to lay a system of tiling which will drain any field after the hardest rain The field should be covered with sod The surface should be level and smooth, so that airplanes can normally land upon and taxi across without injury

5 Approaches

Surrounding obstacles, such as high buildings, high-tension power lines, trees, etc, limit the amount of field available for landing by the amount indicated above, and in addition, provide an element of danger for the pilot in case of misadventure

6 Marking

A white circle, 100 feet in diameter with a band 3 feet wide, has proven by experience to be an excellent distinctive marking for a landing field This can be seen at almost any attainable height with clear visibility By digging out the earth to a depth of about six inches and filling in with crushed rock, a very substantial and economical marker can be made It is necessary to keep the marking clear white to make it show up well This can be done by white-washing from time to time The name of the station should be marked in chalk letters 15 feet long by 3 feet wide A wind indicator, such as the standard aviation wind cone, should be placed at one corner of the field 30 feet off the ground

7 Accommodations

Municipal landing fields should provide communication by telephone, transportation facilities, gasoline, oil and sundry supplies Hangars, guards, and shop facilities will be needed in addition with the development of the use of the field

8 Classification

No classification for municipal landing fields will be published However, for the purpose of consolidating information in a concise form and for the purpose of furnishing statistics, and furnishing pilots information as to cross-country routes, the following divisions will be made

(a) Field from which it is possible for the average pilot to operate every type of machine, even in case of motor failure

(b) Field from which it is possible for the average pilot to operate every type of machine without danger to the pilot so long as the motor functions

(c) Field from which it is possible for the average pilot to operate only certain types of machines without danger so long as the motor continues to function The most skilful pilots will be able to land any type of machine in fields of this classification

(d) Fields which, of necessity, must be classed as "emergency field," inasmuch as they are of such a type that only under the most favorable conditions can successful operations be effected

These specifications were simple and to the point They were based on the experience of the U S Army Air Service and proved to be an excellent foundation for the beginning of commercial aviation a few years later

Fundamental Airport Requirements

Flying is still a new art. It has not yet found its deserved place in our national and international transportation system within which all other means of travel are so well integrated today. Therefore, any landing facilities built today must be planned liberally because they will, of necessity, outlive any type of aircraft design for which they are created.

To be successful, any airport or landing facility must meet four fundamental conditions, which can be stated simply as follows:

1 It must be *planned* broadly and comprehensively.

2 It must be *designed* functionally and practically.

3 It must be *constructed* soundly at reasonable cost.

4 It must be *administered* economically.

These conditions apply to *any* community, whether large or small, and whether such community is embarking for the first time in its civic life on an airport program or is thinking of modifying, modernizing, or extending its existing facilities because of increased air activities.

Each landing facility must be conceived of as a part of a well-integrated system of air activities to provide bases for national defense, in case of military emergencies, airports for commercial air transportation and flying the mail, or landing facilities for the personal flyer.

Airport Authority

The future of aviation demands that the airport problem receive the most serious consideration from every civic-minded organization. Airports constitute a problem for many people. The personal flyer, the air traveler and the airline, the shipper, the manufacturer of aircraft and its distributor, the engineer, the architect, and the taxpayer and many others are all vitally interested in the proper conception and development of airport programs.

Every community which does not already have one should establish an airport authority consisting of its leading citizens. The authority should be a permanent body because, even after its original duties have been discharged, it is most vital that it continue in active service to control the airport management and handle aviation problems which are bound to be posed by the natural growth of the air activities of the community,

as well as to represent it in aviation matters elsewhere. The changes which are occurring and which will continue to occur in aviation are so swift and so significant that any community intending to keep abreast of the times will have to insure its continued progress by keeping in active service men who are informed and who will translate this information into sound improvements in landing facilities.

Survey

The first step of the airport authority should be to prepare a survey to determine the present volume and type of air traffic as well as the ultimate volume which the community could reasonably expect to generate. Whether the ultimate will be reached in ten or twenty years or longer is of less importance than that the greatest possible accuracy in figures be obtained. A change in the length of time it takes to reach the ultimate volume of traffic will merely necessitate a speeding up or slowing down of the project, whereas serious inaccuracy in prediction might necessitate the complete revision of the project.

In preparing the traffic survey, the city, together with the region it serves, should be thoroughly studied. Proper evaluation should be placed upon their interrelation as well as upon the interdependence of one upon the other. This evaluation will disclose the kind and volume of an activity anticipated, thus determining the type and number of aircraft which will need accommodations. It may also reveal that several surrounding smaller communities desiring commercial air service can be better served by combining efforts in the creation of a consolidated airport rather than by each one building its own competitive airport.

It is conceivable that properly located airparks may become the hub of residential areas in a fast-growing congested city, that industrial airports may accelerate the development of slowly progressing factory areas, just as airline airports have served to promote intercity business activities in the past. This is particularly true where other means of transportation have been non-existent or their service has lagged.

Among the specific factors (discussed in Part 1) which influence a survey, the following deserve extensive study:

1 Population of the community and its density

2 Income level. Its relationship to the region and the rest of the world. Distribution by income groups

3 Character of population, increasing or decreasing trend, movement of its center

4 Industry and trading areas, type and volume of business per capita Mail receipts

5 Agriculture Kinds of products and markets

6 Area of community and distance between adjoining cities and airports Population served by existing airports

7. Community interest with adjoining cities

8 Geographical location and local topography as affecting cost of landing facilities to be projected

9 Present local flying and possible trends

10 Existing and proposed ground transportation facilities and travel habits

Another use of the traffic survey will be to enable the air transport operator to estimate the schedules and types of flying equipment needed to meet anticipated commercial air travel demands The flight and performance characteristics of this equipment will, in turn, determine the length of runways required when properly correlated to meet civil air regulations and requirements specified by the CAA

Airport Program

The completion of such a traffic survey will enable the airport authority or civic body charged with the duties of city planning to write a *program* concerning the location and size of the proposed landing area or areas The writing of such a program is of greatest importance since it is the logical means of setting down in an orderly and workable manner all the requirements which the final plan will have to fulfill Furthermore, a written program will consolidate the thinking of the various agencies concerned and cause them to reach an agreement on the subject.

The information obtained from the traffic survey will provide a key to the volume of expected private flying, industrial air activity, commercial air passengers, mail, and cargo which will be handled in any given period It will also indicate peak traffic volume to be accommodated in ratio to total traffic volume, as well as the timing of such peaks during a 24-hour period for each type of air traffic These data properly analyzed will determine the type and number of landing areas required to handle the ultimate need of the community or region as well as their respective location

Specific Airport Requirements

Eight specific requirements must be met to satisfy the development of any sound landing facility·

1 Flexibility of plan

2 Accessibility

3 Adequate size

4 Freedom from obstructions

5 Proper zoning

6 Favorable meteorological conditions.

7 Availability of utilities

8 Proper balance between airfield and buildings.

Flexibility

The exceptional fluidity of aircraft design and its rapid rate of development demand the most careful analysis of design trends and their accurate interpretation to permit farsighted conception of equally fluid landing facilities The conclusion can be drawn from this factual consideration that the first fundamental requirement of any type of landing facility is *flexibility* of arrangement which will allow expansion modification or modernization in keeping with the advancement of aircraft and the increase in their utility

Accessibility

The necessity of locating the airpark, air harbor, or airport as close as possible to the center of traffic generation is the second most important fundamental requirement of landing facilities The utility of these landing facilities depends to a large degree upon their *location*, as the time taken in traveling to and from home or office to the airport must be kept to a minimum for the sake of convenience and expediency This convenient location is mandatory if air transport is to be exploited to the maximum of its potential.

The time-saving advantage of locating airports close to the center of air traffic is shown graphically in Fig 1, in which are plotted "block-to-block" speed curves for a typical transport airplane applicable to local schedule operation and a helicopter By block-to-block speed is meant the average speed from the time the airplane or helicopter leaves the loading apron at one station and stops at the unloading apron at the next scheduled stop This average speed is plotted for various mileages that might represent actual air distances between airports It will be noted that as the mileage between stops drops, so does the average speed. This drop is due to the greater proportion of maneuvering and taxi time to the total flight time as flight distances get shorter

Curve A_1 in Fig 1 represents the resulting average airplane speed from actual departure point in the city to final destination, assuming 15 minutes time from home or office to airport at station of departure as well as arrival. Curve A has been plotted for similar conditions except that 30 minutes ground transportation time was taken at one end and 15 minutes at the other, that is, 15 minutes more ground time than for Curve A_1

Curves *II* and *II*$_1$ represent the same conditions applied to the helicopter. It will be noted that with one-half hour total ground time, the helicopter is faster up to a distance of, roughly, 95 miles. When ground transportation time increases to three-quarters of an hour, this distance increases to approximately 130 miles in favor of the helicopter. Also the speed advantage of the airplane is seriously impaired as the flight distance between stops becomes less. At the

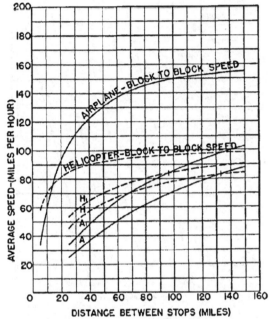

FIGURE 1. EFFECT OF AIRPORT LOCATION ON OVERALL SPEED

lower mileages the airplane offers practically no time saving over other means of transportation, except in large congested areas having heavy surface traffic and few direct expressways.

Thus the success of an airport in a small community, whose air traffic volume warrants only local service, will be predicated to a large extent on a location closest to its traffic-generating center.

In the same line of thought, it is highly desirable that the walking distance from the place where the passenger alights from his car, cab, or bus at the air terminal to the door of the airplane should be as short as possible. There is some disagreement as to what this maximum distance should be, but it may be stated that a maximum of 600 feet is not objectionable. This certainly should be the maximum for two reasons—convenience and time saving.

The necessity of tying in airports with connecting highways, and with rapid transit in the larger cities, is inescapable if the maximum benefits are to be derived from any aircraft landing facility. The airport planner must also bear in mind that the need for rapid means of connecting ground transportation becomes more acute as commercial air traffic increases. This need involves not only a reduction in ground mileage but also the selection of route segments permitting highest safe speed to save ground time. Every new transportation facility must be properly integrated with existing facilities (or new ones, if required) if the airport is to have maximum usefulness.

It can be generally stated that airport income obtained from the renting of building space, landing fees, or concessions is directly proportional to the accessibility of the airport to business districts or residential areas, depending upon the type of airport and its location.

An expensive airport is useless unless it can be reached speedily and at low cost by a volume of people proportional to its capacity. Although an airport can be used as a place of recreation, it is essentially an agency for transportation.

In a region already having airports in operation, proper consideration must also be given to the spacing of a new airport in relation to the others to insure their maximum usefulness and provide unrestricted utilization of the new one.

Size

There is a definite relationship between aircraft performance and airfield size. *Airfield size*, therefore, is the third important airport requirement to be considered. It is dictated primarily by the type of aircraft to be served and the kind of flying to be done.

A common mistake in the past has been to build landing facilities in places where future expansion was economically impossible because of surrounding real estate developments. This shortsightedness has resulted in premature obsolescence of the airfield when air traffic has grown and larger equipment has been needed. Whereas it is unwise to build on too large a scale, it is more so to build too small.

The determination of the size of the airfield portion of an airpark for personal flying is relatively simple, but for an industrial or airline airport it becomes a more complex problem because it is more difficult to predict the growth of manufacturing activities, effects of business cycles, and types of scheduled air service. The best solution so far lies in the selection of the proper area to meet the flying characteristics of the type of aircraft which is expected to be used, particularly those characteristics having to do with landing and take-off. Sufficient land should then be acquired to meet the requirements of the next largest airport classification. This precaution is desirable because, with transport aircraft, for example, there has been a gradual increase in wing loadings, which has had a tendency to increase landing speeds and, consequently, minimum runway lengths for safe operation.

Other factors which influence airport size are elevation of the terrain above sea level and air temperature. The lower air density at altitude means greater length for take-off run and landing run than required at sea level for any particular airplane. It also means a flatter angle of climb. This lower air density reduces the lifting force acting on the wings of the airplane, thus requiring greater speed to obtain the lift available at sea level and, therefore, longer runway lengths. Lower air density also reduces the maximum engine horsepower with unsupercharged engines.

To offset these two characteristics, runway lengths should, as a general rule, be lengthened from basic sea level length by a distance equal approximately to one-fourth the elevation, in feet, of the airport above sea level. Figure 2 shows this relationship graphically for each CAA class of airports.

Obstructions

Freedom from obstruction can be listed as the fourth specific airport requirement. Although airport location and size are of major importance, agencies charged with airport programs must bear in mind that safety of aircraft operation can never be compromised. Therefore, the natural features and artificial obstacles which surround a tract of land being considered for a landing area have a very material bearing on its fitness as an airport and its selection as a site which can be developed to its final stage according to the master plan.

It is difficult to list all the factors governing the selection of a site in their order of importance, but it is obvious that natural topography, which includes mountains, high hills, and ridges, and artificial obstructions, such as tall chimneys, radio towers, high-tension power wires, gas tanks, and the like, in close proximity to the landing area create mental and real hazards, particularly if they encroach on the approach zones to the runways.

Before considering any site, it is mandatory to study this problem thoroughly and to prepare an obstruction map similar to Fig. 3, showing all obstacles, natural and artificial, within a given radius of the proposed site. This radius may vary from 2 miles for airparks

to 5 to 6 miles or more for very large airports, requiring up to 50 to 1 glide ratio in instrument weather, and designed to accommodate aircraft needing large maneuvering air space. Obstructions in the approach zones reduce the effective length of the available landing area if they project through the imaginary approach slope line, and thus a larger area is required than would be necessary if they did not exist. In

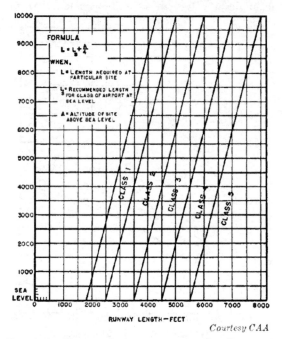

Courtesy CAA

FIGURE 2. EFFECT OF ALTITUDE ABOVE SEA LEVEL ON REQUIRED RUNWAY LENGTH BY CAA AIRPORT CLASS

making the final selection between several possible sites having the same location and size characteristics, it will be found desirable to investigate the cost of removing the undesirable obstructions in order to select the least expensive location. The cost will also determine the practicability of removing such obstructions or reducing their height to a safe permissible height. Freedom from undesirable obstructions must be assured before proceeding further.

Zoning

Next, legal steps must be taken to assure proper zoning, as discussed in Part 6, to prevent the future erection of obstructions which would hamper the safe flight of aircraft in and out of the airport at any later date. The promulgation of *proper zoning* ordinances becomes the fifth specific airport requirement to prevent

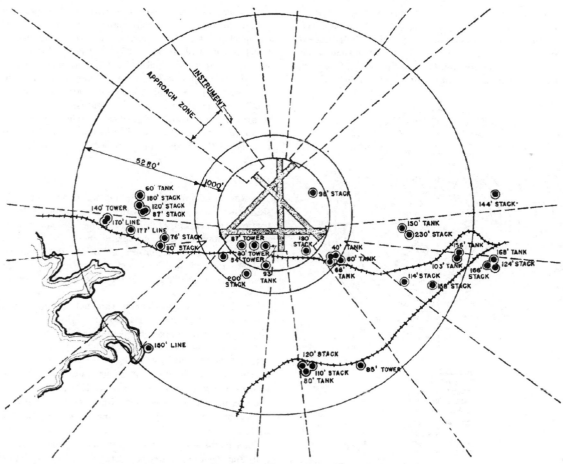

FIGURE 3. OBSTRUCTION MAP

the subsequent erection of man-made obstructions that would reduce the safety or usability of the field.

Efficient land use of the zoned area should be the goal of the airport authority or any agency entrusted with the airport zoning problem. Careful planning will assure full utilization of the approach zones for specific purposes, depending on the type of landing facility. For instance, airpark approaches in residential areas should be devoted to parkways or open-type recreational activities to promote the further development of the neighborhood. Zoned areas surrounding industrial airports should be used for individual commercial activities such as stores, service facilities, storage, and the like. Thus, instead of being detrimental to land values, it is quite conceivable that intelligent planning of zoned areas will improve property values and, consequently, community tax income.

Meteorology

The sixth specific requirement an airport must meet is that the atmospheric conditions prevailing at the contemplated site should be suitable for air operations. *Favorable meteorological conditions* are highly desirable since excessive adverse weather may reduce the percentage of usability to such a low point as to render the project uneconomical. Complete data should be collected on wind directions, velocities, and frequency of occurrence. The data may be plotted in the form of a "wind rose," typically illustrated in Fig. 4. Fog and smoke, as affecting visibility in the vicinity of the landing area, should be studied and their occurrence and intensity recorded.

These and similar conditions are of prime concern to the airport designer as they will affect the orientation and layout of the runway pattern. It has been stated in Part 3 that improved electronic devices and their application to air traffic control will in time be developed to the point where flight operations will proceed irrespective of weather condition, but that time is not yet at hand. Meanwhile, the most dependable service must be provided, utilizing present available methods.

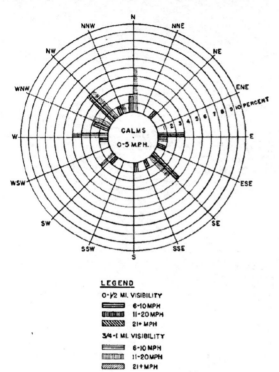

LEGEND
0-½ MI. VISIBILITY
▭ 6-10 MPH
▨ 11-20 MPH
▨ 21+ MPH
3/4-1 MI. VISIBILITY
▭ 6-10 MPH
▨ 11-20 MPH
▨ 21+ MPH

FIGURE 4. TYPICAL WIND ROSE

It must be assumed that even with the universal application of new radio navigational and homing aids, it will always be desirable to operate from fields where adverse atmospheric conditions are at a minimum.

In general, a highland site is preferable to a valley site because valley sites are usually surrounded by terrain obstructions and are more susceptible to fog. Wind conditions are also likely to be more erratic in valleys, rendering prediction of winds and weather conditions more difficult than in highland sites. Valley sites are usually the first ones to "close in" and the last ones to "clear."

Utilities

Serious consideration should also be given to the *availability of utilities*, such as electricity, water, gas, telephone and telegraph, and sewer lines. This avail-

ability may be considered the seventh fundamental airport requirement as it will materially affect the cost of development. It is obvious, for instance, that if water is not available and wells must be drilled to provide a satisfactory supply to fill the normal needs of the airport and emergency requirements dictated by fire protection, a sizable expense may be involved. Similarly, the construction of a central power station to provide an adequate supply of electrical power may be an important cost item. Ample sewage facilities are equally costly if they must be established independently.

Balance

A site having been determined upon, the next consideration is the planning of the airport proper. When the general concept of the scheme has become reasonably well worked out, a *proper balance* must be struck between the interrelationship of the runway pattern and the ground facilities comprising the administration building, passenger station (if separate), aprons, hangars, and others.

For large-capacity airports this balance must also consider the capacity of the airways which serve the airport and which limit the capacity of any one airport. It may be a relatively easy matter to increase the capacity of airfield systems by increasing the number of runways to allow simultaneous landings and take-offs, provided aircraft can be controlled along the airways in proper sequence and with adequate separation to permit their safe operation and control at the airport.

This is the eighth specific airport requirement. It calls for the integration of all the parts of an airport to provide a smooth flow of traffic, to hold taxi distances to a minimum, and to permit shortest passenger walking distances, least handling of cargo, and the efficient administration of all airport functions.

The entire layout when completed should show a proper balance between runway capacity and depot capacity when the airport is operating at peak loads. There should be functional efficiency with economical space utilization. The planner must make every effort to provide the simplest and cleanest design possible, primarily to give optimum service to the air passenger but also to accommodate the visitor.

Airport Economics

Having thus obtained an idea of the size and complexity of the undertaking, the airport authority should next examine the financial aspects of the program involving the entire airport project from the beginning of the design to the completion of the final stages

The first step is to make a rough estimate of the cost of acquiring the land necessary to carry the project to the final stage of the proposed plan and the cost of constructing the complete runway system and buildings This estimate should include grading, drainage, soil preparation, pumping and power stations if needed, fences, roadways, landscaping, insurance fees of architects and engineers, and the like

The next step is to determine how the necessary funds are to be raised and what financial assistance can be expected from federal and/or state governments in order to arrive at the total sum to be raised locally and the annual carrying charges

Maintenance and operating costs should be determined These costs together with the carrying charges and amount of principal to be amortized each year form the sum total to be met by airport revenue and community assessments Airport revenues consist of landing fees, ticket counter and office space rental, as well as hangar rentals which will be charged to the operating airline, industrial operator, or personal flyer Revenue can also be obtained from various concessions, such as telegraph and telephone restaurant, newsstand, soda fountain, and—at the larger airports —souvenir shop, haberdashery, vending machines properly located, dressing rooms, sight-seeing, branch bank, and many others (See Part 9)

A comparison of the possible revenue and estimated expenses and cost amortization will give a fairly accurate idea as to whether the undertaking will be financially sound from the community standpoint or not, also, as to whether the charges to be made to the personal flyer or airline operator will be reasonable enough to permit him to serve the community on an economical basis and progressively develop its air traffic potential

It is at this point that the airport authority must either scale down the project, if too ambitiously conceived, or if the facts warrant that such a goal can ultimately be reached, decide on the number of development stages and the extent of each stage in relation to the complete project

Master Plan

A complete master plan of the proposed airport should then be prepared embodying an evaluation of all the foregoing fundamental and specific requirements and the reasons which led to the conclusions reached It should show a plan of the selected site as it exists and as it is planned by stages

The principal elements of a good master plan are

1 A property survey showing location and orientation of the site with reference to the community, highways, railroads, and rapid transit

2 A topographical survey showing the contour of the terrain and elevation

3 Complete data on meteorological conditions, such as rainfall, fog, smoke, and temperature variations, also a wind rose showing maximum and minimum wind velocities, as well as their direction and frequency of occurrence

4 An obstruction map showing the location, nature, shape and height of all obstructions within a radius of 2 to 6 miles from the boundaries of the proposed airport, depending on its size The map should also indicate the glide ratio over the extended runway zones A statement should be made of the possibility and cost of removing such obstructions to render the site safe for flying on instruments An aerial photograph encompassing the area within a 2- to 6-mile radius is also desirable as a help in the preparation of the airfield plan

5 A study of available utilities to determine the cost of furnishing electric power, gas, water, telephone, and sewage disposal

6 A soil survey to determine the stability of the soil, its character, and the bearing characteristics of its subsoil

7 A plan of the selected runway pattern showing the various stages of construction, location, arrangement, orientation, and length. (An airport data sheet similar to the one on page 91 can be used)

8 A grading and drainage plan to fit the selected runway pattern and building locations

9 A field lighting plan complementary to the various stages of field development

10 An air traffic pattern and control plan showing the handling of the expected peak air traffic for the region and in relation to its airways

11 A building layout plan including administration building and passenger station, also hangars, if any are contemplated

12 A list of locally available materials to be used in the construction of the airport

13 A financial statement outlining the cost of the airport and proposed method of financing

14 An administration and budget plan for the operation of the airport

The capacity, physical and financial, of each stage of development should be properly balanced against the rate of growth of the community to prevent disruption of the city's financial budget A reasonable balance should also be maintained between airport facilities and any geographical region. In other words, airports should be thought of as developments which will bring the greatest amount of service to the largest number of people at the lowest possible cost. In many cases, a sounder program will result from having several smaller communities cooperate in the development of a joint airport for the entire region. This arrangement will be sounder financially as well as operationally since the air transport operator will be able to offer much better service to one airport serving 50,000 persons than five separate but near-by airports, each serving only 10,000.

AIRPORT DATA

1. Identification and Location

Name of airport _____
City or town _____ County _____
Altitude _____
Latitude ° ′ ″ Longitude ° ″
Distance from city and direction _____
Type _____
Activity _____
CAA classification _____
Remarks: _____

2. Topographical Features

Total acreage _____
Dimensions _____
Shape _____
Landing area, expandable _____
Direction and extent _____

3. Runways or Landing Strips

Direction	Length	Width	Surface

4. Buildings

5. Facilities

Hangars	Dimension	Door Width	Door Height

Accommodations, such as fuel and oil, telephone, water, etc.:

Figure 5 illustrates a hypothetical case which may well apply to many communities now contemplating air transport facilities. Here three small communities have collectively solved their problem by joining together to build landing facilities to meet their combined requirements at the lowest possible initial and operating costs. The location of the airport being adjacent to a highway is convenient to each community,

and there is sufficient available land surrounding it to allow for subsequent expansion when increased population, industry growth, and travel habit changes demand enlargement of facilities.

The preceding analysis also applies to industrial airports, except that industrial plants, fixed base oper-

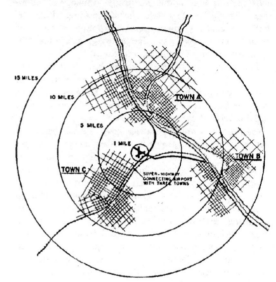

FIGURE 5. TYPICAL REGIONAL AIRPORT PLAN

ators, and non-scheduled cargo operation replace the part played by the airlines.

Airparks or air harbors, on the other hand, may be privately financed somewhat along the lines of country clubs or entirely underwritten by the community they serve as public grounds for the general use of its residents.

As a final check on any plan for landing facilities and ground accommodations, the airport authority of any community should examine its project in the light of its fitness in the overall pattern of our national airway network to appraise fully its worth as a civic improvement and national defense asset.

Bibliography

Airport Management, Civil Aeronautics Authority, U. S. Department of Commerce, Washington, D. C.

Report of the 16th Annual Convention of the American Association of Airport Executives, July 10-11-12, 1944, American Association of Airport Executives, Peoria, Illinois.

"The Development and Forecasting of Airport Requirements," by Edward P. Warner, *Journal of the Boston Society of Civil Engineers*, April, 1944.

Airport Planning for Urban Areas, June 1, 1945, Civil Aeronautics Administration, U. S. Department of Commerce, Washington, D. C.

6

AIRFIELD PLANNING

The airfield, that portion of any landing facility or airport used for the landing, taxiing, and take-off of aircraft, represents a very large percentage of the total capital invested in the development of such landing facility or airport. Its planning and design must be directed to obtain the desired operating characteristics from its runway and taxiway pattern to achieve proper balance with the proposed handling and dispatching capacity of the terminal buildings, and allow the permissible rate of air traffic movement under CAVU conditions, which means "Ceiling And Visibility Unlimited." Although this rate of air traffic movement is much higher than that experienced in instrument landing weather, it is generally agreed that any airfield should be able to handle the capacity of the air space over it and that of the airways it serves, in good weather.

If the capacity of the airfield is designed for instrument landing conditions as they now exist, any improvement in methods of navigation and air traffic control which can permit an increase in air traffic movement rate, bringing such rate closer to that prevailing in good weather, will be equivalent to raising the capacity of the airfield beyond its terminal facilities. It is therefore advisable to design and arrange the runways of scheduled air transportation airports for instrument operation and to provide adequate runway length, width, clearances, and approach zones for such instrument operation. However it may be more economical to design for good weather and increase capacity by multiplying runways if improvements in navigation and control fail to materialize.

Inadequacy of airfield capacity, as witnessed during the past few years, can be prevented in the future by intelligent and imaginative planning. For this sort of planning, the airport planner must have a thorough understanding of the take-off and landing characteristics of the types of aircraft which are to use the landing facilities proposed. It requires an intelligent in-

terpretation of the traffic survey discussed in Part 5 and translation of projected traffic volume into sound airfield design specifications to derive an ultimate plan which can, by stages, meet the progressive steps in the growth of the aviation activities of the community.

Airfield Design Requirements

There are few rules by which an airport engineer can plan and design an airfield because the art is, as yet, too new. His judgment must be good and his thinking rational, and he must keep in mind that once concrete is poured or asphalt is rolled in place, alterations dictated by increased traffic or changes in flying equipment are expensive. A good airfield design should possess the following characteristics:

1. Allowance for landing, taxi, and take-off as independent operations without interference.
2. Shortest taxi distances from gate or loading apron position to end of runways.
3. Safe runway length and separation.
4. Safe approaches.
5. Excellent control tower visibility.
6. Ample loading apron space.
7. Capacity balanced with that of air space over it and capacity of building facilities.
8. Land acreage sufficient to permit subsequent expansion.
9. Lowest possible cost of construction.

Before starting to lay out a runway pattern, it is necessary to have the following data:

1. A survey of the site, showing its size, boundaries, orientation, and topography.
2. An obstruction map within a 2-mile radius, if it is to be an airpark or Class I or II airport, and 4- to 8-mile radius for a larger airport.
3. The number of anticipated aircraft movements, both incoming and outgoing, during the peak traffic hour.

4. The types of aircraft which are to use the field; their landing, take-off, and ground maneuvering characteristics; their overall dimensions.

5. A wind rose showing surface wind velocities, directions, and percentage of prevalence in each of the usual sixteen points of the Weather Bureau wind rose.

The four basic problems to be solved are:

1. Maximum safety in take-off and landing for any aircraft which may use the field. This requires adequate approach clearances, lateral clearances, and runway lengths. The most critical period of any airplane operation occurs during the take-off. This period is divided into three stages: acceleration on ground at full engine power to the point of becoming airborne, gradual climb until sufficient airspeed is gained so the airplane can continue flight in case of partial engine power failure, emergency landing in case the pilot so elects.

2. Minimum taxiing distances possible to expedite the dispatching of arriving and departing airplanes. This requires an efficient taxiway pattern connecting the airfield runway system and the terminal buildings.

3. Efficient handling and parking of aircraft at the apron or terminal building gates. This means the best possible gate arrangement and the shortest travel distances to expedite the orderly flow of mail, passengers, and cargo.

In determining the number of aircraft loading positions it is assumed that one-half hour at the apron for loading and unloading should be sufficient. This appears to be a conservative figure which can be reduced later if the capacity of the airfield can be increased in the future.

4. Arrangement of runways to provide suitable air separation in the air traffic pattern of incoming and outgoing airplanes. This is most important as it determines the airfield capacity when flight movements are made in bad weather and minimizes the need for "stacking" discussed in Part 3.

Types of Runway Patterns

The selection of a runway pattern or configuration is the first step in airfield design. Although the requirements of any landing facility can be met by a given airport classification, either according to the CAA segregation or the ATA classification, the shape of the property, its location with reference to surrounding obstructions, and wind directions will generally demand a compromise between these limitations and the best runway pattern for the type of airport

under consideration. Whenever possible, runways must be aligned in the direction of the prevailing winds to reduce cross-wind operation to a minimum.

The following examples of types of runway configuration are presented without consideration of fixed boundaries. Runway lengths are likewise hypothetical, although they represent what is considered safe practice for each type of runway pattern discussed. Each of the single-runway patterns can be scaled down to meet the requirements of smaller airports as long as the proper clearances are maintained.

Flightstrip

The simplest form of landing and take-off facility is the single flightstrip. This is the "flightstop" or

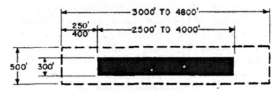

FIGURE 1. TYPICAL FLIGHTSTRIP

single-runway "airpark" shown in Fig. 1. It is the logical pattern where the winds generally blow from the same direction or its reciprocal and when traffic requirements do not exceed 30 to 40 movements per hour. It can consist of a sodded area 2,500 to 4,000 feet long by 300 feet wide, as shown by the black area in the figure. Where land is available, the runway can be made long enough so that one-half can be used to land and the other half to take off, with the station building at its center, thus reducing taxiing to a minimum. Where wind direction permits this simple arrangement, it is a comparatively inexpensive facility which lends itself admirably to local schedule or feeder operation where least time on the ground is a prime requisite to obtain maximum system speed * and low operating cost.

Flightstrips can be used in multiples, arranged in parallel with proper separation for simultaneous take-offs and landings.

Small Airport (Airpark)

The next simplest configuration designed to obtain greater wind coverage consists of two runways, either forming an L, as shown in Fig. 2, or a T, V, or X, depending on the direction of the prevailing winds and the shape of the property. This practical pattern advocated for airparks consists of two sodded landing strips 1,800 to 2,500 feet long and 300 feet wide. Where wind conditions require it, a third strip can be

* The average speed between terminal points of a route.

added. With the development of personal aircraft able to negotiate cross winds 15 to 20 miles per hour or higher, it should not be necessary to require further wind coverage for this type of airport as any one of four permissible shapes of dual strips should be able to accommodate personal flying operations with complete safety.

Sixty-Degree Single-Runway Pattern

With prevailing winds occurring in several directions it becomes necessary to provide wider wind cov-

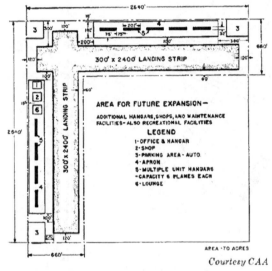

Courtesy CAA

FIGURE 2. TYPE OF AIRPARK

erage to assure uninterrupted operation and a greater degree of airport utility. This can be obtained by using a triangular pattern or 60-degree system having a capacity of 40 aircraft movements per hour, as shown in Fig. 3. This triangular pattern is fundamentally sound and, if properly arranged, allows ample space for hangars and parking areas, keeps all operations compact by having a centrally located terminal building, and keeps taxi distances to a minimum.

The layout need not be equilateral as the angle between any two runways can be chosen so that the long runway is oriented in the low wind velocity direction, and the short runway in the prevailing high wind direction. Thus utilization of land acreage will be the most efficient and usability of the highest degree.

In many locations, the direction which best serves instrument landing operation, because of unrestricted surroundings or high velocity winds during periods of poor visibility, may well be that of the long runway.

Forty-Five-Degree Single-Runway Pattern

When still greater wind coverage is desired for the same airfield capacity as the 60-degree single-runway pattern, either owing to high velocity winds in many directions or strong winds in four major directions, each occurring a large part of the time, a four-runway pattern or 45-degree system should be used. Figure 4 illustrates such configuration with an angle of 45 degrees between adjacent runways. If a square plot of ground were used, the diagonal runways X and X_1 would be 1.414 times the length of the other two runways and should be located in the directions of least wind velocity.

A more conventional layout of a 45-degree single-runway pattern is shown in Fig. 5. The general arrangement is the same as in the 60-degree pattern, illustrated in Fig. 3, and includes 6,000-foot runways, but the acreage required is 820 acres instead of 770 acres. Unless wind conditions, terrain, or surrounding obstructions require a 45-degree runway system, the 60-degree pattern is preferable because of its simplicity and lower cost.

Sixty-Degree Conventional Parallel-Runway Pattern

When the air traffic grows beyond the capacity of the single-runway pattern, additional capacity can be obtained by multiplying the number of runways. Figure 6 illustrates how this is done with a 60-degree single-runway pattern by paralleling it with an additional set of runways without changing the basic configuration of the field. It will be noted that the added runways are longer to accommodate larger and longer-range aircraft which may logically serve the community as air traffic increases. Although the separation of parallel runways should permit one landing and one take-off simultaneously, aircraft taxiing to the outer runway for take-off would cross the landing runway (see wind traffic diagram) in the path of the incoming aircraft. Traffic must, therefore, be regulated so as to prevent any possibility of taking-off aircraft taxiing across the runway used for landing at the time actual landing is made by an incoming aircraft.

In the final stage, this runway layout has a potential capacity of 120 movements per hour.

Sixty-Degree Open Parallel-Runway Pattern

To overcome this drawback, runways can be separated further by arranging them around the terminal area as shown in Fig. 7. This configuration permits simultaneous take-off and landing movements of aircraft without interference at any time. The greater runway separation also permits simultaneous landings if dictated by emergency.

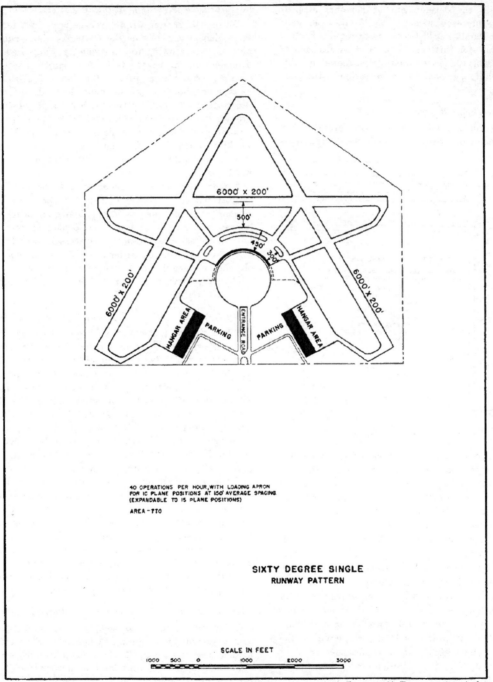

SIXTY DEGREE SINGLE
RUNWAY PATTERN

Other advantages of this scheme are:

1. Improved view of the airfield from the control tower.
2. Less paving and land acreage.
3. Shorter taxi distance.
4. Better land utilization.

Sixty-Degree Dual Parallel-Runway Pattern

When still greater airfield capacity is desired, it can be obtained by paralleling the 60-degree open parallel

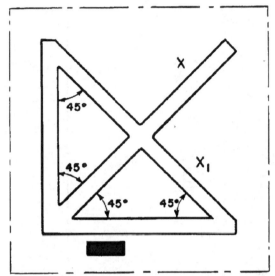

FIGURE 4.   FORTY-FIVE DEGREE SINGLE-RUNWAY
PATTERN

layout, as illustrated by Fig. 8. The first stage of this pattern is similar to that shown in Fig. 7. However, the resultant pattern obtained by paralleling the original set of runway has the same defect as the 60-degree conventional parallel scheme shown in Fig. 6, namely, that of crossing traffic between landing and take-off on each pair of runways. There is insufficient runway separation on each side to permit the use of any pair of runways for simultaneous landings to overcome this objection.

Sixty-Degree Diverging-Runway Pattern

Increasing separation can be obtained by diverging the outer pair of runways of the layout shown in Fig. 8, thus permitting the segregation of landings and take-offs. With any given wind direction, landings can be effected on the converging pair of runways and take-offs on the diverging pair as shown by the wind

traffic diagram in Fig. 9, which illustrates a 60-degree diverging and converging runway pattern.

However, in order to accomplish this, it is necessary to depart from the usual procedure of landing on the inside runways. Landing in this case should be made on the right-hand runway of a pair, and take-off should be effected from the left-hand runways. Thus the movements on the various runways are in opposite direction when the winds are reversed, which complicates air and ground traffic control to some extent.

Sixty-Degree Six-Runway Pattern (First Stage)

A variation of the several 60-degree runway patterns so far discussed is illustrated in Fig. 10. This arrangement is applicable only to cities either having or contemplating a large volume of air traffic. In its first stage, this pattern has a capacity of 120 movements per hour and does not provide good land utilization. It operates substantially as open parallel scheme shown in Fig. 7.

Thirty-Degree Tangential-Runway Pattern

This tangential pattern is the final stage of the 60-degree six-runway pattern shown in Fig. 7. The second stage is obtained by adding runways bisecting the original six runways to arrive at a pattern having twelve runways 30 degrees apart, as illustrated in Fig. 11. This arrangement permits complete segregation of multiple take-offs and landings simultaneously without cross traffic. During peak operating hours it should be possible to complete three landings on one side of the airfield and three take-offs on the opposite side per minute, thus effecting a total airfield capacity of 360 movements per hour. This capacity should be possible, irrespective of wind conditions, as aircraft equipped with tricycle landing gears can land without difficulty at 45 degrees to a 30-mile-per-hour wind.

For a major terminal and base of operation, this layout provides ample space for shops and hangars and their expansion. Its major drawback is that once the size of the central terminal area has been decided upon, it cannot be substantially enlarged without seriously affecting the airfield layout. It also requires greater land acreage, but it is functionally superior to any other scheme where large airfield capacity is needed.

Miscellaneous Runway Patterns

The 60-degree six-runway pattern, shown in Fig. 10, can also be expanded into a 60-degree dual parallel scheme, as shown in Fig. 12, instead of a converging and diverging pattern, but its capacity is one-third less. As there is not a great deal of difference between

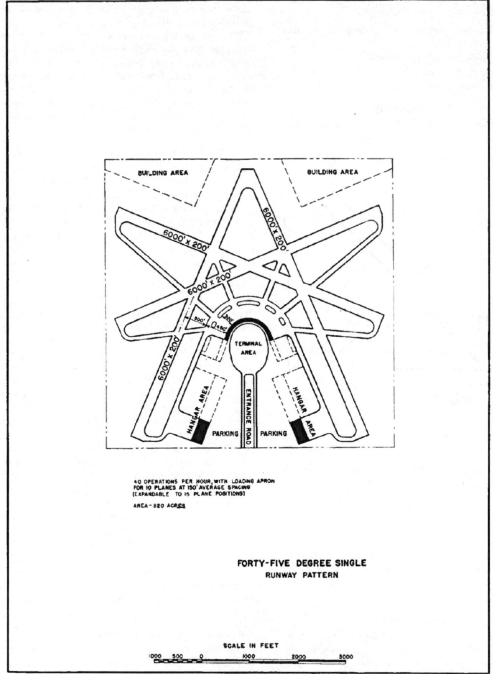

FORTY-FIVE DEGREE SINGLE
RUNWAY PATTERN

Courtesy Air Transport Association

FIGURE 5

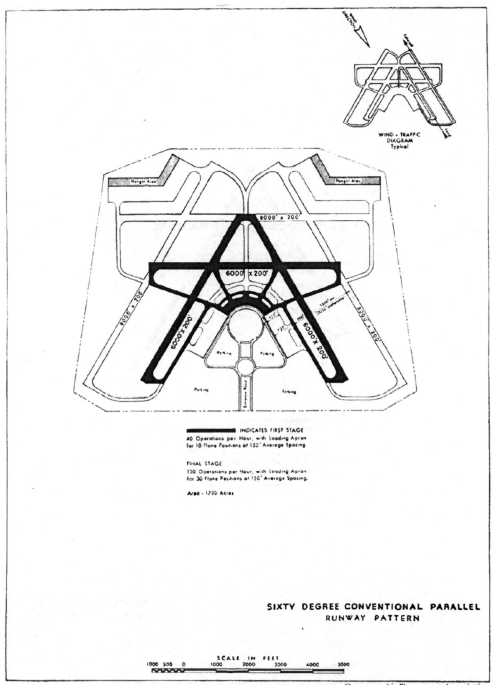

SIXTY DEGREE CONVENTIONAL PARALLEL
RUNWAY PATTERN

FIGURE 6

Courtesy Air Transport Association

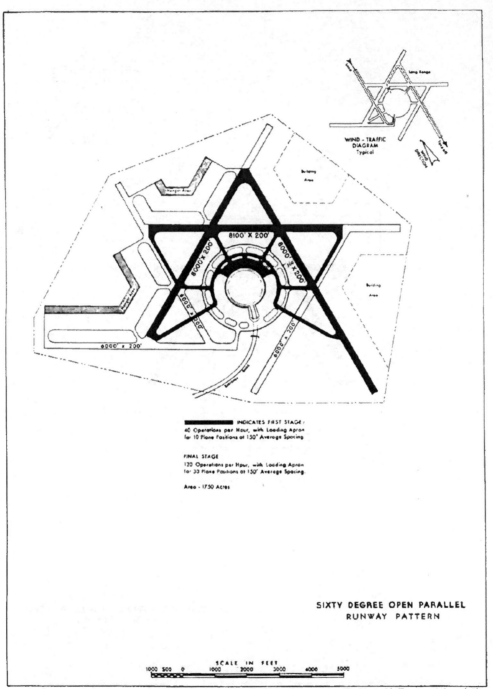

WIND - TRAFFIC
DIAGRAM
Typical

8100' X 200'

8000' X 200'

8000' X 200'

8000' X 200'

8000' X 200'

6000' X 200'

INDICATES FIRST STAGE:
40 Operations per Hour, with Loading Apron
for 10 Plane Positions at 150' Average Spacing

FINAL STAGE
120 Operations per Hour, with Loading Apron
for 30 Plane Positions at 150' Average Spacing.

Area - 1750 Acres

SIXTY DEGREE OPEN PARALLEL
RUNWAY PATTERN

SCALE IN FEET
1000 500 0   1000   2000   3000   4000   5000

Courtesy Air Transport Association

FIGURE 7

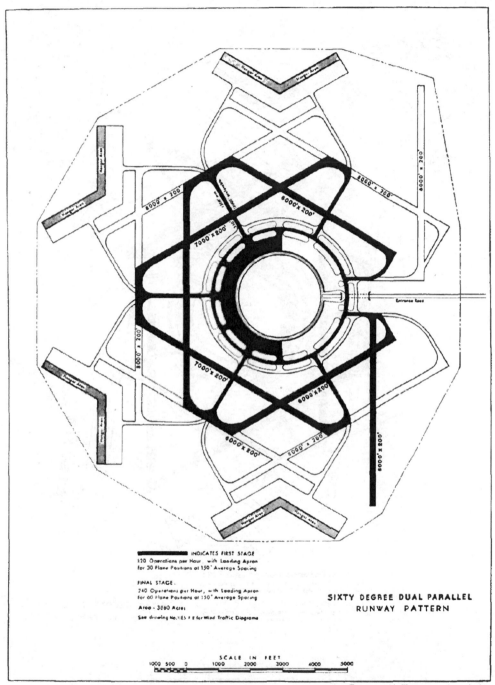

SIXTY DEGREE DUAL PARALLEL
RUNWAY PATTERN

FIGURE 8

Courtesy Air Transport Association

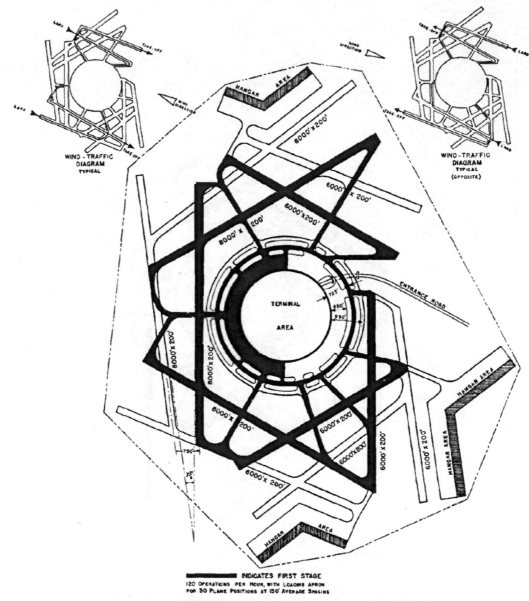

INDICATES FIRST STAGE
120 OPERATIONS PER HOUR, WITH LOADING APRON
FOR 30 PLANE POSITIONS AT 150' AVERAGE SPACING

FINAL STAGE
240 OPERATIONS PER HOUR, WITH LOADING APRON
FOR 60 PLANE POSITIONS AT 150' AVERAGE SPACING

AREA - 3120 ACRES

SIXTY DEGREE DIVERGING
RUNWAY PATTERN

SCALE IN FEET

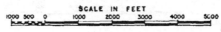

1000 500 0   1000   2000   3000   4000   5000

Courtesy Air Transport Association

FIGURE 9

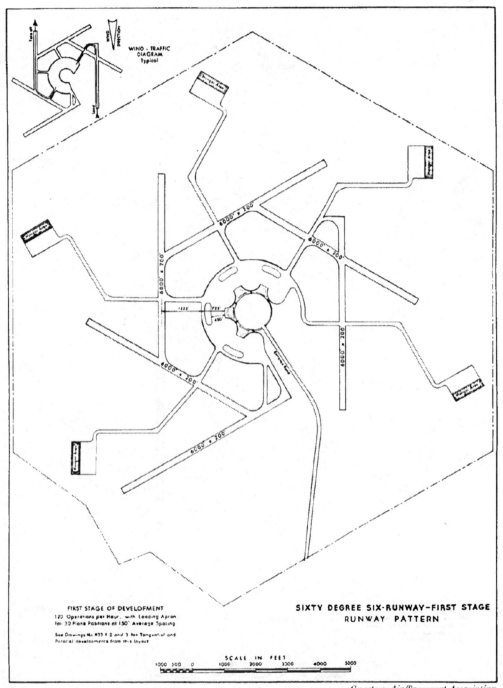

FIRST STAGE OF DEVELOPMENT

120 Operations per Hour, with Loading Apron
for 30 Plane Positions at 150' Average Spacing

See Drawings No. #35 # 2 and 3 for Tangential and
Parallel developments from this layout

**SIXTY DEGREE SIX-RUNWAY—FIRST STAGE
RUNWAY PATTERN**

SCALE IN FEET

1000 500 0   1000   2000   3000   4000   5000

Courtesy Air Transport Association

FIGURE 10

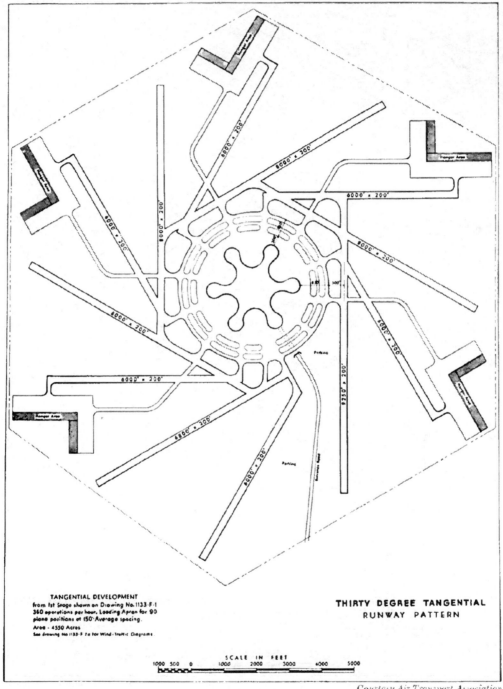

THIRTY DEGREE TANGENTIAL
RUNWAY PATTERN

TANGENTIAL DEVELOPMENT
from 1st Stage shown on Drawing No.1133-F-1
360 operations per hour, Loading Apron for 90
plane positions at 150' Average spacing.
Area - 4550 Acres
See drawing No 1133-F-2a for Wind-Traffic Diagrams

SCALE IN FEET

Courtesy Air Transport Association

FIGURE 11

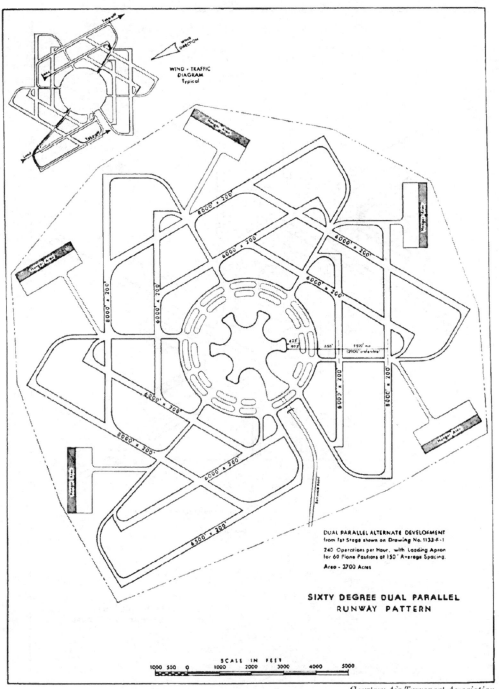

DUAL PARALLEL ALTERNATE DEVELOPMENT
from 1st Stage shown on Drawing No. 1133-F-1

240 Operations per Hour, with Loading Apron
for 60 Plane Positions at 150' Average Spacing.

Area - 2700 Acres

SIXTY DEGREE DUAL PARALLEL RUNWAY PATTERN

FIGURE 12

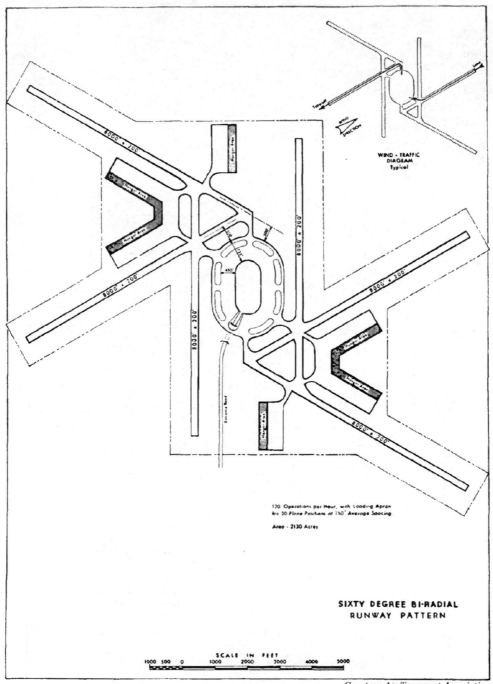

SIXTY DEGREE BI-RADIAL
RUNWAY PATTERN

Courtesy Air Transport Association

FIGURE 13

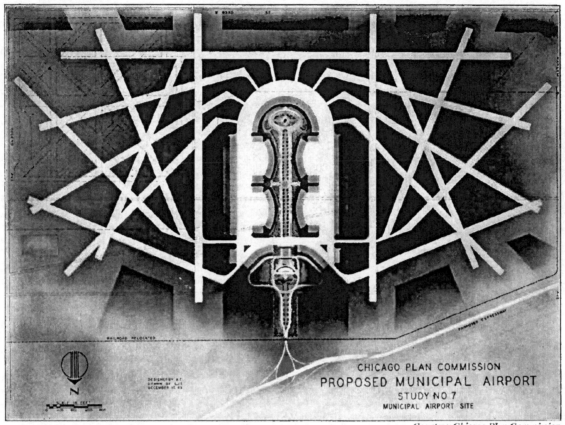

CHICAGO PLAN COMMISSION
PROPOSED MUNICIPAL AIRPORT
STUDY NO. 7
MUNICIPAL AIRPORT SITE

Courtesy Chicago Plan Commission

FIGURE 14. DOUBLE-RUNWAY PATTERN

the area required for each scheme, the land utilization per movement is highly unfavorable to the dual parallel scheme.

All the 60-degree patterns so far discussed can readily be designed as 45-degree systems if the wind rose of a particular location demands it without deviating from the design principles involved or altering the comments made on each scheme except that any 45-degree layout is bound to be more expensive because of the increased paving and larger area needed.

There are many other patterns of single- or multiple-runway layouts which combine the features of basic schemes to solve particular air traffic problems, site topography and development, or financial limitations. Figure 13 illustrates a 60-degree converging and diverging layout with excellent separation. This pattern is applicable where land cost is not a primary factor. Another pattern which overcomes the disadvantage of the fixed central area of the tangential pattern is shown in Fig. 14. In this double-runway pattern, incoming and outgoing aircraft traffic patterns are definitely separated. Access to the center area can be by bridge or underpass to allow aircraft to taxi from one side to the other at the entrance end of the airport.

Typical Airfields

A typical airfield layout for a small city might well look like the plan illustrated in Fig. 15a when most winds blow in the two-runway directions indicated. If greater coverage is required, a third runway could be added. Figure 15b shows a three-runway system and airport layout to permit long runways with a given plot of ground.

Another excellent airfield layout, applicable to a larger community or to serve a region, is shown in Fig. 16. This is a four-runway pattern which utilizes the available area in a most efficient manner. It is designed to serve as a combination airport by providing hangar accommodations and general airport facilities to the personal flyer as well as to industry.

Figure 17 shows how a given pattern capacity can be increased to accommodate two different types of service by practically duplicating the original field on a smaller scale for local schedule operation.

For the larger city commanding a major trunk line stop a more ambitious plan is in order. Its airport development may contemplate a layout such as shown in Fig. 18 which illustrates the runway pattern recommended by a committee of airline engineers to the city of Baltimore, Maryland, for a new airport. Here the

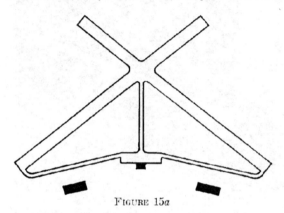

FIGURE 15*a*

first stage consists of the three shaded runways of varying length to accommodate medium-sized transports, such as may be used in domestic operation. The administration building and passenger facilities are also shown shaded for the first stage. Hangar areas are shown separated from the administration and passenger functions of the airport and arranged to allow field expansion when increased activities warrant it. The second stage includes the paralleling of the first three runways with approximately one-half mile separation for instrument landing and take-off operation, thus doubling the capacity of the field. Similarly, the central building can be completed to its original plan to balance the capacity of the airfield. Taxiway layout has been studied to reduce ground taxi distances, and the central location of the passenger station and parking area is conducive to efficient land utilization and expedition of airplane movements.

If the traffic plans envisage long-range operation at a future date, sufficient land should be purchased originally to permit the extension of at least two runways to a length of 10,000 feet in the direction of minimum wind velocity and extension of the others to 8,000 feet minimum.

Realizing that the near future holds great promise for air transportation and faced with the fact that airports in the past have been found inadequate as soon as completed, large metropolitan centers have begun to think of superairports and are planning them on a scale which is expected to meet the needs of scheduled air transportation for some time to come. Among such developments is the Idlewild project, New York City's bid for air supremacy in the East.

Figure 19 shows this superairport that covers an area of over 4,500 acres and is located in the Jamaica Bay corner of Queens, a borough of New York City. Its final cost has been estimated to be more than 150 million dollars. The master plan for this airport is the result of the combined effort of an engineering committee consisting of airline personnel headed by Glenn E. Markt, director of airports for American Airlines, working in conjunction with the Airlines Chief Pilots' Committee and the city officials.

The chief characteristics of the airport are provisions for a substantial expansion and flexibility of stage development to meet any advance in airways control dictated by the application of electronic improvements. It has been planned in three distinct stages, the last stage being a converging and diverging pattern type to provide 360 movements per hour. The central area is made large enough to accommodate 75 to 90 airplane positions, depending upon the building arrangement, assuming an average of 150-foot wing span each. Two-lane taxiing will be permissible at the outer edge of the apron with ample wing tip to wing tip clearance. Service hangars will be located between the runways at the outer edge of the field. A vehicular underpass will be built on the west side to enable full utilization of the apron and minimize taxiing distances when using the runways on the west side of the field.

The taxiways pattern was carefully studied as all airplane traffic between the terminal area and the hangars must use the taxiways, in addition to the airplanes using any one or more of the runways. To eliminate any possible traffic bottleneck, two taxiways are provided from the central terminal area to the hangar areas.

Effect of Meteorological Conditions on Runway Length

To be safe operationally, runways should be long enough to permit aircraft to roll normally to a stop in the event of engine failure during take-off at the point where the landing gear wheels just leave the ground. The other four principal factors which affect runway length requirement for safe operation are winds and

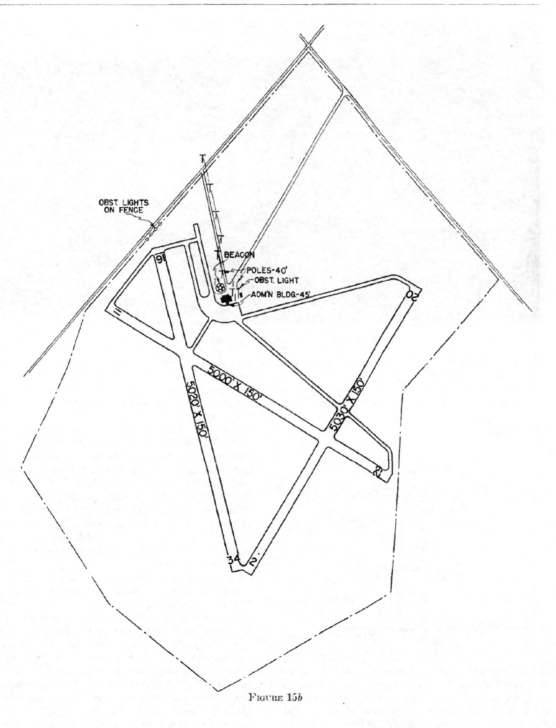

OBST. LIGHTS
ON FENCE

BEACON

POLES-40'
OBST. LIGHT
ADM'N BLDG.-45'

5000' X 150'

5020' X 150'

5030' X 150'

Figure 15*b*

Courtesy CAA

FIGURE 16. WASHINGTON NATIONAL AIRPORT

their direction, elevation above sea level, air temperature, and surface condition.

Winds of noticeable velocity in the general direction of the runway have the effect of reducing the take-off

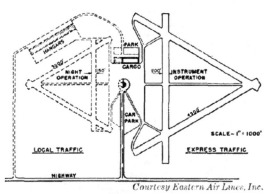

Courtesy Eastern Air Lines, Inc.

FIGURE 17

and landing run. An airplane which normally leaves the ground when it has reached a speed of 60 miles per hour, for example, will take off at 40 miles per hour if traveling against a 20-mile-per-hour wind. In landing, the same holds true. When the "unstick speed,"

that is, the speed at which the wheels of an aircraft leave the ground at the end of the take-off run, and the wind velocity are known, the effect of the wind on runway length required can be determined by multiplying the correction factor derived from Fig. 20 by the runway length for zero wind, as shown in columns 4 and 5 in Table IV of Part 2, for various types of aircraft. This curve assumes that, in landing, the contact speed is the same as the unstick speed in take-off and, therefore, satisfies the definition of safe runway length given at the beginning of this discussion. If these speeds vary, the highest of the two figures should be taken to be on the conservative side. The ground run into wind should be taken with the lowest velocity indicated by the wind data collected over a period of two years if possible.

Tricycle landing gears and higher wing loadings with the use of more efficient flaps permit substantially higher cross-wind values. However, experience indicates that a 12-mile-per-hour beam component should be assumed as the maximum permissible cross-wind velocity for positioning and dimensioning runways for any airpark or airport, except those designed for scheduled air transportation, as airline transports can operate with higher cross winds. Thus the main runway can be used until cross winds at 90 degrees to its direction exceed 12 miles per hour. With only two runways positioned at unequal angles, such as an X,

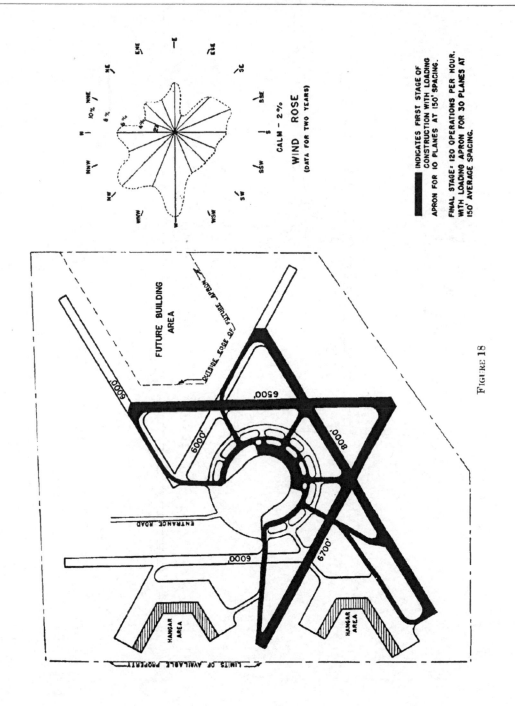

FIGURE 18

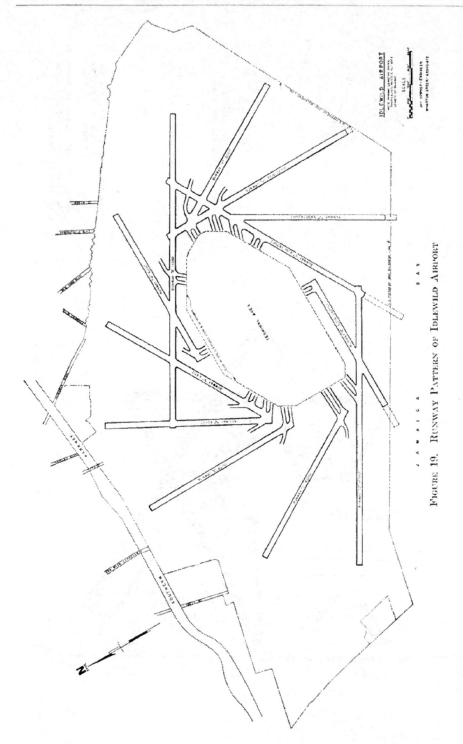

FIGURE 19. RUNWAY PATTERN OF IDLEWILD AIRPORT

for instance, a wind which bisects the larger of the two angles of runway intersection, and which appreciably exceeds 12 miles per hour, will result in excessive crosswind component for both runways. Only the addition of another runway can alleviate this condition, showing the importance of orientating runways in the di-

$$R_W = R_O \times K_R$$

R_W = RUNWAY LENGTH FOR ANY WIND VELOCITY

R_O = RUNWAY LENGTH FOR ZERO WIND VELOCITY

K_R = RUNWAY LENGTH REDUCTION COEFFICIENT

AS OBTAINED FROM CURVE

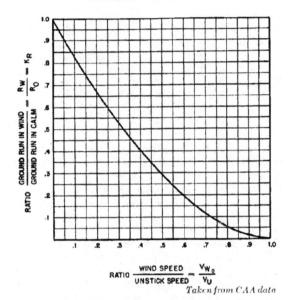

$$\text{RATIO } \frac{\text{WIND SPEED}}{\text{UNSTICK SPEED}} = \frac{V_{W_O}}{V_U}$$

Taken from CAA data

FIGURE 20

rection of prevailing winds to reduce their number and length.

When a two-runway plan is considered, it should first be assumed that the angle between the cross runway and the zero wind or long runway will not be less than 60 degrees. The critical velocity for the cross runway of a two-runway pattern can be calculated as follows:

$$V_c = W_w \times \cos A$$

where V_c = the critical velocity component,

W_w = the main runway beam component,

A = the angle between the cross runway and the wind direction.

This analytical procedure can also be applied to the positioning of runways for a triangular pattern and a quadrilateral pattern. The critical velocity for the second cross runway can be calculated as follows:

$$V_c = V_n \times \csc B$$
$$V_n = V_c \times \sin B$$

where V_c = the actual wind velocity (critical velocity),

V_n = beam component across runway to which operations are to be transferred (approximately 12 miles per hour),

B = runway angle.

An important factor influencing the size of an airport, the zoning of its surrounding area, and the length of its runways is its elevation above sea level. Runways should be lengthened over their calculated length at sea level by approximately one-fourth the altitude in feet, according to the following expression:

$$L_A = L_S + \frac{A}{4}$$

where L_A = resultant runway length at given altitude, in feet,

L_S = runway length required at sea level, in feet,

A = elevation of site above sea level, in feet.

This relationship, shown graphically in Fig. 2, Part 5, is based on standard air, that is, an approximate temperature decrease of 3.6° F per 1,000 feet of elevation. However, there is a possibility that during the summer months, flight operations will occur during the middle of the day when air temperatures of 100° F or higher may prevail, together with subnormal barometric pressures corresponding to as much as 500 feet above the actual elevation of the airport. The effect of these variations * is to increase runway length with altitude, as shown in Fig. 21. These values should be used in planning airfields where these conditions apply.

Another variable element for which allowance must be made in determining field size and runway length is the surface condition of the landing area or runway surface as affected by rain, snow, and/or ice. Although rain has been known to increase the coefficient of adhesion of tire tread to runway surface, the reverse is true as a rule. Snow, if not too light or too wet, provides good retarding action in landing, but ice appreciably reduces the coefficient of braking friction to prevent wheel locking, thus requiring a greater portion of the runway for landing. When the airport has a soft sod surface or the runways consist of loose gravel or

* Technical Report 40, April, 1944, *The Correlation of Aircraft Takeoff and Landing Characteristics with Airport Size*, by A. L. Morse, Civil Aeronautics Authority, U. S. Department of Commerce, Washington, D. C.

cinders, causing greater rolling resistance, the normal take-off run will be appreciably lengthened. Smooth concrete or asphalt surfaces are preferable and are almost universally used except where a hard sod or a well-drained surface is available.

Triangular versus Quadrilateral Runway Pattern

The first problem which usually arises in laying out an airfield is the number of directions to be covered with a runway. Barring localities where the wind practically always blows in one direction or its reciprocal, a selection is generally made between the four-runway and the three-runway system. The four-runway system was favored in the past, partly because of

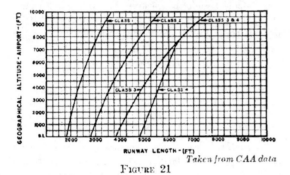

Taken from CAA data

FIGURE 21

airplane characteristics which required landing with the least possible cross wind, because of their relatively low-wing loading and landing gear configuration, and partly because it was felt that a first-class airport should have a runway in the four major directions of the compass.

The choice between a 45-degree and a 60-degree basic runway system with a given wind rose for a certain locality depends primarily on the degree of cross wind which present and future aircraft can safely negotiate during landing and take-off. It is a decision which concerns the designer of large airfields primarily because cost of construction and maintenance is proportional to total runway lineage.

From the common sense viewpoint it is obvious that runway patterns should bear a rational relationship to aircraft operating requirements, such as load factors, for example, bear to aircraft structure design. With a quadrilateral pattern, having each runway arranged at 45 degrees, the maximum allowable wind velocity in a direction 22½ degrees from each adjacent runway is equal to the highest allowable beam component, that is, maximum 90 degrees cross wind to each runway, divided by the sine of 22½ degrees if 100 per cent usability of each runway is to be obtained.

Similarly, with a triangular pattern, having each runway arranged at 60 degrees, the maximum allowable wind velocity in a direction of 30 degrees from each adjacent runway is equal to the maximum allowable beam component divided by the sine of 30 degrees.

Table I is a tabulation of maximum allowable wind velocities for values of beam components varying from 10 miles per hour to 30 miles per hour.

TABLE I

Allowable Beam Component, Miles per Hour	Maximum Wind, in Miles per Hour, Acceptable at These Angles						
	90°	75°	60°	45°	30°	22° 30'	15°
10.0	10.0	10.4	11.5	14.2	20.0	26.1	39.0
12.5	12.5	13.0	14.4	17.7	25.0	32.6	48.2
15.0	15.0	15.6	17.3	21.2	30.0	39.2	57.9
20.0	20.0	20.7	23.1	28.3	40.0	52.2	77.2
25.0	25.0	25.9	28.8	35.4	50.0	65.2	96.5
30.0	30.0	31.1	34.6	42.4	60.0	78.4	115.8

It will be noted from this table that for a similar beam component the 45-degree pattern will allow flight operation with 22 per cent higher wind velocity than the 60-degree pattern, or for the same maximum acceptable wind the beam component can be 22 per cent greater than for the 60-degree pattern. However, it must not be deduced that the 45-degree pattern is superior because the degree of usability for any type of runway pattern depends primarily on the direction of the winds, their intensity, and frequency at such intensity. For winds of higher velocity than those permissible for 100 per cent usability with a given beam component and runway angle, the maximum angle of the wind to the runway will be that angle whose sine equals the maximum allowable beam component divided by the wind velocity. The *unusable wind sector* between two runways, making an angle of 60 degrees, would be equal to 60 degrees minus twice that angle, or $a = 6(60° - 2a)$ for triangular patterns and $a = 8(45° - 2a)$ for quadrilateral patterns. If we call this resulting angle for each pattern b, the percentage of usability for each maximum wind condition becomes

$$100 \left(1 - \frac{b}{360°}\right).$$

An excellent case for the triangular pattern has been made in a paper entitled *Effect of Aircraft Operating Characteristics on Airport Runway Patterns*, by John C. Leslie, Harold E. Gray, and John J. Ford of Pan American Airways. The paper was presented before the

Institute of the Aeronautical Sciences in 1942. Although this presentation dealt primarily with the selection of an airport pattern for transport aircraft, the method of analysis followed is applicable to any type of landing facility.

The trend toward higher airplane landing speeds, partly due to higher wing loadings and also the elimination of stalling speed limitations, will enable large transport aircraft to land and take off with a greater amount of cross wind than now believed permissible. This characteristic may well permit the use of multiple-parallel unidirectional runways for large airports in regions where prevailing winds blow generally in the same direction. It will also be found that in many places where the wind blows prevailingly in a given direction in fair weather, it will blow in a directly opposite direction in bad weather, thus permitting the same runway to be used irrespective of weather. This type of wind direction will result in a greatly simplified air traffic pattern for a region requiring several airports, and should permit a more efficient location of such airports with respect to their function and service to the community. Generally speaking, the average wind velocity should not be used in calculating runway length. Its effect should be considered only as an increased safety factor.

Wind Rose

Wind data are customarily shown by a wind rose. It is a graphic presentation of wind observations tabulated as to direction, velocity, and frequency of occurrence for a period of time, which should not be less than five years in order to strike an average having sufficient accuracy. These observations should be taken at or near the site if possible, as wind conditions vary considerably with location, particularly in mountainous terrain. However, in preparing a report on the probable weather conditions for a particular site from which no observational material is available, it is necessary to use observations from the nearest point and adapt them by weighting the changes that will result from differences in geographical and industrial nature.

It is necessary to develop wind rose illustration of composite winds, extreme winds, restricted visibility, and restricted ceiling winds. Likewise, it is advisable to prepare a computation chart for runway coverage of winds. This chart will often require wind roses by segments of wind velocity to show wind prevalence. These procedures are clearly outlined in the CAA manual, *Airport Design.* Barring violent storms, flying conditions are generally least favorable when there is little wind, and it is in the direction of such low-

velocity wind that the longest runway must be orientated.

Airport Zoning

The zoning of flight approach areas, defined as approach zones, is a matter of utmost importance for the safe take-off and landing of airplanes and for their operation to a height which will permit their returning and landing if the engine fails or the pilot elects to land for any reason. It is a measure of the safety of the field, not only for the passengers and crew of the

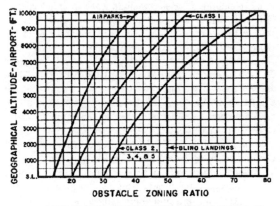

1. ZONING RATIO = DISTANCE FROM OBSTACLE TO END OF RUNWAY DIVIDED BY ALLOWABLE OBSTACLE HEIGHT.
2. TO OBTAIN ALLOWABLE OBSTACLE HEIGHT, DIVIDE DISTANCE FROM OBSTACLE TO END OF RUNWAY BY RATIO OBTAINED FROM APPROPRIATE CURVE.

Taken from CAA data

FIGURE 22

aircraft but also for those who reside or work in adjacent areas.

Airplanes can control their rate of descent within a wide range from a low-angle glide to a steep dive with a pronounced flare immediately before landing. However, their rate of climb immediately after taking off is definitely limited by their wing loading and power loading, and a clear path of low slope and adequate width must be provided beyond each runway for safe operation. The CAA recommends that the approaches to landing areas shall be clear within a glide path of 20 to 1 from the end of the usable area of the field for its Class I landing facilities, and 30 to 1 for its Classes II, III, IV, and V airports with the provision that instrument landing runways shall have a glide path of 40 to 1. These ratios are *minimum,* and it is obvious that the flatter the angle of approach to a runway, the better. In this respect, a minimum of 50-to-1 glide path is not only desirable but preferable for commercial scheduled air transportation.

These glide paths or zoning ratios are for sea level or near sea level altitude fields. As the altitude of the airfield increases, sea level figures must be corrected according to the effect of such altitude on airplane performance. Figure 22 shows graphically obstacle zoning ratios versus airport altitude which should be considered in zoning approaches to runways. It will be noted that the recommended 50-to-1 glide path line for instrument operation crosses the obstacle zoning ratio curve for airline airports at 6,000 feet, and from then on must be increased to 73 to 1 at 10,000 feet. This is as it should be to accommodate the lowered rate of climb of airplanes at that elevation. By glide path or zoning ratio is meant the distance from the end of the runway divided by the obstacle height. A 50-to-1 ratio means a maximum of one foot in height for every 50 feet in length from the end of the runway. Thus, at one mile from the runway, the maximum obstacle height should not exceed 105.6 feet, and so on. All major airports should be zoned for instrument operation in all directions.

Zoning of obstacle height within a given area around the airport must be supplemented by zoning of width. This zone is generally a trapezoidal area extending a few hundred feet laterally each side, beginning at the end of the runway, and increasing in width to a dis-

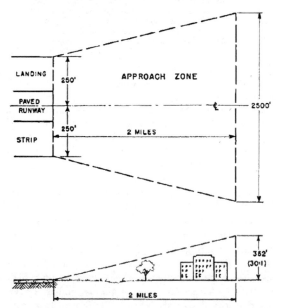

tance of 2 miles from the airport for airparks and Class I and II airports, and 4 to 6 miles for the larger fields.

The ideal zoning can be best described by comparing it to a saucer, the center being represented by the airfield proper and the rim by the glide path ratio desired. Although this condition is attainable and should be made a basic requirement whenever possible, it is rare that sufficient land can be zoned accordingly close to traffic-generating centers, owing either to the topography of the country or to artificial obstructions. A practical compromise, therefore, must be reached, particularly for airparks, many of which are expected to be located within or at close proximity to large communities and major airports.

A suggested zoning is illustrated in Fig. 23. It combines the CAA standards and the runway separation for instrument operation recommended by the ATA Committee on Airport Requirements. The approach zone for each runway used for normal operation is a trapezoidal area in plan form having a width of 500 feet at the boundary of the airfield, and 2,500 feet at a distance 2 miles from the boundary of the airfield. For instrument runways these widths are relatively 1,500 feet and 4,000 feet.

The operating personnel of the airlines is in general agreement that Class IV airports and the higher classifications should be zoned for instrument operation in all directions. The purpose of airport zoning is not only to protect flight paths but also to control the development of the property within the flight approach zones and adjacent or near the airfield, should additional runways located either in parallel or angularly be required later and be dictated by the master plan. Airports should be zoned also to protect the financial investment by preventing the erection of obstacles which would lessen or nullify the utility of the airport. Zoning can also serve to control the quality of development of property surrounding landing facilities, thus preventing the establishment of undesirable structures or the growth of tall trees. It should provide the necessary protection against certain types of manufacturing activities which produce excessive smoke or corrosive chemicals or obnoxious odors. The effect of improper zoning can be understood readily by stating that a 40-foot-high obstacle adjacent to the end of the runway means a reduction of 1,600 feet of effective runway length with a 40-to-1 glide path, and one-half as much with a 20-to-1 ratio.

Every obstruction should be plainly identified for easy recognition during the day and lighted with blinking red lights at night. (Cf. Part 8.)

In orientating runways, care must be taken to align them so that the prevailing flight paths of aircraft will not pass over the most populated or the business districts of the city at less than the regulated altitude.

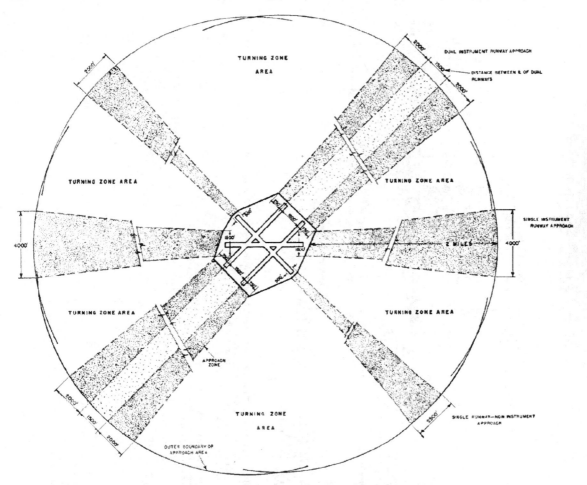

FIGURE 23. RUNWAY APPROACH ZONING

The airfield plan should be properly integrated with the expected growth of the city to prevent future low-altitude flying over dense city areas, and in large regions the airfield must be properly related with all other flying activities.

Effects of Civil Air Regulations on Commercial Airport Design

The civil air regulations for airplanes in the "transport category" require that airports, in design and size, meet the performance characteristics of present and anticipated transport airplanes. These regulations mean, in effect, that:

1. In *taking off*, an airplane should complete the take-off, clear all obstacles, and continue on its flight; or land and come to a stop at the option of the pilot after the occurrence of an engine failure at the critical moment.

2. In *landing*, the airplane should reach the end of the "effective" landing area at an altitude of 50 feet and thereafter land and stop within 60 per cent of the field length.

The "effective" length of the landing area is understood to be the distance from the point where the obstruction clearance line intersects the landing surface to the far end of the landing area. This obstruction clearance line is tangent to all obstructions in the approach zone of any given landing area or runway. It should have a minimum slope of 20 to 1.

The requirements which determine airfield limita-

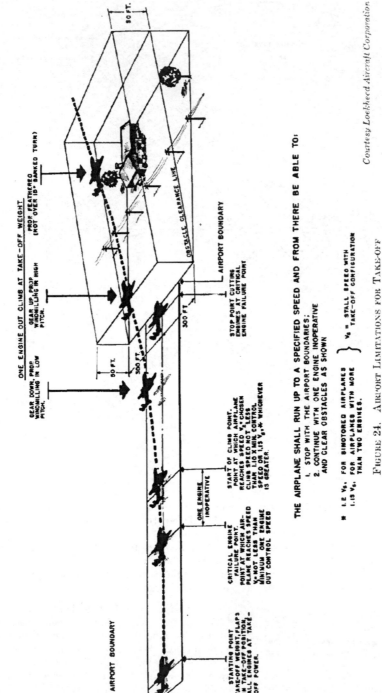

THE AIRPLANE SHALL RUN UP TO A SPECIFIED SPEED AND FROM THERE BE ABLE TO:

1. STOP WITH THE AIRPORT BOUNDARIES;
2. CONTINUE WITH ONE ENGINE INOPERATIVE AND CLEAR OBSTACLES AS SHOWN

* 1.2 V_s, FOR BIMOTORED AIRPLANES
  1.15 V_s, FOR AIRPLANES WITH MORE THAN TWO ENGINES.

V_s = STALL SPEED WITH TAKE-OFF CONFIGURATION

Courtesy Lockheed Aircraft Corporation

FIGURE 24. AIRPORT LIMITATIONS FOR TAKE-OFF

tions for transport aircraft used in air carrier operation are clearly illustrated in Fig 24 for take-off and in Fig. 25 for landing. In the take-off phase, the usable runway length is at least equal to one-engine inoperative (in a multi-engine airplane) climb slope of the airplane with an obstacle clearance slope from its far end This clearance slope might well be 40 to 1 for some airplanes, hence the 50-to-1 glide path recommendation for large airline airports In the landing phase, the required slope is 20 to 1 from the end of the effective area Thus take-off is far more critical than landing for most airplanes, except for those having low-power loading However, with the civil air regulations modified to permit a varying stalling speed according to runway approach conditions and runway lengths, it may well be that the landing distance, which should not exceed 0 6 of runway length, can become the critical factor

For domestic operation, using aircraft with wing loadings of the order of 20 to 50 pounds per square foot of wing area and the necessary power loading to obtain the required rate of climb stipulated by the civil air regulations, the length of runway needed can be expressed by

$$L = 1,000 + \left(150 \times \frac{W}{S}\right)$$

where L = length of runway,
W/S = wing loading

Existing regulations applied to airport runway length at sea level and for zero wind conditions indicate that 3,000 to 4,500 feet of runway is ample for airplanes designed for local schedule air transportation, 4,500 to 6,000 feet for trunk line stops, and 6,000 to 8,000 feet for intercontinental and transcontinental flying with an extension to 10,000 feet or more for long-range transoceanic operation, depending on the nonstop distance to be flown

Paved Runway Specifications

The "effective" length of a runway is the distance required for the take-off or for the landing of an airplane No greater length needs to be paved if it can be practically extended at each end to permit the airplane to land safely after immediately taking off in either direction The take-off or unstick distance is approximately four-tenths of the total needed runway length, and the distance to land is approximately six-tenths of the total runway length Thus the paved area need not be longer than the average distance required to land plus an allowance for surface condition and pilot inexperience, provided there is an available

hard surface portion at each end for overshooting and emergency landing due to engine failure on take-off This partial paving offers a distinct saving in pavement cost without jeopardizing safety of operation

This procedure, however, requires more land since, if only 75 per cent of the distance required needs to be paved, an additional strip of 40 per cent $(1 - 0 6)$ length must be added at each end, making the total landing area 155 per cent that of a fully paved runway. It then becomes a question of balancing the additional land acreage required against the cost of total versus partial runway paving

Runway width depends entirely upon the size of the airplanes which are to use the field and is a function, to a large degree, of their landing gear tread For unpaved airparks, a usable landing strip of 300 feet should be ample This entire width should be usable and graded with a maximum gradient of 1½ per cent It should drain well Widths of paved runways as specified in the CAA manual, *Airport Design*, are considered satisfactory except that runway width for major airports should be a minimum of 200 feet, and possibly 250 feet for superairports called upon to handle the larger transport aircraft which will make their appearance in the near future Runway shoulders should be at least 150 feet wide, built of stabilized material and capable of withstanding the weight of the largest aircraft to use the runway

Runway Clearances

The following general standards are recommended clearances for instrument runways

1 From the center line of a runway to airport boundaries, 500 feet (350 feet minimum) for first-class airports, and 400 feet for all others except airparks

2 From the center line of a runway to any adjacent building, 1,500 feet (1,000 feet minimum) for superairports, 1,000 feet for major terminals, and 750 feet for airports of intermediate size

Separation of parallel runways for simultaneous operation, that is, landing on one runway while taking off from the other, has been subject to much discussion and is still a highly controversial subject A 750-foot center line to center line distance between parallel runways has been found workable in good clear weather, but fails to satisfy the airline operating personnel in instrument flying weather owing partly to lack of accurate instrumentation and partly to the possibility of an incoming airplane's landing on the take-off runway, which might prove disastrous It appears to be the consensus that at least 1,500 feet of

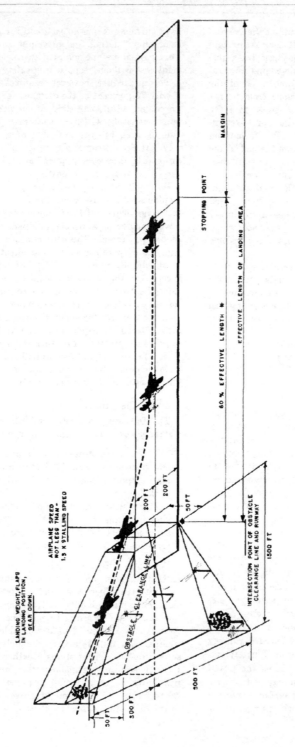

Courtesy Lockheed Aircraft Corporation

* FOR ALTERNATE FIELDS, ALLOW 70 %

FIGURE 25. AIRPORT LIMITATIONS FOR LANDING

separation should be required to carry out simultaneous operation in bad weather One mile whenever possible is desirable

Insofar as simultaneous landing and take-off are concerned, most pilots agree that runways should converge for landing and oppositely diverge for taking off, thus affording maximum air separation when making an approach without fear of collision, as the farther the airplane is from the airport, the greater the separation

Table II lists recommended ground clearances between runways and related portions of the airfield for airline airports

TABLE II

	Instrument Operation	Contact Operation
(1) Separation of parallel runways, center line to center line	1,500 ft	700 ft
(2) Center line of runway to center line of parallel taxiway	500 ft	275 ft
(3) From center line of runway to edge of graded area	500 ft	250 ft
(4) From either end of runway to edge of graded area*	As much as possible	As much as possible
(5) From center line of runway to buildings	750 ft	350 ft
(6) From center line of runway to edge of aprons	500 ft	250 ft
(7) From center line of taxiways to property line	200 ft	150 to 200 ft

* Any rolling area beyond the ends of the runway and up to the available area should be made available as an additional safety measure

Apron Areas

Aprons at both hangars and loading gates should be wide enough to permit the safe movement of aircraft without endangering those parked in front of the hangar or at the loading gate For major airports, apron width at the loading gate should be sufficient to permit two lanes for taxiing without disturbing parked airplanes At the smaller airports having infrequent schedules, one lane for taxiing may be found sufficient Apron width may vary from 125 to 150 feet for the airpark, to 1,000 feet for Class V airports, depending on the type of aircraft to be parked and the frequency of aircraft operations A section of a typical apron for an airport having a capacity of forty operations per hour, that is, having a single-runway pattern, is shown in Fig 26

The loading apron can be 300 feet if traffic does not require more than a one-way maneuvering lane, or 500 feet if two-way taxiing is desired At the apron the spacing of aircraft is shown as 150 feet, which should accommodate any equipment used for local and limited-stop schedules operation Larger aircraft require greater ramp spacing and maneuvering area

Figure 27 is a diagram of the loading apron and maneuvering space requirements for major airports In order to save pavement cost a large portion of the area used for taxiing and maneuvering can be turf as indicated These clearances are flexible and should be determined for each airport by carefully studying the airport layout proper and correlating them with the dimensions of the aircraft which are expected to use the field

Taxiways

The taxiway pattern should be designed to reduce the taxiing distance from the loading gate or administration building to the point of take-off Excessive taxiing is an economic waste which should not be tolerated in airport planning It also results in increased schedule time from point to point and is expensive regardless of type of aircraft For instance, the Douglas DC–3 uses fuel at the rate of 30 gallons per hour while taxiing from loading apron to end of runway This is equivalent to 7 5 cents per minute for fuel only Aircraft are designed to fly not to propel themselves on the ground

Several taxi strip layouts should be made for the runway pattern selected and the best compromise chosen even if it involves a larger total lineage of taxiing distance A wide radius should connect the taxiway with the runway to eliminate unnecessary use of wheel brakes Improper design of taxi pattern may well prove to be a bottleneck in expediting the movement of aircraft during peak traffic hours

The width of taxiways should be approximately twice that of the landing gear tread of the aircraft which are to use it It can be 50 feet for the smaller airports and 100 feet for the larger ones A 50-foot stabilized shoulder should be provided on each side of the pavements to prevent possible landing gear damage should an aircraft run off the pavement

It is hoped that some day it will not be necessary to check the engine or engines immediately prior to take-off, but at present it is necessary to provide warm-up areas at the intersection of a taxiway with a runway These areas should be designed to permit temporary parking in case of delay in take-off without delaying subsequent aircraft operations at high-capacity airports

Apron Turntables

In order to save apron space and to provide simple and accurate parking, as well as to expedite the parking of aircraft, turntables have been successfully used, and their use should be contemplated for every large airport today The problem is to determine the correct

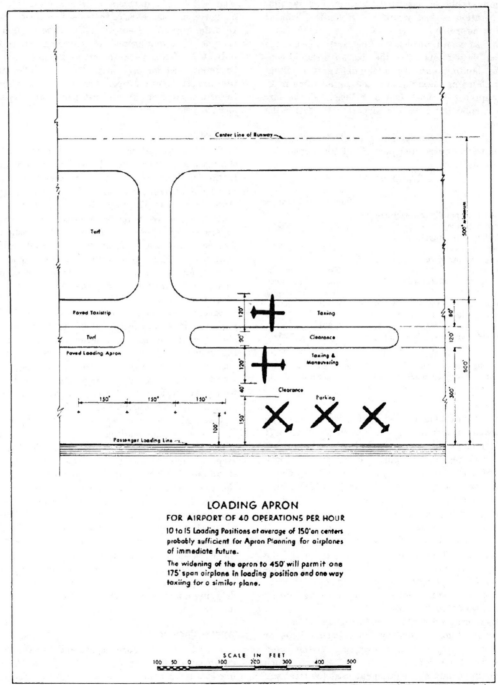

LOADING APRON

FOR AIRPORT OF 40 OPERATIONS PER HOUR

10 to 15 Loading Positions at average of 150' on centers probably sufficient for Apron Planning for airplanes of immediate future.

The widening of the apron to 450' will parmit one 175' span airplane in loading position and one way taxiing for a similar plane.

SCALE IN FEET

FIGURE 26. LOADING APRON FOR SMALL AIRPORT

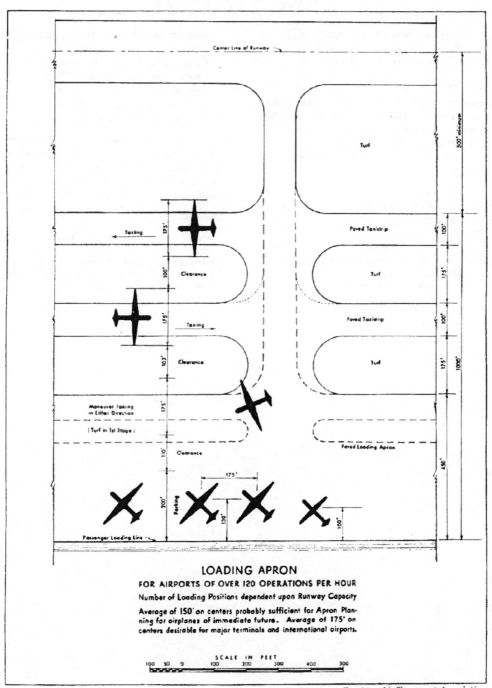

LOADING APRON

FOR AIRPORTS OF OVER 120 OPERATIONS PER HOUR

Number of Loading Positions dependent upon Runway Capacity

Average of 150' on centers probably sufficient for Apron Planning for airplanes of immediate future. Average of 175' on centers desirable for major terminals and international airports.

SCALE IN FEET

Courtesy Air Transport Association

FIGURE 27. LOADING APRON FOR LARGE AIRPORT

turntable spacing to accommodate various types and sizes of aircraft in order to obtain universal and flexible application. (See Part 11 for further discussion.)

Airfield Layout Analysis

Airfield design must be functionally correct. Several runway patterns should be fitted to the available land and each one analyzed and compared with the others to determine the best one for the site. Such comparative analysis should include a tabulation of the following factors:

    Total airfield acreage
    Number of operations per hour.
    Runway pattern type
    Number of runways
    Total lineal feet of runway
    Total square yards of runway paving
    Lineal feet of taxiways
    Total square yards of taxiway paving

    Average taxi distance for landing
    Average taxi distance for take-off.
    Longest taxi distance for landing
    Longest taxi distance for take-off.
    Number of acres per operation
    Runway paving per operation
    Taxi paving per operation

By using this information and cost calculations made from each pattern, the overall efficiency of each scheme can be evaluated by figuring the total cost per operation, either landing or take-off, on the basis of the maximum capacity per hour for each type of pattern under consideration.

Bibliography

Technical Characteristics of Aerodromes, Part I *Siting and Layout of Land Airdromes*, Department of Civil Aviation, British Air Ministry, London, England

7

AIRFIELD CONSTRUCTION

It is impracticable in a book of this size and scope to describe in detail the various phases of airfield construction. Nor does this appear necessary, since many excellent textbooks have been published dealing with drainage design and practice, design and construction of pavements, and allied subjects. It is the intention of the authors to present basic principles of sound construction practice as applied to the airfield. For more detailed information, see the bibliography at the end of this part of the book. The general principles of roadway construction can be applied to the construction of aircraft landing areas.

The landing area of an airfield must be able to support the loads resulting from the operation of any aircraft for which it is designed, indefinitely and without abnormal wear. It should be dustless and well drained. It should have a surface with a high coefficient of friction under all weather conditions to permit efficient braking of aircraft wheels and still cause no undue tire wear when aircraft wheels are being accelerated at the time of contact with the surface immediately when landing and when braked on coming to a stop. The landing area should be clearly recognizable from the air during the day, and suitably lighted for recognition at night. It should be level in all directions used for landing and take-off. Finally, it should be built of materials conducive to low maintenance costs.

Site Analysis

The analysis determining selection of a site to meet aircraft operating requirements has been discussed in earlier parts of this book. Site selection which will allow airfield construction economical in first costs and reasonable in maintenance costs must be the subject of an equally thorough analysis, since the airfield construction costs will represent the major portion of the total investment.

The first point to determine is whether the intended site possesses good natural drainage without steep slopes which will cause excessive grading or erosion. If the site is located on a knoll which slopes gently in all directions or if it slopes to internal valleys, it is likely that relatively little drainage construction will be required. Sites on or near river bottoms should be carefully investigated to determine the level of high or flood waters. Sites on filled ground may require an elaborate drainage system. A general evaluation of the above conditions, as well as a determination of whether a site will require excessive amounts of cutting and filling may be obtained by visual inspection. The necessity of moving tremendous quantities of earth, and particularly rock, may render an otherwise acceptable site economically impracticable.

If it appears that drainage and grading will not present unusual problems, the site should be surveyed topographically and for soil characteristics. The determination of which types of soils may be considered favorable is influenced by the latitude within which the airport occurs and the rainfall. Included generally, in this category are those soils which will induce natural drainage such as gravel, sand, or rock particles combined with a natural binder. Unfavorable soils are those which impede drainage, such as clay, or which have a low bearing power when wet.

The topographical survey and its application in the layout of an airfield have been discussed in Part 6. The soil survey will disclose:

1. The nature of the soil, its profile, its density and moisture conditions. These characteristics will serve as a basis for the design and composition of the subgrade, base course, and surface of the runways. The soil survey should cover the major portion of the site. Screw auger borings distributed over the site and spaced 200 to 400 feet along the center lines of all proposed runways should be made and recorded accurately or the site plan so as to show the various layers in true profile elevation.

Soils should be classified. Drainage characteristics can be recorded at the same time. When a sufficient number of borings have been made, a soil profile can be prepared to obtain an overall picture of the soil conditions for design purposes.

2. Data for construction records and study of subgrades, bases, and surfaces. The soil should be analyzed and tested to determine its granular and cohesive properties. The bearing capacity of a soil mass is one of its most essential properties because it determines the ability of the soil to support and resist applied loads under all climatic conditions. Therefore laboratory tests should be conducted with soil samples from the proposed site to determine its bearing capacity, stability, changes in volume due to moisture variation, compaction characteristics and the required mixtures to obtain a stable soil base.

3. The proper methods of handling the soil and the test requirements which should be included in the construction specifications. Such factors as ground water level and drainability, subgrade supporting properties under all weather conditions, suitability of the soil for stabilization, and suitability as construction material will affect initial cost of construction as well as permanence of any improvements.

The rapid development of soil mechanics in recent years has made it possible to use soil as an engineering material with greater assurance than in the past.

The analysis of this information will indicate the extent to which natural drainage will accomplish the removal of surface water and will give an estimate of the probable amount of artificial drainage required in the form of ditches, subdrains, and culverts. It will indicate the bearing capacity of the soil which, in turn, will be of great importance in designing the runway surfacing. It will have a bearing upon selection of grasses for turfing, representing, usually, over three-quarters of the airfield area.

The topographical survey, together with the soil survey, will influence to a considerable extent the final, detailed location of runways, so that no excessive amounts of cutting or filling need be done and so that cutting will approximately balance filling. The contour map, together with the soil survey, will show the location and size of borrow pits. The local availability of materials suitable for airfield construction will have a material bearing on the final choice of a site since this factor may involve considerable funds.

To sum up, it is advisable to analyze a prospective airport site for its topography, its drainage properties,

its soil characteristics, and its possession of suitable construction materials.

Grading and Fill

The grading plan should be developed by superimposing the airport master plan on a topographic map of the site to determine the amount of fill and grading required for the entire site. Figure 1 shows how this plan was drawn for the Kanawha County Airport at Charleston, West Virginia, and illustrates a typical study of this sort.

The principal controlling factors in the preparation of the grading plan are topography, soil, climatic conditions, orientation of runway system or landing areas, and location of airport buildings. The grading and filling plan should give definite indications of the areas to be excavated and filled, the areas from which borrow is to be taken, as well as the quantities to be moved, the type of materials to be used, and where they are to be placed. The ideal arrangement is one wherein the amount to be excavated equals the fill requirements. When excavated material is insufficient to take care of the fill, the deficiency must be obtained from dredging areas or borrow pits. When too much is available, it should be hauled away to fill approaches. A slope of approximately $1\frac{1}{2}$ to 1 away from the actual landing areas and building emplacements is generally considered satisfactory for all normal drainage requirements without causing excessive erosion. Clay soils may require 2-to-1 slope.

Runway, flightstrip, and taxiway grades should not exceed 1 per cent. The entire area grading should allow an unobstructed view from any point 10 feet above the surface of the runway, flightstrip, or taxiway to any other point at similar height on the airport. The usable area of the airport should be graded so that the entire airport can readily be seen from the control tower location. Deep cuts or gullies should be avoided, particularly at the ends of and along all runways and taxiways.

The preparation of the site will consist of clearing and grubbing. The choice of machinery for removing trees and brush will be influenced by the type of machinery used for subsequent grading work. The entire field area must be cleared, and tree stumps removed from those areas requiring excavation. For other areas, tops of stumps should be cut off not less than 3 feet below finished grade.

The two major steps in the construction of an embankment are the preparation of the foundation and compaction. Just as in building construction, the success of the finished runway will be largely dependent upon a good foundation. Most foundation failures

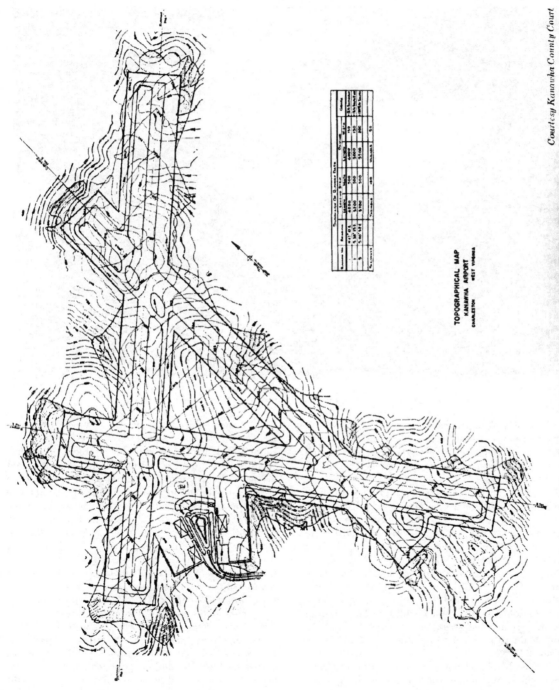

FIGURE 1. AIRPORT TOPOGRAPHICAL MAP—KANAWHA COUNTY AIRPORT, CHARLESTON, WEST VIRGINIA

Courtesy Kanawha County Court

Courtesy U. S. Corps Engineers

FIGURE 2. AERIAL VIEW OF FILL BEING PUMPED ONTO AIRFIELD AREA

may be traced to improper drainage. It is of the utmost importance to determine, on the basis of the topographical and soil surveys, the necessity for and the most effective and economical means of draining subsurface waters.

If fill is to be placed on marshy ground, muck or mud crusts, it will usually be necessary to displace the unstable material by excavation, blasting, or jetting. Even if a crust has a bearing capacity sufficient to carry the contemplated loads, it will not provide a satisfactory foundation material since there will be shifting of the crust causing breaks in the pavement.

Where fill will be placed on steep slopes, steps should be cut to hold the fill. Where fill is to be placed on previously compacted areas, such as old highway beds, these should be scarified to provide a good bond with the new fill.

Soil must be placed and compacted with great care, thoroughness, and under constant experienced supervision. Embankments placed hydraulically, in a semi-liquid state, or composed of sand or earth mixed with large stones require no compaction. Where hydraulic fill is taken from the bottoms of bodies of water, its suitability must be carefully determined since some types require a long period of time to attain required firmness. Great care must be exercised to prevent the occasional pumping of sludge onto the fill since sludge will form pockets of an impervious membrane which will never dry out and will be a constant source of trouble. Where sand fill is used, the depth of the embankment may be unlimited.

Most embankments are compacted with rollers. Good practice in this case limits successive layers to a compacted depth of no more than 6 inches. Since the most favorable condition for placing and compacting soil occurs at the moisture content at which that particular soil offers the greatest resistance to change, proper moisture control is of the utmost importance. Before work is begun, field tests should be made to determine the optimum moisture content of the various soils involved. The results of these tests should be checked against sample areas that are compacted in accordance with the findings of the tests. This

check assumes that proper selection of soils has been
made on the basis of the soil survey.

Soil from the cuts or borrow pits must be wetted
(or more infrequently dried) to be brought to or on
the dry side of optimum moisture content, hauled to

Courtesy "Construction Methods"

FIGURE 3.   EXCAVATION OF EMBANKMENT

the area under construction, properly placed, and then
rolled until the desired degree of compaction has been
attained.   Frequently, the compaction of filled areas
is accomplished by allowing the soil-hauling vehicles
to travel over fill to reach their destination.   This
method, while economical, is not the best practice inasmuch as the vehicles tend to travel more heavily over
certain defined paths, resulting in uneven compaction.

Courtesy "Construction Methods"

FIGURE 4.   ROUGH GRADING

The following general points should be observed in
grading design and placement:

1. Proper drainage should be accorded to subsurface water to insure stability of the embankment.

2. Subgrade soils should, insofar as practicable,
be of a uniform character to insure uniform subgrade support.

3. Soils should be compacted in thin layers with
uniform rolling over the entire area, using sheep's-
foot or rubber-tired rollers.

4. Grading plans should be laid out to carry away
surface water from runways, taxiways, apron areas,
and building sites.

The choice of equipment for grading and compacting, as with the equipment for clearing, will be determined by the nature of the material involved, the size
of the job, local practice, construction time factor, and
other considerations.

Courtesy "Construction Methods"

FIGURE 5.   LEVELING OPERATION IN FOREGROUND; WA-
TERING TRUCK IN CENTER BRINGING SOIL TO PROPER
MOISTURE CONTENT; COMPACTION IN REAR

Drainage

Almost every airfield will require drainage of water
arising from one or more of the following sources:

1. Surface water from rainfall or snow.
2. Subsurface water.
3. Water draining into the airport area from adjoining land.

Wherever possible, airfield design should allow for
natural drainage to accomplish the above.   Artificial
drainage must be designed and installed to take care

Courtesy "Construction Methods"

FIGURE 6.   CLOSE-UP OF COMPACTION BY MEANS OF
SHEEP'S-FOOT ROLLERS

of water removal in excess of that hauled by natural
means.   Since an elaborate drainage system may represent a large portion of the cost of airfield construction,
it becomes important to analyze the prospective site
for its drainage characteristics.

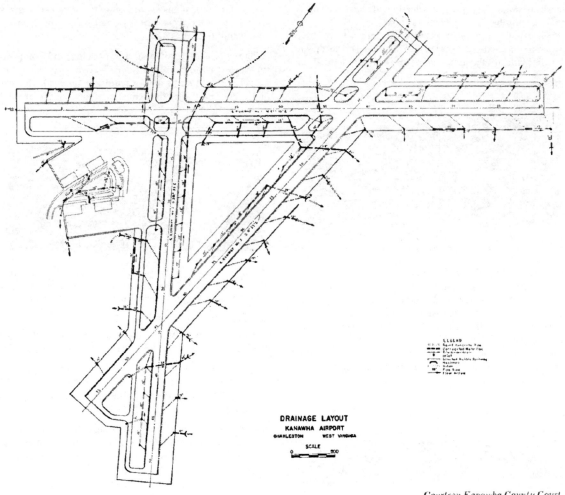

DRAINAGE LAYOUT
KANAWHA AIRPORT
CHARLESTON   WEST VIRGINIA
SCALE

Courtesy Kanawha County Court

FIGURE 7

Surface waters can be removed in only three ways: by evaporation; by percolation through the soil; by conduction. In airfield design, the first way may be disregarded since, to have an all-weather field, surface water must be removed immediately and, therefore, no time can be allowed for evaporation. Whatever water is not absorbed by the soil itself through percolation must be carried away by drainage devices, such as ditches or subdrains.

The foregoing paragraphs on *Grading* have indicated the necessity of making a comprehensive soil survey of the site so that embankments may be properly placed and compacted. The same soil survey should be used in the design of the drainage system to indicate the nature and extent of the drainage system required. The soils must be analyzed for their porosity. Furthermore, the various strata of soils must be charted and analyzed, since a shallow layer of porous soil underlaid by strata of clay will allow for surface drainage only to the extent of the top layer and, therefore, will cause subsurface drainage problems.

It becomes apparent, therefore, that the airport designer must have a survey showing the following: extent of principal soil types; available outlets for natural drainage; contour intervals. On this map should be superimposed the runway, apron, and building layout, indicating elevations of principal points. Cross-sectional and longitudinal profiles of runways and aprons must be drawn. Soil profiles, ground water profiles, and information on infiltration capacities of the soils in question must be available. In addition, the designer will require data on rainfall and snowfall collected over a 5- to 10-year period taken from

Courtesy "Construction Methods"

FIGURE 8.   TRENCH DIGGER USED IN LAYING SUBSURFACE DRAIN

Weather Bureau observations in surrounding territories. And finally, temperature data, including the maximum depth of frost, should be available.

Subsurface drainage may be required to accomplish the lowering of the water table of the area and to drain waters resulting from percolation of surface waters through the soil. Determination of both these conditions may be made from the soil survey. Water which may drain into the airport area from surrounding territory should be disposed of by means of proper grading, ditches, or drains beyond the immediate runway area in order to prevent a possible loss of subsoil stability, or to keep the water table of the airfield area down to a safe level.

Whether runways are to be paved or sodded, surface waters must be removed quickly so as not to impair the operating efficiency of the field. Further, they must be removed in such a manner as to prevent erosion of the soil, and to prevent impairment of the stability of the embankment subsoil by softening. Runways should be crowned in the center sufficiently to discharge surface water to their sides. Concrete gutters, topped with removable concrete covers pierced with holes to admit drainage, may be placed alongside the runways. These gutters are connected to subdrains which carry off the water to discharge points. This method is expensive to install and is infrequently

Courtesy U. S. Corps Engineers

FIGURE 9.   COMPLETE SECTION OF DRAINPIPE BEFORE BACKFILLING

used. Another more common method is to carry the water from the runways across the shoulders to a shallow ditch running along either side of the runway; subsurface drains are placed under the ditch with inlets suitably spaced. A third, and the least expensive, method is to carry the water from the runway across the shoulder to a valley or ponding area where the water may collect (as in a catch basin). From this point the collected water may be carried away more slowly by means of subdrains. In addition to economies resulting from the use of smaller drainpipe sizes, this method allows for utilizing removal of water through the soil. However, care must be exercised to prevent soil erosion and soil softening when this method is used. This method is of particular advantage wherever large amounts of water, precipitated at a high rate (such as tropical showers), must be disposed of quickly. A fourth method of removing surface water from runways is by the installation of vitrified clay Web Skip-Pipe continuously along both sides of a runway. This pipe is comparatively easy to install, is low in cost, and is designed to withstand the heaviest aircraft wheel loads (Fig. 10).

Experience has proved that French drains will not perform satisfactorily for the removal of surface water from large areas such as airports because of their tendency to become filled with silt and because they may freeze in cold weather. Perforated corrugated steel pipe (with or without bituminous covering) may be used for subdrains where the action of the soil will not be corrosive. The subdrain may consist of corrugated iron, vitreous clay, or concrete pipe reinforced under

Courtesy Robinson Clay Product Company

FIGURE 10. CLAY PIPE SURFACE DRAIN USED AT EDGES
OF PAVEMENT

runways, taxiways, ramps, and shoulders. All drainpipes should be of ample size to insure satisfactory performance under any conditions of peak water removal.

Manholes, spaced at suitable intervals, should be provided to allow for removal of silt from the drainage system. All drainage pipes should be pitched sufficiently to prevent the collection of silt at any except predetermined points.

The methods of estimating run-off, sizing, and spacing of drains and inlets, and design of pipe are subjects beyond the scope of this book.

The surface drainage system should be kept entirely separate from that used for subsurface drainage. Subdrainage should be designed to discharge directly into outfalls. There are a number of common soil combinations which will indicate the necessity of providing subdrains. Where pervious soils occur above and impervious below, water will seep through the top layer, collect on the impervious, and form unstable soil unless removed. Where soils are impervious above and per-

vious below, trenches may be dug through the top layer allowing the water to drain to the pervious layer, where it may be removed naturally or by drains. Irregular strata of pervious or impervious soils may allow the collection of water in pockets or springs, which will require separate drains leading to the main drainage system.

Courtesy American Rolling Mill Company

FIGURE 11. CORRUGATED IRON DRAIN

If the water table is close to finished grade, it may imperil the stability of the surface, cause frost heaves, or cause flooding of the field during periods of excessive rainfall or spring thaws. A subdrainage system should then be installed to lower the table. If the porosity of the subsoil is such that subdrains will not produce proper drainage and, therefore, permit the appearance of frost heaves, such soil should be removed and replaced with soil of the proper characteristics.

Various systems of subsurface drainage are in common use, and are illustrated in Figs. 11 and 12. Pipes which may be used for this work are concrete pipe, vitrified clay pipe, unglazed drain tile—all laid with open joints; also corrugated metal pipe. Pipes are laid in open trenches surrounded with gravel or crushed rock. The back filling of these trenches should be compacted with the same care as that given to the construction of embankments in order to prevent future settlement.

In designing any drainage system, it should be borne in mind that the most frequent pavement failures in

Courtesy "Construction Methods"

FIGURE 12.　CLOSE-UP VIEW OF LARGE CONCRETE DRAIN

runways, taxiways, and aprons may be traced to the loss of stability of the subsoil, resulting from poorly designed, improperly placed, or inadequate drainage. Drainage problems should be given the most careful study not only to protect the initial investment but also to insure reasonable conditions of maintenance.

Surfacing

The selection of the type of surfacing for any given landing area and its design will be influenced by the following considerations:

1. Safety of aircraft operation.

2. Nature and density of anticipated air traffic.

3. Characteristics of the soil on which the landing facility is to be built.

4. The degree of permanency desired and the size of the budget.

5. The climatic conditions of the area, such as humidity, rainfall, and temperatures.

6. The load requirements which will affect the thickness of the pavement and the preparation of the subsoil to obtain proper stabilization.

7. The availability of materials and construction equipment. (A good gravel deposit near by or an acceptable grade of sand on the airport site will serve to provide construction materials at low cost and will result in an economical development. Although availability of materials should not necessarily be the determining factor in the selection of a site which is acceptable, location and airway wise, it will influence the choice to be made between two such sites for a given locality in permitting the reduction of overall construction costs.)

8. Reasonable maintenance costs.

Runways may be either turfed or paved. If all-year, all-weather operation is required, the choice will be paving. There are two main types of paving, "rigid" or concrete paving, with or without reinforcing, and "flexible" paving, which includes macadam, asphaltic concrete, and the bituminous types. The experience and knowledge gained in highway paving may be applied generally to runway paving. The two are essentially similar, with the exception that paving types which depend upon the kneading action of traffic to maintain their required density cannot be used for runways, and designs employing softer asphalts should be used in their stead to provide against hardening to a point where cracking could occur.

Runway surfacing should be constructed so that when completed it is free from all loose particles which can be picked up by the propeller wash, since this may cause serious damage to control surfaces. Runway surfacing should be free from dust. The surfacing should be of a color or have a refractive index which will allow it to be readily distinguishable from the surrounding countryside. Where night operation is contemplated, the surfacing should have good light-reflecting qualities. If it can be accomplished at no marked increase in cost, it is highly desirable to have the color of the runways in contrast to the color of all other airport paving. This distinctive color will provide a definite safety factor for the inbound pilot.

Effects of Aircraft Wheel Loading

The loads imposed by aircraft through their landing gear wheel tire contact on the landing area are of two kinds, static loads while the aircraft is at rest at the loading apron, and dynamic loads while the airplane is taxiing, checking its engines prior to take-off, taking off, or landing. Static wheel loadings are given in Table II, Part 2, for various types of transport airplanes in operation today or anticipated for the near future. Tire footprint and unit loading are also given for each of these airplanes. Static wheel loadings of

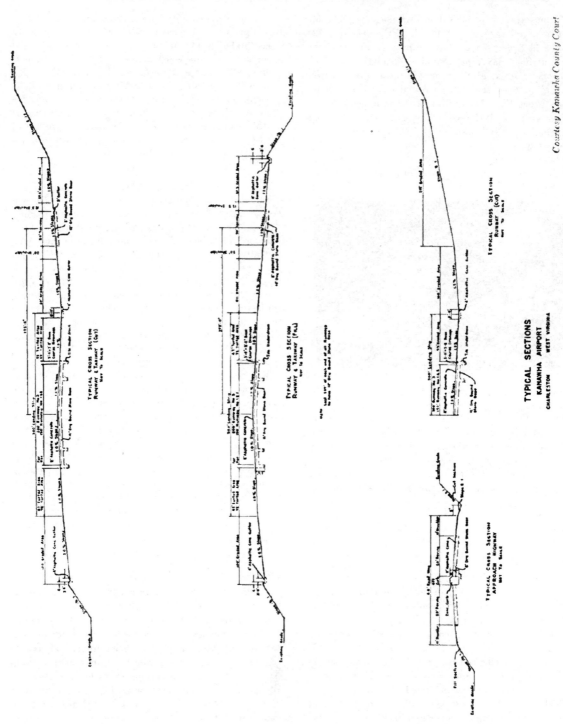

FIGURE 13. SECTIONS THROUGH RUNWAYS—KANAWHA COUNTY AIRPORT, CHARLESTON, WEST VIRGINIA

Courtesy Kanawha County Court

personal aircraft are similar to those of the larger private cars

The area of contact of the tire on the runway surface with pneumatic tires can be approximated by the following formula

$$A = 0.9 \times \frac{W_L}{P_I}$$

where A = area of contact or tire footprint,
W_L = wheel load,
P_I = tire inflation pressure

It will be found that the values obtained by applying this formula will be within 10 per cent of the actual tire footprint area for any given tire, as tire pressures often vary for the same size and capacity tire according to individual tire manufacturer recommendations

The tire contact area is generally oval in shape, but it may be assumed to be circular for pavement stress computation This assumption will always give safe results because calculated stresses are greatest for a circular shape Pavement design is not an exact science, and theoretical calculations must be liberally interpreted by the engineer to arrive at a satisfactory and permanent pavement solution

Airplane tires are generally of the semi-low-pressure type and cause less damage to pavement than automotive vehicle tires, however, they transmit heavier loads with the larger aircraft

The most severe condition to be met occurs during engine warming-up and during engine checking prior to take-off, when the airplane is standing still and the engines are run up either to bring them to operating temperature or to check them immediately before taking off These areas are in front of the hangars for engine warm-up, at the junction of the taxiways with runways and at the end of the runways for engine checking. These areas require not only the heaviest type of pavement to withstand the pounding resulting from vibration, but, in addition, a shear resistant type of pavement laid on stable subsoil base to prevent grooving or cupping when the frequency of operation is high The loads used for design should be increased 25 per cent over the maximum static aircraft loads for these areas These areas of pavement must also be of a type which will not be affected by possible oil drippings from aircraft engines

Impact loading at the point of contact of the landing gear wheel tires with the runway surface, that is, when the airplane ceases to be airborne and lands, is not serious except in the case of a very hard landing, which will cause damage to the airplane landing gear structure itself In a normal landing the airplane gradually transfers its weight from air lift to the pavement over a distance which varies with its rate of descent and landing speed The major force vector is horizontal, since the airplane moves forward faster than it descends and the shock-absorbing system of the airplane landing gear absorbs much of its kinetic energy In a hard or crash landing, however, the impact loading can be as much as four to five times the weight of the airplane. Some of this impact is absorbed by the landing gear system and tires with the result that the unit pavement loading seldom exceeds approximately one and a half to twice the normal static load Normal runway paving design, therefore, is based on the actual static wheel load of the heaviest aircraft which is regularly expected to use the runway The safety factor in the design of rigid pavements will allow for the occasional use of the pavement by aircraft imposing stresses in excess of the design load and approaching the modulus of rupture without causing pavement failure

Pavement wear occurs primarily on these landing areas owing to the absorption of the kinetic energy required to accelerate the landing gear wheels to the airplane landing speed at the time of contact with the ground This wear is reflected mostly in the abrasion of tire tread rubber caused by the grinding effect against the pavement, which itself also suffers a slight amount of abrasion each time An examination of the landing areas will show numerous black streaks, indicating that airplanes seldom land twice on the same spot However, repetition of such landing loads and abrasion, together with higher loads with heavier airplanes, requires that pavement design include a factor to meet these conditions

There is a tendency on the part of aircraft designers to provide prerotation of landing gear wheels for larger airplanes in an effort to gear them to the pavement at the point of contact, thus reducing pavement wear and surface shear loading as well as rubber tread wear Rubber tread wear can become a very important economic factor with large transport airplanes making numerous landings.

Rigid Surfacing

Since rigid paving exerts a bridging action over subsoil pockets, this type of surfacing should be used only where there is little likelihood of future subbase settlement. Where such tremendous quantities of paving are involved, as in an airport, it would be uneconomical to design a slab for considerable bending resistance Uneven settlement of subbase would result in the cracking of pavement with attendant high maintenance costs.

Where the subbase is stable, concrete paving may be expected to give long service at very low maintenance costs. The light-reflecting qualities of concrete are excellent; pigments may be added to the mix to produce

Courtesy "Construction Methods"

FIGURE 14. FINAL GRADING BEFORE LAYING OF CONCRETE; STEEL FORMS AT SIDE PROVIDE TRUE LEVEL OF FINISHED SURFACE AND TRACKAGE FOR GRADER

any desired color. The surface texture may be accurately controlled and varied, if desired, for different areas which are subjected to different uses.

In the design of concrete pavements the proper design and layout of joints is of the utmost importance. Joints must be designed to allow for expansion, con-

Courtesy U. S. Corps Engineers

FIGURE 15. CONCRETE RUNWAY PAVING. ALTERNATE STRIPS ARE LAID, ALLOWED TO SET, AND THEN AREAS BETWEEN PAVED

traction, and warping of the slab. Joints at the intersection of two runways, or a runway and a taxiway, should be laid out so that one runway may move independently of the other.

Pavement scaling may occur with ordinary concrete where rock salt is used to reduce ice formation on the surface. Air-entraining portland cement concrete is recommended since it will tend to eliminate pavement scaling.

Concrete pavements probably attain their greatest usefulness for engine warm-up, engine checking, and other areas of heavy service because of their natural resistance to oil and gasoline drippings and because of their rigid surface, which will prevent cupping due to excessive traffic.

The average life of concrete paving, if properly designed and placed, may be expected to range from 15 to 25 years. During this period the only maintenance required should be inspection and repair of joints. Joints may be sealed satisfactorily with a soft bitumen mixed with a mineral flour to prevent flowing in warm weather. Broken areas or spalls may be repaired satis-

FIGURE 16. "CURING COMPOUND" BEING SPRAYED ONTO FRESHLY LAID CONCRETE PAVING

factorily with concrete. During this period the light-reflecting qualities inherent in concrete will deteriorate only slightly. If repaving is required at the end of this period, the original paving will furnish an excellent base course. Repaving may consist of either additional concrete or a bituminous wearing surface.

During the war the technique of laying concrete runways in freezing weather was perfected. It is laid by heating the ingredients of the mix before mixing, preheating the base course (consisting usually, in such cases, of sand), and by protecting the finished slab with hay and tarpaulins. The significance of this development is that if careful evaluation of all factors indicates the choice of concrete, construction need not be delayed by freezing weather.

A number of materials have been developed which afford protection to "green" concrete during the required period of curing and which are sprayed onto the surface immediately after finishing of the concrete. They create an impervious membrane, preventing the surface evaporation of water during the critical initial curing period. The application of these materials leaves a film which becomes colorless or wears off in a short time and, therefore, does not affect the color of the finished surface.

The principal advantages of concrete paving are its permanence, its strength, its resistance to oil and gasoline, its low maintenance cost, and its high light-reflection characteristics. The principal disadvantages are the relatively higher initial cost and the time required for curing (upwards of seven days), during which time

Courtesy "Construction Methods"

FIGURE 17. WINDROWS OF SAND AND GRAVEL BEING MIXED WITH ASPHALT PREPARATORY TO SPREADING AND ROLLING

the area paved is unusable. This period may be reduced by the use of high-early-strength concrete.

Flexible Surfacing

In contrast to the rigid types, the bituminous pavements make 100 per cent use of subgrade support. If this support is good, the pavement thickness may be decreased; if low, a base course of local materials, such as calcide, slag, gravel or broken stone, or other high-support material, may be placed over the subgrade and this covered with an asphalt pavement. Bituminous pavings need be designed only for the traffic anticipated in the near future—not the ultimate—since the original paving can easily be strengthened with the addition of an extra course of asphalt.

The light-reflection characteristics of asphalt paving, being dark, are naturally low. Any desired color may be attained with the application of a surface treatment. In wet climates where a rougher texture of white-grained particles is required to allow the surface to appear white when wet, the use of white sand, lime rock, or granite particles as aggregate in the seal coat will give the desired effect. Any particles which are added to the surface must be thoroughly bonded

to the surface. If they become loosened, they may constitute a hazard to operating aircraft. In dry climates the surface may be given a wash coat of Medusa or Atlas white cement. Both these treatments will require renewal to preserve the desired degree of whiteness, increasing maintenance costs.

Asphalt paving requires no joints, since the inherently flexible nature of the material allows it to expand and contract without cracking. Bituminous as well as rigid paving may be easily maintained and repaired, using asphalt patching mixtures having delayed curing properties. The patch may be feathered at the edges to leave no ridges, and the patched area is immediately available for use.

Flexible pavements will be lower in initial cost than rigid paving, particularly where sand, gravel, or slag is available locally. They have a higher maintenance cost than concrete but are easily maintained. Where the subgrade is of such material that one cannot predict with certainty absence of settlement, it is advisable to select a flexible pavement, which will settle in large areas rather than with sharp cracks.

Courtesy "Construction Methods"

FIGURE 18. ASPHALT RUNWAY PAVING

Shoulders—Dust Treatment

Major airports should have paved shoulders for a width of 75 feet on either side of runways. This width provides a safety factor should a sudden air gust force an aircraft off the edge of the paving while landing. Such paving should not be designed on the same basis as the runways, since the traffic will be extremely intermittent. If the soil has good bearing power, the objectives will be attained with soil-stabilization, using either cement or asphalt.

Soil stabilization is also recommended for runways and taxiways at secondary airports and emergency landing fields where low first costs are an important factor and where traffic is light.

This form of paving is made in the following manner. The soil is first pulverized to the required depth and then bladed to approximate grade. If cement is used, this material is spread uniformly and mixed with the pulverized soil. Water is incorporated with a pressure distributor to attain the required moisture content. The mixture is compacted, the surface shaped, and finished with rollers. If asphalt is used, it is applied to the pulverized soil under pressure, and the surface is then shaped and rolled. The soil cement should be surfaced with a bituminous leveling course after exposure of the former for several months.

Some areas of this country will not permit the growth of a good stand of grass over the area not covered by paving. Since some treatment is required to prevent the blowing of dust or sand, bituminous materials are worked into the soil to a depth of 2 to 3 inches, followed by rolling.

In arid regions where soil stabilization is not economically justified, where a stand of grass is needed to hold the soil and prevent dust storms, the soil may be given a very light oil spray after seeding which will hold the moisture content in the soil and prevent the blowing of seed. This treatment will be of value for the first germination only, since the presence of oil will render the soil unsuitable for future plantings.

General Paving Comments

Experience indicates that the flexible pavements show less resistance to the forces generated by engine warming and testing and by taxiing than the rigid types. Also, the rigid types have greater resistance to the drippings of oil and gasoline. On the other hand, the impact loads developed during landing or take-off forces are resisted equally well by either type. For these reasons it would appear that a balanced paving design, taking all factors into consideration, might call for construction of runways of flexible surfaces, with rigid paving for taxiways and aprons and at the ends of runways. This distribution of paving types would automatically produce the desired differentiation of color between runways and all other paved areas. The asphalt could be finished with an aggregate of white sand for light reflection. The difference in the index of refraction of this light seal coat on the asphalt and of concrete would give the appearance of different colors for the two materials and would identify the runway portion of the field.

The standard method of estimating runway construction and maintenance costs is given in the table that follows. By this method the different types of pavement are evaluated on the basis of annual costs.

ANNUAL COST OF VARIOUS ROAD SURFACES
(Grading, Drainage, and Right-of-Way Costs Not Included)

(See explanatory notes for each item immediately following this table.)

	Type of Pavement		
	Type A	Type B	Type C
Assumptions			
(n) (a) Useful service life			
(b) Salvage value			
(r) (c) Prevailing interest rate			
(E) (d) Periodic resurface and repair (one during life of surface)			
Annual Investment Charge			
(A) 1. First cost (construction) per mile			
(S) 2. Less salvage value			
3. Depreciation			
4. Annual depreciation or retirement cost			
Annual Interest Charge			
(I) 5. Average annual interest charge on outstanding indebtedness			
Annual Maintenance Cost			
(B) 6. Regular surface maintenance per year			
$\left(\dfrac{E}{n}\right)$ 7. Necessary periodic resurface and repair			
8. Total annual cost			

EXPLANATORY NOTES

Assumptions:

(a) The *useful service life* of each pavement type can be estimated from a knowledge of conditions within a definite territory. It is possible that in many states this estimate can be made from facts presented by the report of the State-wide Planning Surveys.

(b) *Salvage value* will vary greatly with the type of surface. It should be considered as the first cost less the estimated cost of replacing the pavement to original standard at the end of its estimated useful life.

(c) *Prevailing interest rate* will depend on general market and local conditions.

(d) The item of *periodic resurfacing and repairing* will probably be the hardest item to estimate. As a rule this work is done by the maintenance crews, all the jobs being lumped in the maintenance report at the end of the year so that it is difficult, if not impossible, to obtain the cost per square yard. However, in many cases enough resurfacing is done by contract so that an estimate can be obtained which is approximately correct. If other means fail, the engineer of maintenance can usually give a very close estimate of the cost based upon his knowledge and experience.

Items of Cost (per Mile)

The Committee on Highway Transportation Costs of the Highway Research Board in 1929 developed a comprehensive method of computing the annual cost of highways This method is thoroughly explained in the report of this committee which is published in the *Proceedings* of the Ninth Annual Meeting of the Highway Research Board

The formula so developed was modified by Professor C B Breed of the Massachusetts Institute of Technology This modification appears in his paper "Analysis of Road Costs on the State Highways of Worcester County, Massachusetts," which appeared in the *Proceedings* of the Thirteenth Annual Meeting of the Highway Research Board The formula as developed by Professor Breed is

$$C = \left(\frac{A+S}{2}\right)r + \frac{A-S}{n} + B + \frac{E}{n}$$

in which C = average annual road cost,
A = original capital cost,
B = annual maintenance cost,
r = rate of interest
n = estimated life, in years, of the surface before renewal is required,
S = estimated salvage value of highway at the end of n years,
E = any periodic maintenance required during life n

1 *First cost* is the bid price or original construction cost for the surface Items such as grading and drainage structures are not included so that cost figures are on a comparable basis for all types Estimate of this cost should be based on the average bid prices for several similar projects in the same general vicinity The first cost is item A of the formula above

2 *Salvage cost* is the estimated worth of the pavement at the end of estimated life This cost is difficult to determine but can be obtained from analysis of past performance of various types and from reconstruction costs where records are available The best sources of information on this item are the road life studies of the State-wide Highway Planning Surveys This is item S of the formula used

3 *Depreciation* is considered the original cost less the salvage value at end of estimated life

4 The average annual *retirement cost* is the amount of depreciation during the useful life of the pavement divided by the years of estimated life It represents the amount which each year must be set aside as a reserve fund to retire the estimated depreciation or it may be used to retire bonds if the original project was constructed with borrowed money In the formula developed by Professor Breed it represents the item $(A - S)/n$

5 To avoid the use of financial tables not always readily available, an approximate method of figuring the annual *interest* charge is used Since it is used for all types, the small inaccuracy will not affect the comparison The approximate formula is

$$\left(\frac{A+S}{2}\right)r = I$$

where A = original cost (item 1),
S = salvage value,
r = prevailing rate of interest,
I = annual interest cost on indebtedness

The above approximation is obtained in the following manner
The original cost (A) less the salvage value (S) equals the amount to be depreciated during the useful life of the pavement, as discussed in item 4 Half of this amount, $(A - S)/2$, represents the

average sum, or indebtedness, upon which interest is to be paid during that life This average is based upon the assumption that at the end of the first year interest is paid upon the amount ($A - S$), but at the end of the useful life $A - S$ equals zero and, therefore, the interest paid is zero because of the deduction of the uniform annual depreciation of item 4

In this assumption the salvage value (S) is not amortized during this term of years As a result, interest must be charged upon it in full each year

The resulting total interest charge at r rate of interest would then be $\left(\frac{A-S}{2}\right)r$ plus S times r, or as an equation

$$\text{Annual interest} = I = \left(\frac{A-S}{2}\right)r + Sr =$$

$$\left(\frac{A-S}{2} + S\right)r = \left(\frac{A-S+2S}{2}\right)r = \left(\frac{A+S}{2}\right)r$$

This item of interest is the first term of the formula for annual cost developed by Professor Breed

6 *Regular maintenance* should be taken from actual maintenance records if item for pavement surface is separated in cost statement If costs are not on comparable basis, the figures may be taken from our maintenance cost studies This is the item B in the formula

7 Some states omit the *period retreatment and repair* costs of certain types of pavement surfaces Since this reconditioning may occur more than once within the estimated life of that pavement type, it should be considered as an annual cost item and distributed over the life of the pavement Periodic maintenance is the item E in the formula

8 The final *annual cost* is derived by totaling items 1 to 7, inclusive It is represented by C in the formula described above

Paving Maintenance

Maintenance work on paved areas should be done systematically and periodically by trained personnel Since airport paving is similar to highway paving, and since well-equipped and well-stocked highway maintenance shops are situated over the length and breadth of this country, it would seem logical for the airport manager to contract with his state highway department for the inspection and maintenance of all paving This policy could apply to all airports except those situated in the largest cities, which would probably have enough work to warrant keeping a trained maintenance crew on the payroll continuously

Inspection should occur at least twice a year—in the spring and in the fall It should cover all shoulders as well as runways and taxiways Periodic inspection will disclose whether the drainage originally provided is sufficient and in the right places, or whether additional run-off gutters are required to prevent erosion

Turf

The paved areas of an airfield seldom exceed one quarter of the total, which means that 75 to 100 per cent of the area of every airfield will have to be protected with turf or by some form of erosion and dust control. Turfed areas for airfields fall into three general use classifications

1. Landing areas require a thickly matted, tough, wear-resistant grass, growing in a soil which possesses excellent drainage properties and at the same time contains sufficient plant nutrients. Sodded areas are entirely suitable for the type of landing areas exemplified by airparks, flightstops, and CAA Class I airports, where the frequency of airplane movements is relatively low or the traffic consists mainly of small privately owned airplanes having low wheel loading

2. Turf in areas infrequently used, such as shoulders adjoining paved runways, may be of a less dense growth than indicated in item 1 above. The root system should be strong and deep to prevent erosion, since the shoulders will act as a watershed to the paved runways

3. In "pasture" areas, or areas which will support no traffic, the principal function of the grasses is to hold the soil, preventing erosion and dust.

The type of grass to be used as well as the best soil preparation to nurture the growth of vegetation must be considered along with the initial soil and topographical survey described earlier in this part

The soil survey will determine the acidity or alkalinity of the soil, which, in turn, will be one of the factors determining the choice of grass. The survey will also disclose types, amounts, and location of topsoil available for finished grading. Intelligent use of these data will prevent the loss of valuable topsoil by mixing with embankment materials. In addition to being guided by Weather Bureau statistics on rainfall, temperature, sunshine, length of daylight during days of different seasons, one should also examine types of grasses grown in near-by localities to determine the choice of turf. Grass types should not be planted too far from the region or regions in which they are known to thrive best. Finally, the grass selected should be available locally in quantity in the form of seed, plantings, or sprigs

To attain low maintenance costs, grasses having maximum coverage, a strong root system, and minimum rate of growth are most suitable. Grasses must be selected to fit the climatic conditions of the region and the soil characteristics of the site. For instance, Bermuda grass is best suited to anchor sandy topsoil and grows exceedingly well in warm and humid localities. Bluegrass, on the other hand, is preferable in more temperate climates. Species able to stand adverse moisture and temperature conditions are highly

desirable. It is known that drought-resistant grasses remain dormant during a dry period and resume growth when rain falls again. Such grasses are generally deep rooted, thus possessing the advantage of providing better anchorage for loose soils and shifting sands

The growth of turf should not be attempted in arid regions where the average annual rainfall is less than 15 to 18 inches. Where it is impossible to grow grass because of poor soil, arid climate, or the high cost of planting and subsequent maintenance, the area may be dustproofed by spraying with a mixture of crude oil and a suitable bonding element to settle the dust. This procedure, however, tends to render the soil unusable for any future plant growth

Maintenance of Turfed Areas

Personnel which has had experience in the caretaking of large areas of turf, such as golf courses, will be well qualified to conduct the maintenance of turf for an airport. Grass should be cut no lower than 2½ to 3 inches above ground. (Mowing machines are discussed in Part 11.) Grass cuttings should be left on the field to rot and help fertilize and mulch the grass. Worn spots may be patched by disking, with the disks set vertically, followed by seeding and rolling. After the spring thaws, the turfed areas should be rolled to make the grass firm and keep the ground surfaces smooth for drainage. From time to time it may be necessary to apply a top dressing of fertilizer, either alone or in combination with lime, sand, or peat, in order to keep the turf in top condition

Bibliography

Airport Design, Civil Aeronautics Administration, U S Department of Commerce, Washington, D C, April, 1944

Airport Engineering, by H O Sharp, G R Shaw, and J A Dunlop, John Wiley and Sons, 1944

Design Manual for Airport Pavements, Civil Aeronautics Administration, U S Department of Commerce, Washington, D C, March, 1944

Handbook of Culvert and Drainage Practice, The Shelt Company, Elmira, N Y, and Harrisburg, Pa, 1937

Joint Airport Users Conference—Proceedings, the National Aeronautic Association, Washington, D C, July 24–25, 1944

"Observations on Airport Construction," by Bernard E Gray, Air Commerce Section of *Flying* for June and July, 1944, The Ziff-Davis Publishing Company, Chicago, Ill

Principles of Highway Construction as Applied to Airport Flight Strips and Other Landing Areas for Aircraft, Public Roads Administration, Federal Works Agency, Washington, D C, June, 1943

Publications issued by the Asphalt Institute, New York, N Y

Publications issued by the Portland Cement Association, Chicago, Ill

8

AIRPORT LIGHTING

The principal reason for installation of airport lighting is to permit night flying operations with the maximum degree of safety Every phase of the planning and installation of the lighting system must be carried out with this main objective constantly in mind. As air traffic on an airport increases, the complexity and extent of the lighting installation will also increase Thus the work should be planned in stages complementary to those of airfield and building expansion

The CAA has established standard specifications governing all types of airport lighting equipment It is also carrying on a continuous research program developing improved devices Every airport lighting plan should be submitted to the CAA for checking and approval before construction is begun

The major components of an airport lighting plan are airport identification, boundary marking, runway lighting, taxiway lighting, and ramp and apron floodlighting. The inclusion of these several components and their nature will be determined by the extent and type of night operations for which each individual airport is planned, plus the extent of the budget for initial investment in this facility and its later maintenance

Personal-Flying Airport Lighting

Since it may be assumed that the dependability of both personal aircraft and private pilot technique will improve, it is fair to presume that there will be an increase in activity in night flying for this category. Every personal-flying airport should be planned with at least minimum facilities for night operation, which include boundary marking, illuminated wind direction indicator, rotating beacon, code beacon, and ramp and apron floodlighting

Beacon

The rotating beacon at an airport, the beam of which is visible for miles, indicates to the flyer that the field is equipped for night operation It should be mounted higher than any surrounding obstruction. The bottom edge of its beam, when set horizontally, should clear all obstructions If mounting it on the roof of a hangar or the terminal building does not give the required clearances, the beacon should be elevated by mounting it on a separate tower

The beacon should be rotated at six revolutions per minute It should project beams of light in two horizontal directions, 180 degrees apart One beam should flash a clear light, the other a green light (For marine airports which provide landings on water only, one beam should be clear and the other yellow) The Bartow type of rotating beacon has four horizontal lenses with two alternate ones tilted at 12 degrees to the horizontal, the alternate ones producing a flash of lower candle power In addition, it has a top lens tilted 7 to 12 degrees from the vertical, producing a wabbling beam of low intensity This beacon, with its more continuous flashes, provides better visibility at high altitudes

Code Beacon

Every airport should be equipped with a code beacon which continuously flashes a Morse code signal designating the airport (The code signal is assigned by the CAA) This beacon should be mounted high enough so that its beam also will clear all obstructions It should be equipped with two 500-watt lamps and a green color screen A motor-driven cam, cut to order for each signal, operates the metal contacts producing the flashes

Wind Direction Indicator

The wind direction indicator for the personal-flying airport will, normally, consist of a standard wind cone (36 inches in diameter and 12 feet long) illuminated by four 200-watt angle reflectors placed 6 feet above the top of the cone, providing continuous lighting at any position of the cone

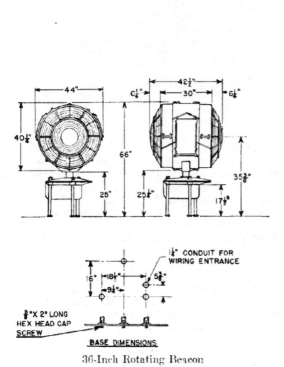

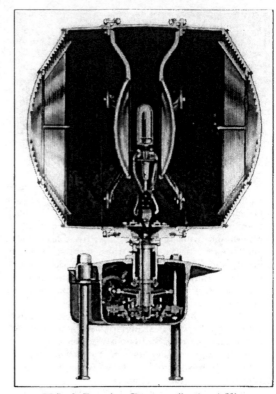

36-Inch Rotating Beacon   36-Inch Rotating Beacon—Sectional View

FIGURE 1. AIRPORT BEACONS. (*Courtesy Crouse-Hinds Company*)

The lighted wind tee (12 feet by 21 feet, 4 inches), replacing the wind cone, is painted orange for daytime true wind indication; green lamps are mounted for night-time indication. It should be located on the field in an area remote from buildings and free from false wind current where no eddies will occur. It should be visible from all parts of the field. The tee should be mounted on a concrete base and surrounded by a 4-foot-wide circle of white crushed rock, 40 feet in outside diameter. If desired, the tee can be electrically and automatically controlled by a remote operator.

Boundary Lights

Boundary lights should be placed to indicate a true outline of the entire landing area of the field. A unit should be placed at each angle of the boundary, and units between angles should be placed approximately 300 feet apart, and no more than 330 feet apart. Wherever there is a fence along the edge of the field, the lights should be placed 10 feet inside the fence. They should be mounted approximately 2½ feet above

the ground, and in no case more than 5 feet. The height of the mounting will be influenced by the geographical location of the field. For example, in areas of deep snow the light should have a greater mounting height.

For smaller fields, where the perimeter is less than 12,000 feet, operation of boundary lights by multiple circuits is generally considered more economical than series circuits which operate at higher voltages. Boundary lights should be mounted on an orange-colored cone of either the rigid type or the tip-over disconnect type; the color of the globe should be clear. Boundary lights which mark a hazardous approach should have red marker lights rather than clear. Either Fresnel or prismatic globes may be used for boundary markers. Boundary lights of the flush marker type may be used in locations where there is no snow or where snowfall is light. Flush markers used for boundary lighting emit a vertical as well as a horizontal light beam in contrast with flush contact lights which do not have a vertical beam.

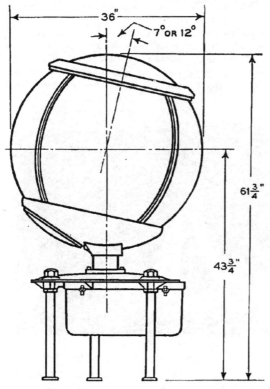

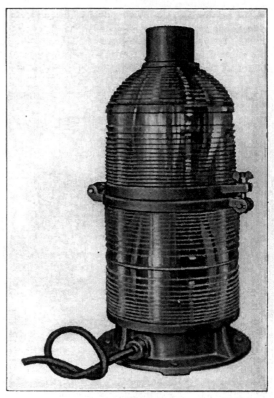

36-Inch "Bartow" Type Rotating Beacon   Code Beacon

FIGURE 1. AIRPORT BEACONS. *(Courtesy Crouse-Hinds Company)*

Floodlights

Both hangar and building aprons may be flood-lighted efficiently with 750-watt, 240-millimeter Fresnel floodlights spaced 50 feet apart. The mounting height should be 20 feet, with a sharp top cutoff of the beam to prevent glare in the pilot's eyes. In addition to providing necessary lighting to carry on the business of loading, unloading, and servicing planes, apron floodlighting provides the incoming pilot with an additional device by which he may orient himself and obtain a better perspective of his situation with respect to the ground.

The above series of elements is the minimum required to provide for night operation for an "all-way" airfield. The next step in field lighting is the installation of floodlights to provide for even distribution of light over the entire available landing area. Landing field floodlights are available with interchangeable lenses which will vary the horizontal spread of the beam. By arranging the lights in banks and selecting

the proper lenses, the desired distribution may be obtained. These lenses are further designed so that the vertical beam spread is narrow. This spread, together with the low mounting heights required for safety, will allow the light to be confined to the area to be lighted and will reduce glare to the pilot. Landing field floodlights are available in 1,500-watt and 3,000-watt lamp sizes.

This type of lighting provides a good initial investment for the small airport since, if runways are added later, the lights may be relocated at the ends of runways to provide runway lighting. Adjustments in lens types and focusing will, naturally, have to be made for the converted use, since the distribution requirements for runway lighting will differ from all-way lighting. Field floodlighting should be laid out so that the pilot can make a landing in any direction with the source of light behind him or at such an angle as to produce no glare.

For an airfield having runways, it becomes necessary to designate the particular runway which the pilot is to use as well as to provide sufficient illumination so that he may make a safe landing thereon.

The simplest and most economical method of providing runway lighting and identification is by the installation of two or more landing field floodlights at the

FIGURE 2. TETRAHEDRON WIND DIRECTION INDICATOR

ends of each runway. Each bank of lights is separately controlled from a central control panel located in the control tower (or in the Operations Office for terminal buildings having no control tower). Only the floodlights at the end of the runway from which the land-

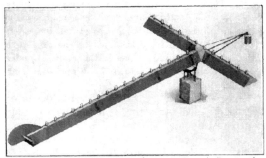

FIGURE 3. WIND TEE

ing is to be made are turned on, the rest of the runways remaining in darkness, thereby illuminating a single runway at a time. No glare will be experienced by the pilot, since the source of light is shielded from or behind him. In addition to lighting the runway proper, the distribution of light should be such as to illuminate

the 500-foot-wide landing strip area of which the runway is a part.

Landing field floodlights are usually mounted in pairs with a double unit obstruction light placed on top of the pair. Where more than two floodlights are used in a group, each end group should be marked with a double obstruction light. For perfectly level

FIGURE 4. BOUNDARY LIGHTS

fields floodlights should be mounted 8 to 12 feet above the ground. Fields or runways having humps require greater mounting heights to provide for complete illumination. Thus the profile of each runway must be considered in designing a system of floodlighting. Floodlights are usually mounted directly on top of the transformer housing in order to bring the lights as close to the transformer as possible to reduce line losses. If air-insulated transformers are used, a steel housing may be provided; if the transformers are oil

FIGURE 5. TIP-OVER DISCONNECT FITTING

insulated, a reinforced concrete housing should be used.

A major defect of floodlights is their poor performance under conditions of fog. The relatively wide beam distribution lights up the myriad particles of moisture constituting the fog and causes a "blob" of light rather than a clearly defined path. In locations where fog is present a fairly high percentage of the time, runway lighting by means of Bartow beam-controlled lights is recommended since this type produces a pin-point source of light.

Scheduled Commercial Airport Lighting

The accurate completion of scheduled flights under adverse weather conditions demands the installation of a field lighting system of greater precision than re-

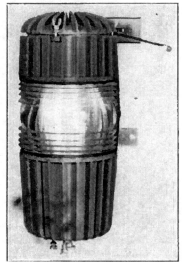

Courtesy Westinghouse Electric Corporation

FIGURE 6. APRON FLOODLIGHT—750-WATT 240-MILLI-METER FRESNEL

quired for personal-flying airports. In addition to the elements described before, plans for a scheduled commercial field should include contact lights, range lights, approach lights, and traffic control lights. An illuminated tetrahedron should be substituted for the wind cone or tee.

Contact Lights

Contact lights replace runway floodlights for indicating and outlining the runway a pilot is to use, with the floodlights reserved for emergency use. The lights for each runway should be on a separate circuit controlled by the control tower operator.

CAA standards call for installation of units every 200 feet along both sides of each runway. For major terminals it has been proposed that contact lights be installed 110 feet apart. Alternate lights would be wired to separate circuits, which would permit turning on lights spaced 220 feet apart in normal weather,

and 110 feet apart in bad weather. Furthermore, this arrangement would provide a safety factor since, if service to one circuit were disrupted, runway marking could still be provided at 220-foot spacing.

Two types of contact lights are in general use: flush marker and Bartow beam-controlled. The first type has the body of the unit set into the concrete base with only the lens and cap projecting above the surface, a distance of 2 to 2¾ inches. Most of the light is concentrated in two beams 180 degrees apart with the beams directed at and toeing in slightly toward the center line of the runway. The units should show a clear light to the pilot, except those for the final 1,500 feet of each runway, which should show a yellow light. Therefore the contact lights for the 1,500 feet at each

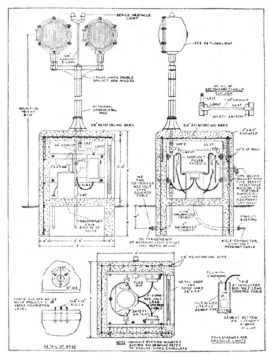

Courtesy Crouse-Hinds Company

FIGURE 7. RUNWAY FLOODLIGHT

end of each runway are equipped with 180-degree yellow screens to show a clear light from the approach end and a yellow light from the opposite end. Flush marker lights should be set in a 4-foot-square concrete base at the edges of rather than on the runways.

Flush marker lights are designed to resist heavy wheel loads passing directly over the unit, but will not resist the forces of a wheel turning on a unit; nor are they proof against snow plows. For areas of heavy

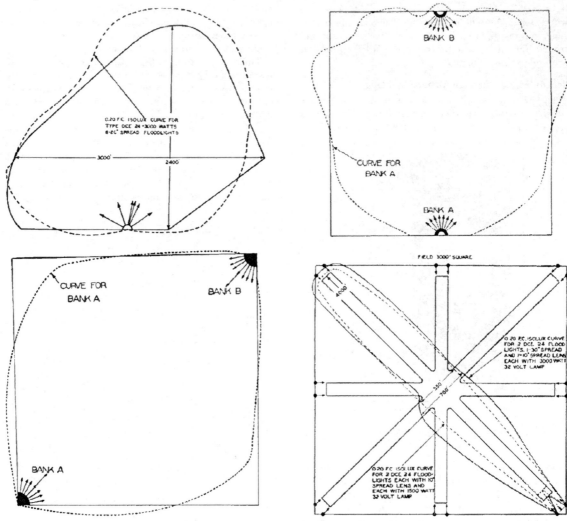

FIGURE 8. AIRFIELD FLOODLIGHTING. (*Courtesy Crouse-Hinds Company*)

snowfall, flush markers present a problem since each unit must be cleared by hand or with a rotary brush snow remover. In such an event, orange painted poles may be stuck in the ground on the off-runway side of each unit to indicate its location to the snow remover.

The Bartow beam-controlled unit is set on a standard giving a total projection of 25 inches above the surface of the runway. It provides a pin point of light of predetermined intensity. Beams are adjusted so that when a pilot is making a landing, all the lights appear to be of equal intensity, providing him with a clear perspective upon which to base his judgment of height.

In addition, a point source of light rather than a more diffused light source has greater fog-penetrating value.

It is recommended that Bartow beam-controlled runway lights be installed 15 feet beyond the edge of each runway. Thus a runway 200 feet wide would have its lights spaced 230 feet on centers. The spacing should be such that the outboard propeller of a plane traveling with its outboard wheel at the edge of the runway will not strike the light. As a further precaution, the units should be mounted on a tip-over disconnect type of fitting which will allow the light to tilt over when struck and simultaneously unplug it from the electri-

Exterior View

TYPES I OR II

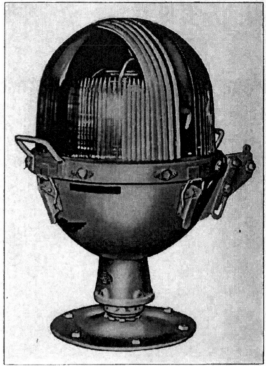

Section

FIGURE 9. CONTACT LIGHT. *(Courtesy Westinghouse Electric Corporation)*

eal circuit. The candle power of the beam-controlled light can be varied permitting highest intensity during adverse weather conditions, and lower intensity during clear weather thus preventing excessive glare.

The Bartow beam-controlled runway light is recommended over the flush marker light as a contact light for three principal reasons. First, the performance of the light as a landing aid to the pilot appears to be

Courtesy Line Material Company

FIGURE 10. BARTOW BEAM-CONTROLLED RUNWAY LIGHT

superior, particularly during conditions of fog. Second, the light will continue to provide illumination under all except the severest snow conditions and also during low-swirling dust or sand storms. Third, the installation and maintenance of any fixture which is above ground are simpler than of one which is flush with the ground.

Range Lights

Range lights with green globes are used to indicate the ends of runways and to code them, the same number of lights being used at both ends of a runway, and the greatest number of lights used to indicate the best runway. They should be set in a line at right angles to the center line of the runway. Range lights should

Day View

Courtesy Bartow Beacon Company

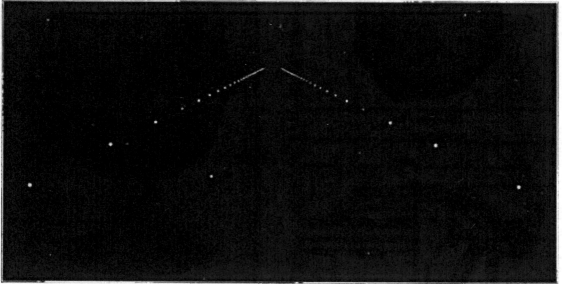

Night View

Courtesy Bartow Beacon Company

FIGURE 11. INSTALLATION OF BARTOW BEAM-CONTROLLED RUNWAY LIGHTS

be located 100 feet beyond the ends of runways and spaced 50 feet apart. If two runways converge near a boundary line, the two groups of range lights must be separated from each other by one clear light, even if this reduces the spacing. Where a runway ends 300 feet or more from the boundary, auxiliary range lights with yellow globes are located at the boundary line.

Either of two types of globes may be used, Fresnel or prismatic. Either of two types of mounting may be used, tip-over disconnect assembly or rigid cone assembly with the cones painted white and orange. The former type of globe and mounting is preferred. Range lights may be connected in series with boundary lights.

Taxiway Lights

The next step in developing a comprehensive lighting installation is the inclusion of taxiway lighting and traffic control lights. Taxiway lights are flush marker lights with a blue screen. They are mounted either on both sides of a taxiway or on the side of a taxiway which will be at the left of an incoming plane. They are spaced 200 feet apart for all except scheduled commercial airports, for which the spacing should be 100 feet.

Traffic Control Lights

Traffic control lights for taxiing planes should be located at the intersection of each runway with a taxi-

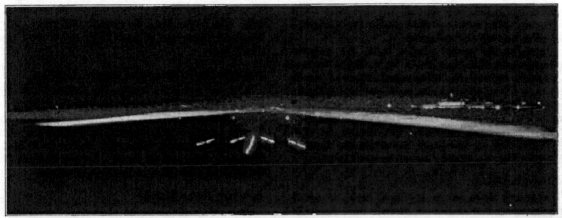

Green Arrow

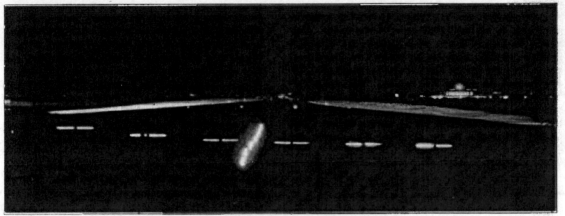

Flashing Red Cross

Installation

FIGURE 12. TRAFFIC CONTROL LIGHTS. (*Courtesy Westinghouse Electric Corporation*)

way and be individually controlled by the control tower operator. They consist of flush marker lights mounted in pairs, one red and one green.

Recommended traffic control lights for airborne planes consist of a green arrow and flashing red cross, one arrow and one cross being placed at the end of each runway. Neon elements are used, each one individually controlled. The lighting of a green arrow indicates a clear landing on the designated runway, giving both clearance and direction. The flashing red cross indicates that an emergency has developed, warning the pilot that the landing cannot be made safely.

Approach Lights

Approach lights are an additional device to enable the incoming pilot to line up properly with the designated runway. There is today no standard system of approach lighting. Several more years of intensive experimentation will be required to develop a system acceptable to all interested agencies and users. One system consists of a row of 8-foot-long red neon elements set at right angles to the center line of each runway. They are spaced 100 feet apart and extend 1,500 feet beyond the end of the runway. The center line of the row of approach lights is spaced 85 feet to the left of the center line of the runway. Another system being developed currently by the Bartow Beacon Company is illustrated by the diagram. The system employs 750-watt, type D-1, beam-controlled units throughout.

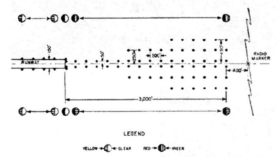

LEGEND

ploys 750-watt, type D-1, beam-controlled units throughout.

Wind Tetrahedron

The illuminated wind tetrahedron replaces the wind cone or tee as a wind-indicating device for larger airports. As its name implies, it is tetrahedral in shape. It is painted orange and white for daytime recognition and is illuminated with green and red lamps outlining its edges for night operation. The fixture should be mounted on a concrete base and in a location such as defined for the wind tee. Three types of tetrahedrons are in use: free-swinging; remotely controlled; a com-

bination of free-swinging with devices for remote control. The fixture may be covered with fabric, sheet metal, or waterproof plywood, with fabric most commonly used.

Non-Scheduled Commercial Airport Lighting

In extent and type, lighting for non-scheduled commercial airports falls somewhere between lighting for personal and for scheduled commercial airports. The type of operation to be carried on, frequency of night operation, and other influencing factors must be individually analyzed (as, in fact, for any airport) and the lighting plan fitted to these requirements.

Auxiliary Power Supply

Since safe night operation of aircraft depends upon continuous, uninterrupted electric service, it becomes extremely important to provide an auxiliary source of power upon failure of the primary source. The best provision, if available, is to run two separate feeder lines to the airport from separate sources of power. Where only one source is available, emergency auxiliary equipment should be provided in the form of a diesel- or gasoline-driven generator of sufficient capacity to handle the bare minimum requirements. In either case, change-over to the auxiliary source should be accomplished automatically, and should provide current of equal voltage and phase characteristics as the primary source.

The question of lamp failure should also be considered in the layout of the lighting plan. The plan should allow safe operation even with the sudden interruption of any single lamp. As an illustration, runways should never be lighted with only a single floodlight, since the failure of the single source of light would plunge the runway into darkness at a time which might be extremely critical for a safe landing.

Control

Control for all field lighting should be centralized, both in location and equipment. For airports having

Courtesy Westinghouse Electric Corporation

FIGURE 13. CONTROL PANELS—SURFACE MOUNTED

one the location is the control tower. For others, control should be located in an operations office, commanding a clear view of the available landing area and approaches.

Control panels vary from simple surface-mounted desk panels to elaborate control desks or panels. The former include a convenient arrangement of switches, enabling the operator to switch on and off manually the various elements comprising the field lighting layout. The latter are arranged so that the operator may preset the particular lighting arrangement required for

Courtesy Crouse-Hinds Company

FIGURE 14. CONTROL DESK

each individual case and then, by a master switch, turn on that entire portion of the installation. This panel will include a reproduction of the runway layout in miniature with indicating pilot lights, meteorological instrument indicators, control switches, circuit breakers, and contact light brightness switches.

Obstruction Marking

The requirements for obstruction marking around an airport and along airways have been codified by the CAA. The recommendations of the administration should be requested as to the extent of obstruction marking required at every airport being planned. In addition, various governmental agencies, such as the U. S. Army Corps of Engineers, Federal Communications Commission, U. S. Coast Guard, have requirements for marking facilities under their jurisdiction.

The purpose of night marking—either fixed or flashing—is to warn pilots of the presence of objects which constitute a hazard to their safe operation. This warning requires such marking for a given area surrounding each airport, along airways, and over or along areas which may expect night traffic.

The following general rules indicate the type of hazard that requires obstruction marking:

Hazards within 3 miles of a landing area:

Marking of a hazard may be necessary if:

The structure is over 150 feet above ground or water level at the point of location.

Or the top of the structure is above a 60-to-1 glide angle from the nearest landing area boundary, measured from a point 500 inside the boundary.

A structure may become a menace to air navigation if:

The structure is over 200 feet above ground or water level at the point of location.

Or the top of the structure is above a 50-to-1 glide angle from the nearest landing area boundary, measured from a point 500 feet inside the boundary.

Hazards over 3 miles from a landing area:

A structure over 3 miles from a landing area becomes a potential hazard when it is over 150 feet above ground or water level and is not shielded by other construction or natural features at least as high.

Marking of a hazard may be necessary when situated:

In or over open water used as a natural course for aircraft.

On a prominent hill or in open country.

Near a railroad or highway used as a course by aircraft.

Elsewhere and exceeding 200 feet in height above ground or water level.

To avoid becoming a menace to air navigation, structures should, as far as possible, conform with the following guide:

Height above Ground or Water Level	Minimum Distance from Center Line of Airway, an Aid to Air Navigation or Nearest Landing Area
Over 400 feet	10 miles
Over 300 feet	5 miles
Over 200 feet	3 miles

The marking must be so installed as to provide warning lights visible to the pilot from any angle. In remote locations such lights should be controlled by a light-sensitive switch. A transfer relay should be used providing instant change-over to reserve lamp when the service lamp fails for locations where relamping is difficult. Fresnel or prismatic red globes may be used, either singly or in pairs. Pairs are recommended for marking isolated obstructions, such as landing field floodlights; single units are used to outline the contours of a building or other spread-out structure.

Day obstruction marking of hazards serves the same function as night marking and is usually accomplished by painting the structure alternate bands or squares of international orange and white. As in night marking, the extent of marking required is determined by the CAA.

Runway Marking

Three types of runway marking are recommended: to indicate the direction of the runway with respect to the compass; to indicate the approximate length of the runway; and to indicate the center line of the runway. Numbers one-tenth of the magnetic compass reading to the nearest whole number are painted on the ends of each runway. Numbers and length symbols are painted with non-reflective black or white paint. Center line stripes are painted with reflective white paint. In addition to the above, markers may be painted with reflective white paint, indicating a distance of 1,500 feet from the ends of each runway. Standards for these symbols are shown in Fig. 16. If the center lines of taxiways are marked, reflective yellow paint is used.

General Comments

The basic elements available for airport lighting have been described together with the function of each element. To the factors already mentioned which must be considered in planning the lighting layout—budget for installation and operation, type and extent of night operations anticipated, geographical location—the following should be added: proximity to near-by airfields and location with respect to lighted airways. If an airport is situated near a major terminal and is designated as an auxiliary landing field, its lighting facilities will be more inclusive than if it were remotely located. Similarly, if a private flying field is situated along a lighted airway and is designated as an emergency landing field, it will be desirable to install light-sensitive automatic switching devices for the airport marker beacon, rotating beacon, wind cone, boundary

and range lights. This will insure the automatic switching on of minimum lighting at dusk and switching off at sun-up without operational personnel in attendance.

The lighting devices described and their order of presentation indicate the possibility of progressive in-

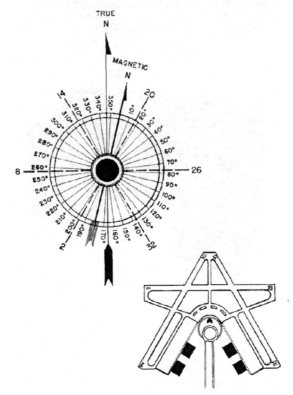

FIGURE 15.   COMPASS DESIGNATION

stallation of more adequate equipment as required. Thus, as for runway and building planning, the lighting installation should be planned in balanced and coordinated stages.

Bibliography

Airport Lighting Manual, The Civil Aeronautics Administration, U. S. Department of Commerce, Washington, D. C.
"Let There Be Light," by Davis Tuck, *Air Transport,* October, 1945.

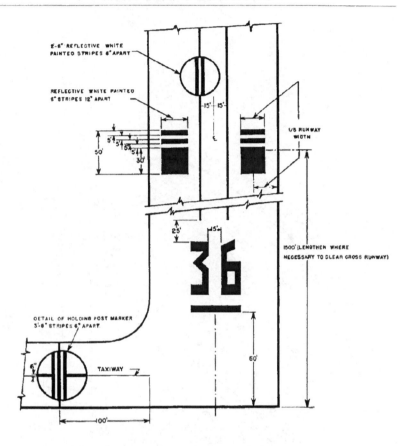

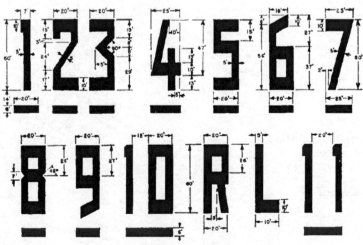

FIGURE 16. RUNWAY MARKING STANDARDS

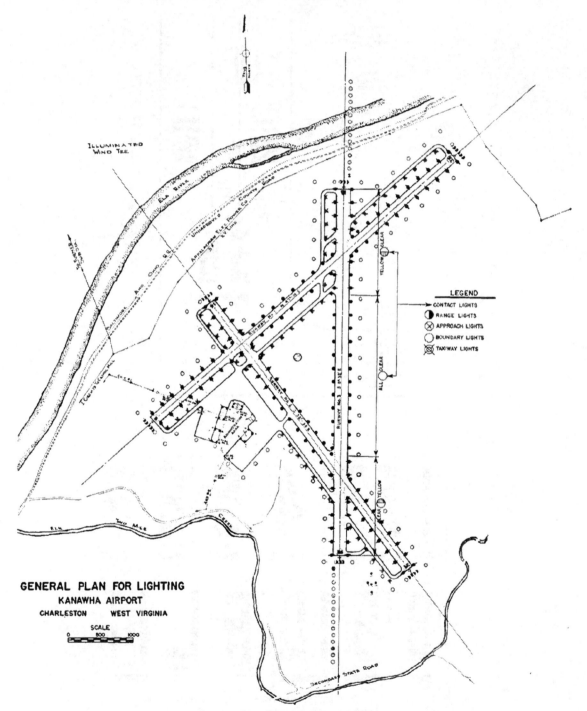

GENERAL PLAN FOR LIGHTING
KANAWHA AIRPORT
CHARLESTON   WEST VIRGINIA

FIGURE 17. AIRFIELD LIGHTING PLAN

9

AIRPORT BUILDING DESIGN·

FUNDAMENTALS

The "terminal building" which served the beginnings of aviation consisted of a corner of a hangar, partitioned off from the rest, heated with a pot-bellied stove, and containing a desk, a few chairs, and sometimes a telephone. From these humble quarters the entire business of an airport was transacted—charter flights, flying instruction, sales and maintenance of aircraft. The evolution of airport terminal design from its primitive stages to such a structure as the Washington National Airport Terminal is as fundamental as the development of aircraft, though of a much less spectacular nature. Contrasted with the design development of mechanical devices, the history of architecture shows that the tendency to design buildings on the basis of past concepts has always been stronger, unfortunately, than the will or liberty to design on the basis of true functional analysis. It would be fatal to the full development of flying to permit concepts of sound airport design to become frozen at this stage. The technique of design for airport buildings must keep pace with the technique of aircraft design. The full exploitation of the latter is dependent upon progressive planning of attendant ground facilities.

Today, specialization of aircraft according to use is reaching undreamed-of refinements. Examining airport buildings, one finds a similar specialization in the process of development. But this development is still in its primary stages, and its culmination will be reached only when the potentialities of flying have been completely exploited. In planning these structures the designer must remain on guard against premature standardization of planning concepts to a greater degree than with any other phase of airport design. The planning of every new airport presents a challenge to examine faithfully the best solutions to the problem which have been made and then to im-

prove on these, thus insuring continuous progress on the ground as well as in the air.

Site Location

In the past the planning of a landing facility began with the disposition of the runways. When their location had been determined, one or more areas—circumscribed by runway clearance and property lines—were left over. The most suitable of these was then developed for airport structures of all types. As often as not the "left-over" areas were decidedly unsuitable for terminal or hangar development by present-day standards.

Although the primary concern must still be with correct positioning of runways, the growing realization of the importance of sound terminal development, together with clearer conceptions of *balance* between runway and terminal capacity, indicates a more rational approach to site location. The master plan discloses approximate volumes and types of traffic to be planned for. The traffic, in turn, will indicate—roughly—the area required for terminal development. The determination of this area must proceed simultaneously with determination of runway size. Then, as the planning of the runways proceeds, the requirements of building sites must be kept constantly in view. The final location of the runways must be attended by a complementary designation of adequate building areas.

The suitability of any one such area as a site for terminal building development should be evaluated in accordance with the following requirements. The site should provide:

1. Ample area for first stage of building development and future expansion thereof.
2. Ample area for roadways.
3. Ample area for car parking.
4. A configuration such that items 1, 2, and 3 may

be brought into correct functional relationship with each other

5 Convenient access to main highway and other transportation means serving the landing facility.

6 Central location with respect to runways

7 Proximity to and ease of installation of utilities —electric power, water, gas, sewage, telephone

8 Favorable orientation with respect to topography, prevailing winds, compass

9 Good subsoil characteristics including natural drainage

Site Area

The determination of ground areas required for airport buildings of the nature and size to serve immediate needs is a relatively simple process. To determine now what these requirements will be in twenty years is beyond the capacity of the human mind Common sense dictates that the unpredictability of this type of development be met by providing space and still more space surrounding every airport building

There was a marked tendency in the past to crowd all airport buildings—administration, hangars shops, school—close together The result has been that when expansion of any one of the elements was required it could be undertaken only by moving or demolishing existing structures If the surveys of the master plan indicate the slightest possibility of future traffic growth (and practically every plan does), it will be sound to plan these elements with open "buffer" areas between them For major terminals entirely separate areas should be designated for each element.

It should be borne in mind that technological developments may allow a greater utilization of runways than predicted at the present time In such an event, more movements per hour will be accommodated with existing runways, necessitating increases in apron and building size, or additional buildings For example, landing aids may be perfected during the next decades to a degree which will render present conceptions of proper balance between runway and depot capacity entirely inadequate

Other developments may occur which will reveal the necessity of providing additional building space or acreage The personal-flying landing facility may be enlarged with a school, clubhouse, tennis courts, or arena The non-scheduled commercial airport may require the addition of facilities for police patrol, cropdusting, or a host of different agencies In scheduled commercial fields, the increases in facilities may occur in the form of a hotel, or an "airplane row" of showrooms In other words it is not increase in runway capacity alone which may call for enlargement of orig-

inal plans It may be one of any number of facilities which will have to be provided for, and in many cases, their exact nature or scope is too unpredictable to plan for intelligently at the present time

Car Parking—Roadways

Ample car-parking areas (based on an average of 300 square feet per car) are a basic element of every air terminal program Their size and relationship to the building group will differ according to the class of airport under design. Roadway design will likewise differ both in nature and layout.

For the personal-flying field, it may be assumed that the great majority of vehicles coming to the field will be bearing people who will spend some time at the port The first desire and act of the student, the private flyer, the club member, or the visitor will be to park his car and then proceed to the terminal on foot—proceed over the shortest and most direct path Accordingly, the car-parking areas must be well integrated with the main ingress and egress roads, and the roadway leading to the front door of the "central" building may be designed for relatively light traffic Car-parking facilities and roadways for working personnel may be grouped with those used by the public

The roadway system of a personal-flying field will not have to be designed for intense traffic movement, since the daily morning and evening peaks are relatively light compared with those at the commercial airport All elements of the building group should be linked together with roads—for convenience, service, and fire protection For the smaller field, a two-lane, two-way road will be sufficient For the larger, the main access road to the central building should be designed for one-way traffic only, service roads may still be two way

For the commercial port, the main emphasis should be placed on getting the taxicab, bus, or the air passenger's motorcar as close to the point of embarkation or debarkation as possible Car parking, in this case, is distinctly secondary to roadway access The roadway system must be designed to handle heavy peak loads with maximum fluidity of movement Car parking must be classified in several ways. The area closest to the entrance will be used as a taxicab stand A more remote area will be for short-time parking, to be used by the enplaning or deplaning passenger or his family or friends Still more remote will be the area for commuter parking, and beyond that space for the airport sightseer This last one must be designed to handle heavy weekend and holiday travel Separate areas will be needed for parking cars of working personnel. Different parking rates, varying according to the walking distance, will be the major controlling factor in keeping lots available for the designated type of parker.

For the smaller commercial airport, the separate areas may be combined into one lot, segregation being achieved by means of painted lines, signs, curbs, or fences The larger airports will require a number of lots for each classification.

Separate road access and truck courts must be provided for mail, express, and service trucks at the larger terminals All but the smallest commercial ports should also have separate road access and parking areas for each hangar area It is of obvious importance that passenger traffic be kept moving steadily and at fair speeds, cargo and service should also be allowed to move over unobstructed roads Wherever possible, the main roadway classifications of passenger, cargo, and service should be kept separate.

"Service" will include the activity of the hangars as well as the more commonly known requirements of service at the terminal building; there will also be an interrelation of service between hangars and plane-parking positions which should be provided for with roadways rather than permitting service vehicles to use aircraft maneuvering areas

For industrial airports, cargo being substituted for passengers, the primary concern will be to provide direct roadway access for the entering or departing trucks The extent of car-parking areas (principally for working personnel) will depend on the degree of integration with adjacent manufacturing activities It is conceivable that the industrial airport terminal may include in its program a showroom to exhibit products being manufactured and flown by the company This showroom will necessitate a car-parking area reserved for visitors and buyers.

It is only natural that the main emphasis of this book, as far as "traffic" is concerned, should be placed upon design for air traffic. Nevertheless, the most careful analysis must be made of anticipated vehicular movement The two types of traffic—air and ground—must be in proper balance, otherwise, the airport will not function at maximum efficiency

Central Location

Irrespective of the size of a landing facility, every effort should be exerted to place the plane apron area centrally with respect to the runways in order to reduce plane taxi distances Although this subject has been treated in Part 6, it is appropriate to re-examine it at this juncture.

Excessive taxi distances are an economic hardship on the personal flyer as well as the commercial operator.

Furthermore, the time lost in such maneuvering will lessen the interest of the personal flyer, and increase the schedule time of the air passenger Inasmuch as the tendency of all types of airfields is to increase in size rather than decrease, it becomes progressively more important to reduce taxi distances to the minimum In certain instances previous planning methods may be entirely reversed. The best area for terminal development will be chosen first and the runways then arranged around this area In the planning of Idlewild—New York City's new superairport—this concept has been carried to the point where the terminal area is an "island" completely surrounded by runways and connected to the "mainland" by a vehicular underpass

The customary location of control tower surmounting the administration building has many inherent advantages, permitting close integration of this facility with communications, air traffic control, and other agencies A site located centrally with respect to the runways will allow this interrelationship to be maintained and at the same time will provide optimum visibility over all portions of the airfield

Balance with Runway Capacity

In order to function at maximum efficiency, all the elements composing a landing facility must be in balance with each other If any one of these elements is too small, it will become the source of operational "bottlenecks"; if unnecessarily large, it will become a financial liability It would be unthinkable to plan a railroad station of 24-track capacity with a 20-foot-square waiting room, or a way station with a waiting room 200 by 100 feet The airport terminal development and all attendant facilities—plane-docking areas, building proper, access roads, car-parking areas—must bear a correct space relationship to the traffic which may be accommodated by the runway system

Space Requirements

Irrespective of size or nature of operation, all airport terminals may be considered to consist of two major elements, the aircraft parking apron and the terminal building proper The starting point for determining the size of building is an evaluation of the maximum number of planes which can be docked at the apron simultaneously, the number based on runway capacity From this figure an analysis may be made of the traffic which will flow through the building resulting from these planes

For the personal-flying field, it may be assumed that the maximum runway capacity will be 80 movements per hour for a single-runway system The average time which each aircraft spends at the apron should not exceed 30 minutes. In occupying an apron position each craft accounts for two movements Thus, to determine the maximum number of parking positions required, the runway capacity per hour is divided by 4, resulting in the figure of 20 positions for a personal-flying field of single-runway design

The scheduled commercial landing facility will have a runway capacity approximately one-half that of a personal flying field This reduction is brought about by the differing operational characteristics of the larger craft using such a facility The time spent at the apron should not exceed that for personal aircraft Thus a single-runway layout for a scheduled commercial airport (having a maximum capacity of 40 movements per hour) requires, theoretically, 10 plane-parking positions at the apron In actual practice, this figure is usually increased by 3 to 5 positions, since empirical operating standards cannot always be attained in commercial practice, particularly when one airfield is served by a number of airlines

The runway capacity of a non-scheduled commercial airport will fall between those of the two foregoing categories The types of aircraft operating during a peak traffic hour must be estimated This will become the basis for estimating runway capacity. The average time spent at the apron will probably be greater than for the other classes, being determined again by the expected nature of operation Since all these factors will vary for each airport of this category, no design data can be established at this writing (As an example, however, if it is determined that the runway capacity will be 60 movements per hour and the average time at the apron 40 minutes, the number of plane-parking positions required at the apron will be 20)

The space allotted for each plane dock is determined by the turning radius of the larger size of aircraft using the field plus wing tip clearances (cf. Part 2), and is usually designated by a circle of the proper diameter For personal-flying fields this diameter is 50 feet, for scheduled commercial fields designed for domestic operation it is 150 feet The largest airplanes engaged in transoceanic travel require 250 feet For non-scheduled commercial fields it will be determined, as for runway capacity, individually, and will be a figure between 50 and 150 feet. For the last category, supporting as it does the greatest variety of plane sizes, it is well to design the average plane dock size on a modular basis If 55 feet is taken as the module, one module will serve personal aircraft, two modules, or 110 feet, will serve planes of the DC-3 class, three modules, or 165 feet, will serve planes of the Constella-

tion class In this way any combination of all types of aircraft may be accommodated

Stage Planning

It has been stressed earlier that every landing facility should be planned in stages to accommodate increases in traffic This means that every element of landing facility design must be planned in a flexible coordinated manner so that, as increases occur—and by whatever manifestation—all these elements may be maintained in balance progressively

With this in mind, it should be emphasized that the determination of numbers of plane-parking positions required (under "Space Requirements") refers to the *maximum* number which will balance the capacity of a given runway under present methods of operation The number actually required at any one time will be determined on the basis of the traffic analysis of the master plan

Taking as an example a hypothetical community requiring a scheduled commercial airport, the master plan discloses that 7 plane docks are needed immediately, 12 will be required in 4 years, 18 in 6 years, and 26 in 10 years. A single-runway system will suffice for the first 5 or 6 years, with an increase to parallel indicated for the years following The terminal area must be planned for the ultimate capacity which a parallel runway system can generate, although the actual building which will take place at the start will be relatively modest

Varying plane sizes will, obviously, have an important bearing on the traffic which will have to be accommodate by the terminal area A doubling of passenger-carrying capacity doubles the number of people passing through a terminal building with no increase in plane-parking positions. This variable, as well as others, must be acknowledged in preparing the original traffic survey The safest rule to follow is to plan every terminal area for the maximum number of people which may conceivably use the facility, and to do so in a manner which will allow ready progression from the initial stage to the ultimate No airport terminal building exists which is too large, in fact, no terminal exists which is, today, large enough

Planning for Expansion

The importance of planning every building on every airport with a view to possible expansion having been established, the method whereby such expansion may be brought about at reasonable cost should be discussed at this time. One fundamental rule is that rectangular buildings may be added to with less loss of space and at lower cost than odd-shaped circular or angular structures Another rule is that the nuclear structure should be clear spanned or have sufficiently large spans so that when the need for expansion arises, partitions may be easily moved, or the original cell may be cleared of partitions entirely and function as the central lobby

Floor and ceiling treatments of the first cell should be carried through, and partitions should occur within the finished floor and ceiling lines This simple rule allows for maximum flexibility in partition rearrangement with least waste of material and cost The partitions themselves should be of "dry-wall" construction so that they may be moved easily Fenestration should be arranged on a modular basis to further the cause of mobility in planning

Many airport buildings are one-story structures built directly on the ground with little or no basement The most comfortable and most flexible heating system is circulating hot-water radiant heat with wrought-iron piping embedded in the concrete floor slab The initial cost is somewhat higher than for direct radiation or unit heaters but will prove to be a sound investment Partitions may then be moved at will without affecting the heating layout

In most cases the shape of the available building site is determined by the direction of the adjacent runways The first inclination is to "hug" these boundary lines and design a V-shaped, circular or semi-circular building If the lot is not too restricted in size, this temptation should be avoided and the most simple form—a rectangle—adopted The counter argument may be raised that wings may be added to the V-shape to take care of future expansion True, but they will take care of expansion in only one direction If it should come about that the central area has to be increased in depth as well as width, trouble may occur in reworking the odd-shaped plans If the central lobby of an odd-shaped plan is built large enough, originally, to take care of any possible expansion, the financial structure of the airport will be burdened with a "great hall" which will not begin to be used to capacity for many years

In every case the ultimate plan as well as the first stage should be drawn at the outset This initial investment in slightly higher architect's fees will be more than paid for as the years go by

Direct Access to Aircraft

The primary purpose of any airport building is to perform a necessary intermediate function between the traveler's arrival at the airport by ground transport and his departure by aircraft The most direct access must, therefore, be provided (in time as well as distance traversed) from the point of arrival, through the building, and into the aircraft For the deplaning traveler, the intermediate function may differ or be omitted entirely, and his course may be routed differently The different routes of an enplaning and a deplaning traveler will be of more significance as the traffic through the building increases, and will have greatest value in the larger commercial airport buildings

The intermediate function of the building differs for the various categories of airports For the personal-flying field or airpark, it is filing a flight plan or checking on the condition of the weather For a commercial airport it is ticketing and baggage checking For the cargo section of a commercial airport or for an industrial airport, products are substituted for passengers, and the intermediate function is the consolidation or sorting or packing of cargo But in every case the most successful plan is the one where the least amount of time and energy will have to be expended in loading the aircraft

Frequently today the primary circulation is circuitous, time consuming, and often leads to a lessening of interest on the part of the air student or private flyer, or delayed schedules for the commercial traveler Not only must the traffic circulation be direct, but it should also be further enhanced by means of suitable, legible placards illuminated for night use Well-designed directive or informative signs increase the usefulness of any public building and add to its functional attractiveness

Concessions

Concession areas, properly designed and located, have an extremely important bearing upon the final success of every airport building program Although first thoughts must be directed at planning for maximum efficiency in handling the public's flying activities, this same public must be accommodated with a wide variety of incidental services or "concessions" They may range from cigarette and candy vending machines at the smallest airpark to a hotel or newsreel theater at the largest airport, but the relationship of concession to flying activity must be clearly understood

Some airport terminals have been planned around the revenue-producing potential of concessions rather than around the convenience of the air traveler This approach has resulted in such an obfuscation of circulation within and about the building that the air traveler (who is the prime motivation of the building's existence) is hard-put to find the way to his airplane No airport building will give proper service to the pubhe or be a financially sound undertaking unless concessions are present in volume and kind compatible with the type of airport in which they appear. At the same time no airport building will function successfully which allows the concession areas to encroach on the functioning of the building as part of an airport. The solution lies in a careful analysis of the types of concessions which each airport may be expected to support, the area which should be devoted to each concession, and the location of each concession with respect to its neighbor and to the primary areas devoted to flying activities.

Certain types of concessions, their area requirements and their location have been indicated in the programs presented in the second half of this part of the book. As the plans will demonstrate, it is entirely possible to locate concessions so that they will not interfere with primary circulation and, at the same time, to make them convenient to the public. A restaurant may, for instance, be placed on an upper floor and thereby command a much better view of flying activities than a first-floor location would. The person who patronizes a restaurant has a reasonable amount of leisure time to spend and will not mind the walk up a flight of stairs. The "snack bar," on the other hand, should be on the main floor; it will be patronized by the person whose time for refreshment is limited. By the same token, his ability to see the field is of distinctly secondary importance to obtaining food in a hurry. By placing this element on the off-field side, valuable space is made available for functions dealing directly with flying activities which must be on the field side. This illustration is cited as an example of the location analysis which must accompany the planning of every concession.

The financial relation of concessions to the financial structure of the entire airport development is discussed on page 162.

In many cases a large proportion of patrons of airports are visitors or sightseers. Their circulation should be segregated from that of the air passenger. Concessions may be located so as to deflect this secondary stream from the primary one, resulting in a better plan from the air passengers' viewpoint and in increased income to the concessionaire.

Economics

The transport of persons by air, either personally or commercially, is still in its primitive stages. Contrast the one hundred years of railroad development or the forty years of motor vehicle development with the short span of air transport development. What ingenious devices the mind of man will conceive to simplify air transport or even to revolutionize existing means no one can foretell. The best that can be done with airport building design, therefore, is to plan on the basis of the most advanced knowledge currently available. And the best, as far as economics are concerned, consists in thinking of the shortest possible life expectancy compatible with sound business practice.

If airport buildings can be built of relatively inexpensive materials and financed in such a manner that they can be torn down to make way for more advanced designs within a period of fifteen to twenty years, the entire field of air transport will have gained an immeasurable advantage over any other mode of transport. For it will not be the designer of aircraft who will arrest the progress of development in the air. It will, if it occurs, be the tremendous investment in obsolete ground handling facilities which will retard or even halt development in the air. The watchword of the aircraft manufacturer has always been to regard with suspicion inflexible tooling for limited production, since a large fixed tooling investment tends to freeze design and retard progress. The same thinking must be applied to "tooling" the ground facilities of aircraft—their airports.

At every stage of planning, a financial take-off of the project should be made. It will include estimates of the following costs:

Land acquisition
Elimination of obstructions
Grading and drainage
Landscaping
Roadways and parking lots
Building construction
Utilities
Architects' and engineers' fees
Amortization of mortgages (for different periods).
Insurance
Maintenance

Against this must be balanced estimated income, which may include the following:

Hangar rentals
Landing fees
Dues from club members
Office rentals
Concessions
  Restaurant and bar
  Vending machines
  Telephones and telegraph
  Barber—beautician
  Valet
  Car parking

SHEET 1

	July	August	Sept.	Oct.	Nov.	Dec.	Jan.	Feb.	March	April	May	June	Total
Rentals													
Terminal Building	2,988.33	2,844.60	2,702.80	2,702.81	2,577.80	2,882.63	2,852.58	2,683.58	3,602.15	2,717.05	2,780.72	2,780.72	34,115.86
Hangers	5,763.22	5,763.22	7,255.69	10,348.38	5,439.07	9,153.23	6,986.24	6,986.24	6,985.52	6,986.96	6,986.24	6,986.24	85,640.25
Temporary Buildings	30.00	30.00	30.00	30.00	30.00	30.00	30.00	30.00	30.00	30.00	30.00	30.00	360.00
Total Rentals	8,781.55	8,637.91	9,988.49	13,081.19	8,046.87	12,065.86	9,868.82	9,699.82	10,617.67	9,734.01	9,796.96	9,796.96	120,116.11
Landing Fees	2,127.50	2,230.00	2,375.00	2,325.00	2,675.00	2,325.00	2,622.83	2,835.00	2,647.50	2,660.00	2,925.00	2,927.50	30,675.33
Ramp Service													
Scheduled Aircraft	1,040.00	1,150.00	1,130.00	1,180.00	1,220.00	1,220.00	1,180.00	1,300.00	1,260.00	1,260.00	1,360.00	1,360.00	14,660.00
Itinerant Aircraft	115.46	92.75	87.25	70.00	178.38	95.75	137.00	118.60	114.50	141.63	175.00	237.37	1,563.69
Aircraft Storage	30.00	30.00	30.00	60.00	60.00	60.00	60.00	90.00	145.00	60.00	106.00	87.50	818.50
Total Ramp Service	1,185.46	1,272.75	1,247.25	1,310.00	1,458.38	1,375.75	1,377.00	1,508.60	1,519.50	1,461.63	1,641.00	1,684.87	17,042.19
Charter & Sightseeing Service													
Air Carrier													
Goodyear Guarantee												2,000.00	2,000.00
Total Charter & Sightseeing Service												2,000.00	2,000.00
Gasoline Concession													
Gulf Oil	12,500.00	12,500.00	12,500.00	12,500.00	12,500.00	12,500.00	12,500.00	12,500.00	12,500.00	12,500.00	12,500.00	12,500.00	150,000.00
Taxicab Concession													
Airport Transport	938.81	1,008.03	1,019.31	1,038.60	994.65	1,067.55	1,072.07	980.93	1,041.24	1,130.50	1,239.78	3,568.53	15,100.00
Bus Concession													
A. B. & W. Transit Co.	47.10	54.70	53.40	56.28	55.53	55.44	56.30	52.87	58.22	48.57	53.99	157.60	750.00
Air Terminal Services													
Restaurant	967.71	1,181.87	1,031.46	986.92	842.89	634.71	792.47	811.99	928.61	1,357.34	1,461.33	1,464.92	12,343.22
Coffee Shop	1,687.61	1,756.70	1,694.86	1,650.78	1,447.30	1,382.85	1,423.90	1,392.13	1,512.32	1,627.62	1,672.49	1,679.97	18,828.53
Employees' Cafeteria	654.92	626.22	728.70	700.58	653.95	677.14	614.13	540.42	566.02	492.68	467.37	500.78	7,221.91
Hangar Café	412.66	393.30	420.99	419.27	423.50	420.10	430.80	377.14	426.43	353.87	395.73	416.28	4,900.07
Meals Aloft	855.57	1,028.37	1,126.29	1,055.72	1,065.99	945.74	936.06	804.36	928.60	1,587.23	1,847.25	1,836.23	14,015.41
Soda Fountain	748.82	773.96	718.99	711.29	670.59	671.42	632.90	554.93	591.88	658.47	874.58	837.31	8,455.23
Automatic Soft Drink Vendors													
Cart Vendors													
Vending Machines	425.94	425.95	447.45	6,021.83	636.53	552.13	522.31	588.44	692.35	567.02			10,789.95
Tobacco & News Stand	347.60	351.96	366.66	360.91	352.42	337.77	338.79	325.40	390.51	358.62	378.65	395.38	4,303.77
Souvenir Stand	70.84	85.90	72.99	70.77	70.80	92.91	87.02	88.27	95.87	103.07	87.93	73.73	1,000.10
Barber Shop	61.82	61.89	62.09	71.58	72.62	76.00	67.69	69.71	72.13	65.00	73.25	68.53	822.31
Lockers	.83	.82	.74	.92	.93	.79	1.05	1.05	.78	1.11	1.21	1.51	11.74
Scales													
Rest Rooms			1.25	1.25	2.50	1.25	1.25	2.50	1.25	1.25	1.25	1.25	15.00
Miscellaneous													
Box Lunches	93.86	83.48	75.99	101.40	101.01	99.40	122.95	129.26	157.13	147.45	134.62	107.23	1,353.77
Parking Lot Stand	46.37	13.66											60.03
Public Roads Cafeteria				1,167.45	81.81	76.99	84.59	78.50	83.67	74.63	92.19	99.13	1,828.96
Surcharge on Excess Receipts													
Total Air Terminal Services	6,214.54	6,783.18	6,748.46	13,318.67	6,422.84	5,969.20	6,056.00	5,764.10	6,352.55	7,425.36	7,423.85	7,471.25	85,950.00

FIGURE 1. FINANCIAL STATEMENT OF SCHEDULED COMMERCIAL AIRPORT—INCOME

	July	August	Sept.	Oct.	Nov.	Dec.	Jan.	Feb.	March	April	May	June	Total
Turnstiles	1,068.90	1,614.20	1,790.00	1,228.40	799.30	280.30	480.90	393.90	615.40	1,748.30	1,800.00	2,450.00	14,359.60
Miscellaneous													
Paper Cups	20.79	21.86	28.33	13.86	8.06	4.64	11.47	8.26	8.39	15.96	21.81	23.73	187.16
Napkin Dispensers	21.05	17.15	10.55	26.30	18.85	23.30	18.80	28.75	33.75	15.75	24.90	31.05	270.20
Conducted Tours		1.00			.90		1.00					4.90	7.80
Work Orders	1,161.63	384.03	200.27	1,035.28	561.73	108.36	200.28	287.15	117.36	218.76	262.81	4.00	4,541.66
Miscellaneous		8.66		2.77									11.43
Total Miscellaneous	1,203.47	432.70	239.15	1,078.21	589.54	136.30	231.55	324.16	159.50	250.47	309.52	63.85	5,018.25
Utilities, Sale of													
Telephone	500.05	595.01	564.12	561.90	570.27	583.35	580.75	584.10	567.85	625.04	603.80	601.65	6,937.89
Steam	747.23	776.89	587.39	1,646.05	2,502.83	6,907.31	4,631.14	2,171.46	2,502.31	1,506.08	307.93	305.28	24,591.90
Electricity	2,689.16	3,284.35	3,083.44	1,373.90	5,171.73	5,227.12	2,051.69	2,528.76	3,734.26	3,390.15	3,701.07	3,248.91	39,484.54
Water	520.75	497.25	507.28	307.66	475.56	257.30	238.06	222.93	265.60	226.22	297.23	628.50	4,444.34
Total Sale of Utilities	4,457.19	5,153.52	4,742.23	3,889.51	8,720.39	12,975.08	7,501.64	5,507.25	7,070.02	5,747.49	4,910.03	4,784.34	75,458.69
Total Receipts	38,524.52	39,686.99	40,703.29	49,825.86	42,262.50	48,750.48	41,767.11	39,566.63	42,581.60	42,706.33	42,690.13	47,404.73	516,470.17
Total Receipts—Year Ago	34,341.47	33,530.68	34,818.44	35,194.06	36,722.18	38,297.83	40,773.50	37,321.10	39,157.38	38,159.33	37,516.63	38,068.94	443,901.63
Total Receipts—Prior Years	33,026.58	38,214.53	35,827.47	33,126.36	30,911.79	28,082.62	28,680.18	27,854.14	35,553.44	38,522.45	37,097.12	36,349.24	403,253.92

Spectators' gallery.

Newsreel theater.

Drugstore

Florist

Bank

Hotel

Laundry

Plane servicing, gas, oil; aircraft parts and accessory sales

Others.

Simple mathematics will determine over what period of time the structures may be amortized to provide a sound investment Such studies, if made intermittently throughout the planning stages, will quickly disclose which factors, either of revenue or of expense, appear to be getting out of line

Since the number and size of the concessions which may be expected to flourish will have an important bearing on the size and, therefore, the cost of construction, their inter-relation must be carefully balanced. It will be found frequently that adding more concessions will more than make up for increased first costs, and the problem then becomes one of raising additional funds

The financial statement shown in Fig 1 is the actual record of one of the major commercial airports in this country

FIGURE 1   FINANCIAL STATEMENT OF SCHEDULED
COMMERCIAL AIRPORT—EXPENDITURES

Expenditure	1945
Personnel Services	$369,943
Travel	71
Transportation of Things	177
Communications	12,005
Utilities	47,975
Other Contractual Services *	42,303
Supplies and Materials	34,127
Fuel	81 511
Equipment	5,623
Transfer of Funds Between Government Agencies	—51,535
Net Expenditures	542,230
Revenues	594 725
Profit or Loss	+52,495

* Repairs and Maintenance performed by outside agencies

Fundamentals have been discussed in this part which are of importance by themselves They are site location, effective planning for expansion, direct access to aircraft, proper choice, design, and location of concessions, functional planning An adherence to these fundamentals will contribute materially to the economic success of the airport project

Construction

The simplest construction materials will most adequately meet the fundamentals of economic planning and non-monumental, functional nature

The airpark or air harbor buildings, codes permitting may be built of wood frame sheathed with wood (clapboard, weatherproof plywood, flush siding) Experience in building millions of structures of wood indicates that this material fulfills most requirements of reasonable life span, easy alteration, low maintenance costs, reasonable first costs, pleasing appearance Hangars designed to accommodate personal aircraft may be built of wood as long as satisfactory fire protection is provided The trusses being of timber are slow burning, and the remainder of the wood required may be treated to acquire non-combustion supporting characteristics if deemed necessary

The larger personal-flying airport buildings and those for commercial fields should be built of incombustible materials But again, simple, inexpensive materials should have first choice A steel or reinforced concrete frame may well be faced with select common brick where this material is locally available For the smaller structures where fire protection is desired and first costs must be kept to a minimum, wall-bearing concrete block is an entirely satisfactory material

Since the ground floors of a large number of airport buildings consist of a concrete slab laid directly on the ground, integrally colored and hardened cement or asphalt tile is a satisfactory floor finish Where more funds are available or where a dense flow of traffic is anticipated, terrazzo flooring will be indicated

Roof structures for the simplest buildings are of wood joists For the larger, fireproof buildings, steel joists covered with gypsum slabs or precast concrete beams covered with precast concrete slabs are satisfactory The largest spans, naturally, are framed with steel or reinforced concrete *

Large areas of glass should be used for the exterior walls of airport buildings (double-glazed in cold climates) The nature and use of this type of structure demand a close integration of the interior with the outdoors A clean-cut, impressive, and functional effect may be obtained by using simple materials, by having them express local function and character, and by having well-proportioned masses of structure—masses which bear a relationship to the ground upon which they are built The final choice of building materials rests on local availability of both materials and the labor to erect them, and the size of the budget

* The authors hold no brief for any one building material Specific materials are mentioned herein merely as examples of materials which they consider appropriate

Mechanical Services

Heating

Generally, heating for airport buildings follows conventional design practice. A central plant generating high-pressure steam should be considered for the larger airports. The steam is delivered to all buildings on the airport, hangars included, at pressures of 40 to 50 pounds. At each building it is reduced to ±5 pounds and then distributed to the heating elements. The steam at high pressure is used directly to generate 180° F water for dishwashing in the various restaurants and cafeterias. Steam at lower pressures is used to generate domestic hot water for toilet rooms and showers. This system has been satisfactorily employed at the Washington National Airport.

Since chimneys cause obstructions at airports, the top of any stack should not exceed the height of an adjacent roof by six feet. Where the total stack height resulting from this limitation is insufficient to produce an adequate natural draft, a forced draft should be provided. The chimney should be located so as to cause no interference in visibility to the control tower operator or interference in the accurate reading of meteorological instruments.

Air Conditioning

The control tower and airway traffic control offices must be air-conditioned. Various concessions, such as restaurants, usually are air-conditioned. Whether other offices are conditioned must be determined by individual tenants. Public lobbies and waiting rooms are usually not air-conditioned; forced ventilation should be provided in every case.

The only radical departure from normal practice is the provision, which should be built in, for supplying warmed air in the winter and conditioned air in the summer to the airplanes parked at the apron. (This provision applies, naturally, only to commercial aircraft.) Mobile units have been used in the past to accomplish this but they have not proved to be entirely satisfactory. The most practical solution appears to be the use of a service pit on the apron to which the tempered air has been brought and from which direct connection to the plane may be made. Since the forcing of air through very long ducts results in excessive losses in either heat or cold, it will be more efficient to place a combination unit heater and air conditioner in the building near the apron opposite each of the plane parking positions rather than to attempt the job from a central plant. Ducts approximately 75 feet long may then be placed under the apron from the unit to the pit. Steam will be brought to the unit for winter heating, and either brine or a refrigerant may be circulated to the unit for summer cooling.

The air-conditioning load for a 48-passenger plane will be approximately 3½ tons. When larger airplanes of 100-passenger capacity make their appearance, this load will be doubled. At that time it will be more efficient to install a second 3½-ton unit with its own duct to another pit than to increase the size of the original unit. The ducts have two points of attachment to the larger plane; if they were served from a single pit, the length of connecting hose would be excessive.

The possibility of having an air-conditioning engineering firm install and operate all phases of air conditioning at the airport on a concession basis should not be overlooked. Such an arrangement might prove lucrative to the airport management and most efficient for the tenants.

Other Services

The design and installation of electric power, lighting, and plumbing for airport structures follow conventional practice and, therefore, no discussion of these services has been included. It is strongly recommended that all plumbing plans be submitted to the District Sanitary Engineer, U S Public Health Service, for approval before the start of construction.

Special attention should be given to the layout of communications—telephone, public address system, teletype, and pneumatic tube installations. The requirements for each of them must be obtained from the various tenants occupying the building. They should be obtained at an early stage in design so that provision for the facilities may be built in, and later cutting and patching be reduced to a minimum.

Compressors for delivering compressed air to the ramp service pits should be located in proximity to the heating plant so that piping and electrical supply may be reduced to a minimum and maintenance engineering personnel may be most efficiently employed.

An incinerator should be included in the planning of every airport terminal building. This equipment should be accessible to all principal users of the airport for the treatment of refuse which cannot be disposed of by means of sewers or garbage collection. The size of an incinerator will be determined by the number and type of users.

Functional Planning

A short plea is entered here for designing airport structures on a strictly functional, non-monumental basis. From every conceivable point of view it may be demonstrated that such an approach is the only practicable one

From the financial point of view, one certainly need not call to mind the number of monumental buildings which are today burdening the treasuries of almost every community. Firehouses with church steeples, school buildings in the "collegiate gothic" with tons of cut stone façades—none of these millions spent on superficial ornamentation have contributed to stamping out a fire or increasing the perception of the student The same approach must not be allowed to contribute financial hardships to a community in its airport construction program

From the aesthetic viewpoint, one need only cite the clean, functional contours of our modern aircraft to indicate where inspiration for design should come from The thought of an airplane covered with flush-riveted aluminum alloy sheet parked in front of a "Mount Vernon" or "Mission" airport should produce even in the most casual observer a sensation of uneasiness

Many volumes have been written in the last few decades on modern architecture, large amounts of energy have been expended in arguing the appropriateness of modern forms In airport building design no argument is necessary The question of "tying in with local tradition" is non-existent since airports, by their very nature, must appear on isolated sections of land As to function, they are housing the most modern means of transport and, logically, should complement this mode And last, there are today relatively few airports, thus liberating the designer from the bonds of habit, dogma, and tradition The progressive community will find real satisfaction in building a new kind of monumentality into its airports—clean, functional building design

PROGRAMS

The master plan will disclose anticipated amounts and types of air and ground traffic for a proposed landing facility On the basis of such information, a program may be drawn up of the elements which will form the airport terminal development, and an approximation made of the square foot areas required for each element The charting of such a program will serve two important functions First, it will cause the persons interested in and entrusted with the responsibility of organizing the local endeavor to come to agreement as to just what should be planned and built Second, it will become an instrument which will permit those charged with the actual planning and construction of the building to proceed with their work in a progressive and orderly fashion

This section, therefore, is devoted to a presentation and discussion of programs which might be encountered in the planning of various types of airport buildings Just as the types of airfields fall into three major categories—personal, non-scheduled commercial, and commercial—so, also, may the types of airport buildings be classified

It is intended that these programs, and their accompanying plans, will serve as a suggestion of the type of plan which might be incorporated into a complete airport design They should not be regarded as final, complete, and capable of being transplanted, *in toto*, to the local scene The solution of every planning problem must be solved locally, since it is influenced by local conditions

Personal-Flying Airports

First Stage

> Central lobby
> Field manager's office.
> Operations office
> Toilets
> Locker rooms
> Showers
> Heating plant

This is the simplest form of terminal building for an airpark, air harbor, or small airport The central lobby would function as a clubroom, where local air enthusiasts could gather, its atmosphere should be warm and inviting The field manager's office and the operations office should open onto the lobby and be interconnected In the offices accounts would be kept, weather information dispensed, flight plans filed, and arrangements made for whatever aircraft servicing might be required Locker rooms and showers would, of course, be optional but highly desirable

The entire building would be a simple, one-story rectangle It would be clear-spanned in width, and all partitions would be made removable so that as much of the whole rectangle as required would function as the lobby for the second stage The heating plant should be large enough to accommodate an additional unit to take care of future expansion of either the original building or of a new, separate near-by building, or both

Second Stage

In addition to items enumerated under the *first stage:*

> Larger lobby
> Additional offices for manager and operations.
> Lunch bar
> Separate room for local flying club
> Separate toilets for public and personnel
> School room.
> School office
> Storage room

At this stage, flying activities have grown to the point where the patrons have banded together to form a flying club Transient trade is accommodated by having space for increased airport personnel Facilities for serving food are indicated Flying instruction is being offered A storage room is provided where transients or others may check personal effects

The lunch bar, the separate room for the local flying club, the school room, and the school office will bring in rental revenue to help strengthen the financial position of the airport

Third Stage

At this stage, traffic through the building has increased, and flying instruction requires room for expansion Therefore a separate structure is built to house school activities The space vacated in the original building may be used to house a restaurant (operated in conjunction with the lunch bar), increased office requirements, or to enlarge the central lobby still further

The new school unit might contain.

> School offices
> School rooms
> Library
> Small shop for mechanical instruction
> Toilets
> Lockers

If it should develop that the activities of the flying club require expansion, it might be housed in another

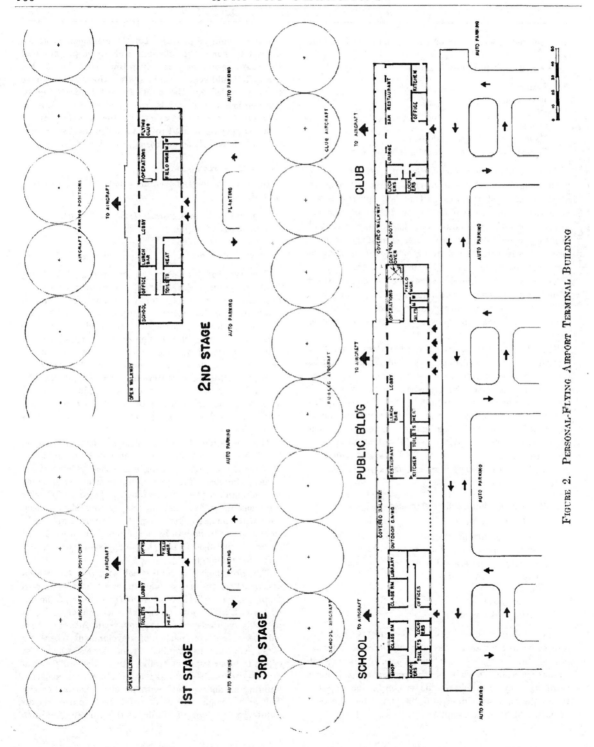

FIGURE 2. PERSONAL-FLYING AIRPORT TERMINAL BUILDING

unit on the opposite side of the original one from the school

The new club unit might contain

> Lounge
> Restaurant
> Bar.
> Offices
> Toilets, locker rooms, showers
> Squash courts, tennis courts, bowling alley, etc.

This might become the recreational center for the entire neighborhood, thereby promoting both the health of the local inhabitants as well as their interest in air activities The removal of club facilities to separate quarters would free additional space in the central building to accommodate the increased traffic concerned more directly with actual flying or new types of agencies, such as air taxi or "fly-yourself" service

The new units might be constructed either as wings added onto the first, or as separate buildings connected with it by covered walkways under which could be run heating, plumbing, and power lines from the central plant

The advantage of housing these activities in separate buildings is that the different types of traffic would be more definitely segregated By reducing interference between the activity of a transient air traveler and a local club member, each would be served more expeditiously and completely Driveway access and car parking could be similarly segregated Intercommunication between these activities would still be direct and protected from the elements Buffer space would be provided for the further independent expansion of any unit

Non-Scheduled Commercial Airports

Industrial—First Stage

> Airport operations offices
> Shipping space and office
> Receiving space and office
> Communications and weather.
> Pilots' room.
> Control tower
> Toilets, lockers, etc

This building would serve as the link between the flow of production of the factory and the flow of transport at the flying field It would occupy a somewhat similar position to that of the conventional factory shipping and receiving rooms, bridging the gap between the railroad siding and the plant, but the program would be more complex

Space would be provided for the management of the airport proper The scheduling of air shipments, and the coordination of this scheduling with that of the aircraft, would require office space. Rooms would have to be provided for the pilots to rest between flights Located between the pilots' room and the room devoted to airport operations would be the communications room, supplying needed information to the field operations office as well as meteorological data to the pilots.

Industrial—Second Stage

In addition to items enumerated under *industrial, first stage:*

> Increase in areas of *industrial, first stage.*
> Executives' lounge
> Executives' toilets
> Display rooms

This type of industrial airport terminal building would be planned for a larger operation than the *industrial, first stage.* It would contemplate a shift in emphasis from the entirely utilitarian plan of the *industrial, first stage,* to include rooms where executive personnel, riding the company's air freighters or transports, would be able to wait for the next plane or entertain visitors This room should be nicely finished, be outfitted for conference work, and, if possible, should have a view of the field. It should also adjoin a sales- or showroom where the products being manufactured and flown to all parts of the globe would be on display.

The utilization of these programs is dependent upon the development of aircraft which will haul shipments at rates low enough to bring about real volume of air cargo Engineers are now planning prototypes which will accomplish this Therefore the planning of their complementary facilities on the ground should keep pace with them, so that when these aircraft are ready to fly, there will be buildings available which have been designed specifically for the purpose—to handle air cargo for industry

The programs for industrial airports have been visualized on the basis of an industry having its own flightstrip or airfield as an integrated part of the entire plant The attainment of such an objective is probably not destined for the immediate future There will be an interim period of development where air cargo will first be handled at an airport which also caters to other types of traffic In this event, the programs—modified—will take their place as a separate building on such a field with its own roadway access This arrangement will be desirable both to preserve an uninterrupted flow of traffic to the various buildings

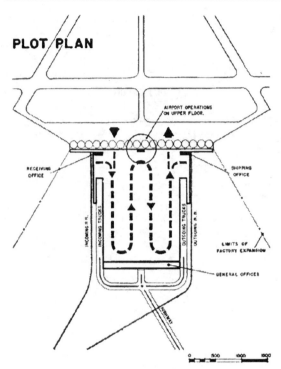

Figure 3. Industrial Airport Terminal Building

at the field serving various functions and to permit segregation of traffic by type, since the major ground traffic to the cargo section will consist of trucks and the rest will be passenger vehicles.

Another development will be that the cargo airport will serve as a major distribution point of air cargo for the larger communities. Its function will parallel that of the railroad freight yards with their terminal warehouses. The programs outlined before will parallel the railroad siding which serves the industrial plant directly.

Special Services

    Central lobby.
    Operations office.
    Manager's office.
    Service rooms and offices.
    Toilets, lockers, storage, etc.
    Heating plant.

Such a building, serving as the focal point of an airport having only non-scheduled commercial operations, would provide both space for operation of the field and space for the users of the field. These users might include companies or agencies engaged in flying instruction; charter or taxi operation; crop dusting; aerial photography and survey; police—state or local; fire patrol; government agencies (Civil Aeronautics Authority, Federal Bureau of Investigation, Department of Commerce, etc.); and Red Cross. The number of service rooms and offices (see *special services* above) required will depend upon the number of users of the field. Their individual layout and square foot area requirements must be determined individually.

If the entire field consists of a flightstrip, remotely located, used for a single purpose—fire patrol or police patrol—the program would be cut down by eliminating the central lobby and the operations office. If the field is used for both personal and non-scheduled commercial flying, its program will consist of a combination of *personal, third stage* and *special services*, and it will be good practice to segregate these activities by housing them in different buildings. In such a case, one structure will be the focal point—operationally—of the field and, therefore, the manager's and operations offices will be eliminated from the other.

Scheduled Commercial Airports

Two philosophies have developed for the planning of terminals serving scheduled commercial airports: one for "centralization" and another for "decentralization."

In the centralized plan all passengers, baggage, and cargo are funneled through a central building and are then dispersed to their respective plane gates. In the decentralized plan the passenger and baggage arrive at a point near the departing plane; all airline functions are carried on adjacent to the plane; airmail and cargo are handled through a central interairline cargo room. The amount of space required for docking planes at a Scheduled Commercial Airport is the primary factor governing the type of plan which should be employed. Thus, where the number of plane gates required is such that the overall walking distance exceeds approximately 600 feet (or the approximate distance encountered at larger railroad stations), a shift from centralization appears to be in order. Increases in cost brought about by greater roadway requirements and dispersed building design indicate that the decentralized plan will be used only for very large terminals.

Present analysis indicates that whenever plane gate requirements for individual airlines at one airport exceed six plane-parking positions, the completely decentralized plan begins to become operationally uneconomical. At this point, therefore, another shift is indicated toward the centralizing of each individual airline's operations, resulting in a series of centralized airlines' spaces arranged in a decentralized fashion.

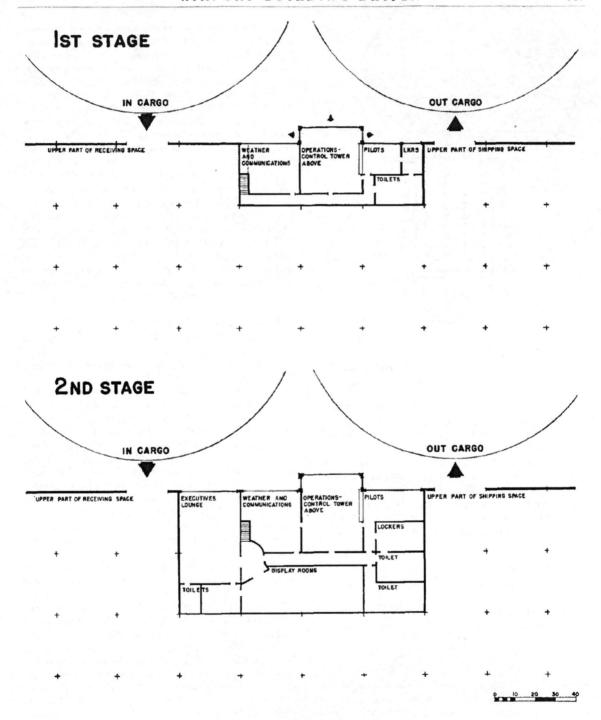

FIGURE 3. INDUSTRIAL AIRPORT TERMINAL BUILDING

The evolution of an airport from centralization through decentralization to decentralized-centralization is illustrated in the four schematic diagrams shown in Fig. 4. It should be noted that in the fourth case the volume of traffic through each airline terminal becomes sufficiently great to warrant the inclusion of extensive concession areas at each of these points. These areas add to passenger convenience and provide additional revenue by having concessions placed where they will be directly accessible to the greatest number. It should also be borne in mind that in the latter scheme two airlines, each requiring less than six plane gates, may combine waiting rooms and other facilities capable of being shared, and, together, occupy an individual airline unit.

The activities which must be housed in the apron terminal area of a decentralized plan are of considerable extent and variety. Practically all the functions customarily performed in a central building are moved to this new location. In addition, a number of services usually performed at the hangar are transferred. Since hangars might be ½ to 2 miles away from the loading apron, it would be uneconomical—both in time and actual expense—to have an airplane traverse such distances to change a spark plug, for example. Minor repairs, fleet service, commissary service, and other similar work will be taken care of at the apron. Recent developments in aircraft power "egg" assemblies, permitting a complete engine change in 30 minutes or less, indicate the scope of work which may be performed away from the hangar and at the loading apron in the interest of greater utilization of aircraft.

The detailed working arrangement of the decentralized plan is discussed more fully under *decentralized*, page 180.

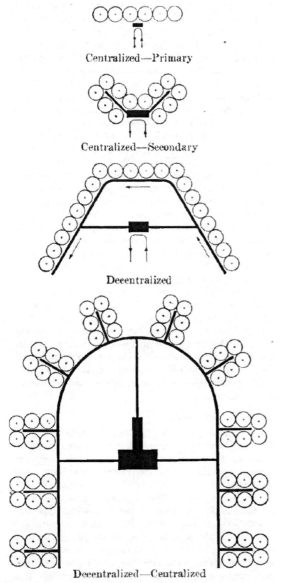

Centralized—Primary

Centralized—Secondary

Decentralized

Decentralized—Centralized

FIGURE 4. EVOLUTION OF SCHEDULED COMMERCIAL AIRPORTS

Centralized—First Stage

    Central lobby and waiting room.
    Manager's offices.
    Airline counter space.
    Airline operations offices.
    Airmail and express room; post office window.
    Lunch bar.
    Toilets.
    Heating plant.
    Building service.
    Control tower.
    (Concessions).
    (CAA).
    (Weather Bureau).

As in the first stage of the design for personal-flying terminals, this structure would be planned with an eye to expansion by starting off with a fairly large clear-spanned rectangle, the entire area of which would be used as the lobby in the final stage, but which could be subdivided, initially, providing office space and a smaller lobby. The program outlined would be a minimum layout for the initial period of commercial airline service. Items in parentheses would be included if warranted by traffic volume. Airline requirements (areas, arrangement, counter details, etc) would have to be obtained directly from the companies serving the community These elements are developing and changing so rapidly that standard details would soon be obsolete However, for purposes of general planning, it may be assumed that a standard ticket counter length will vary from 4 to 5 feet, width will be 2 feet, 6 inches, and height, 3 feet, 6 inches, baggage scale wells will be 2 feet, 6 inches wide

Centralized—Second Stage

In addition to *centralized, first stage ·*

> Restaurant.
> Separate post office
> Separate railway express.
> CAA
> Weather Bureau.
> Concessions
> Separate public and personnel toilets

This program would be applicable to airports served by several major airlines and, perhaps, one or two feeder airlines Areas would be greater, and separate quarters would be provided for mail and express The amount of space devoted to concessions would be the result of local analysis of factors influencing such a decision, as it must be in the planning of every airport terminal

The building for the Winston-Salem Airport is a good solution of this problem Particularly commendable is the clean-cut impression which the design offers

Centralized—Third Stage

In addition to *centralized, second stage:*

> Separate lobby and waiting room
> Spectators' gallery
> Airline cargo and baggage room.
> Pilots' lounge
> Incoming-baggage rooms
> Facilities for handling international traffic.

Plans for the new San Antonio Airport are an excellent example of this program The major difference from preceding programs is that this is a "two-level" scheme as opposed to a "one-level" The main driveway ramps up at the entrance to discharge passengers and visitors at a level one story above grade All trucks—for mail, express, food, and like service—approach the building at grade level The passengers remain at the upper level and board the planes over movable gangplanks which offer protection from the elements All operations in conjunction with servicing the aircraft, as well as baggage and cargo handling, occur at grade level. Thus there is a complete segregation of passenger handling and operations, allowing each to function at maximum efficiency

Another noteworthy feature is that the customary plan of having a clear straight view from the entrance through the lobby and out onto the field has given way to a more functional plan, placing airline ticket counters opposite the entrance This plan accomplishes two desirable objectives first, it places the ticketing areas where they will do the best job for the air passenger as well as the airline, second, by providing no spectacular viewing place for the general public at this level, it steers the casual sightseer to the waiting room on the second floor where a better view of the field can be had More important, it accomplishes segregation of passengers and spectators, which is essential if the traveling public (for which the building is primarily provided) is to be speedily handled Locating the waiting room on the second floor also enhances the concession value of the adjacent restaurant

A central airline cargo room is provided on the ground floor where airmail, express, and baggage may be consolidated by flight and dispatched directly to each plane by means of tractor trucks towing baggage carts Incoming-baggage rooms are provided at each end of the lobby so that arriving passengers may claim their baggage and proceed into the city without having to back-track through the lobby

The facilities for handling international traffic are located at one end of one of the "fingers." A separate driveway is provided The usual customs and immigration quarters are provided plus a waiting room, which may be shut off from the general circulation, for passengers who have not yet cleared immigration, or for those who are not terminating but who merely get off the plane during its stop and are technically "out-of-bounds"

Centralized—Fourth Stage

The program for such a building is similar to the one for *centralized, third stage* However, since this would be a plan for a major terminus, the various elements present themselves in greater volume, complexity, and area, with greater space devoted to concessions

The terminal at the Washington National Airport is a well-conceived terminal of the centralized type It is two level throughout all its circulation, with the exception of the final boarding of the plane at which point passengers have to go to the grade level and walk across the apron Although the main lobby is exceedingly impressive, it is not considered as functional a solution with respect to passenger handling or airline

Howard Lovewell Cheney, Architect
Benjamin Lane Smith, Associate Architect

Winston-Salem Airport

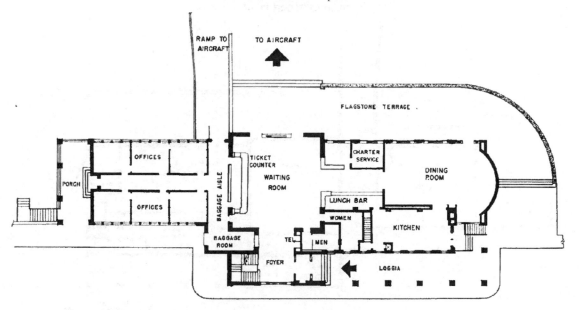

FIRST FLOOR PLAN

FIGURE 5.   SCHEDULED COMMERCIAL AIRPORT TERMINAL—CENTRALIZED—SECOND STAGE

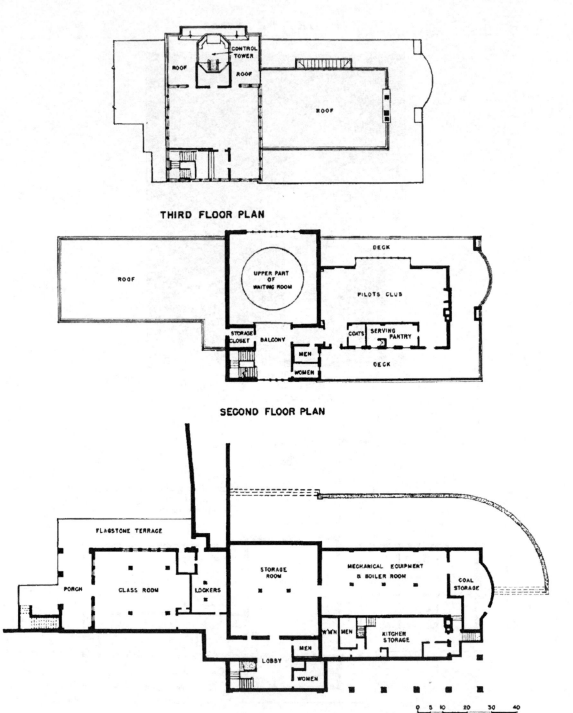

THIRD FLOOR PLAN

SECOND FLOOR PLAN

GROUND FLOOR PLAN

FIGURE 5. SCHEDULED COMMERCIAL AIRPORT TERMINAL—CENTRALIZED—SECOND STAGE

173

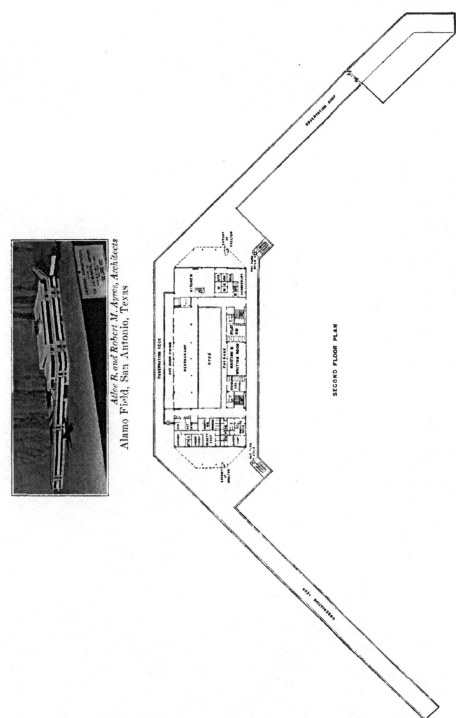

Adloe B. and Robert M. Ayres, Architects
Alamo Field, San Antonio, Texas

SECOND FLOOR PLAN

FIGURE 6. SCHEDULED COMMERCIAL AIRPORT TERMINAL—CENTRALIZED—THIRD STAGE

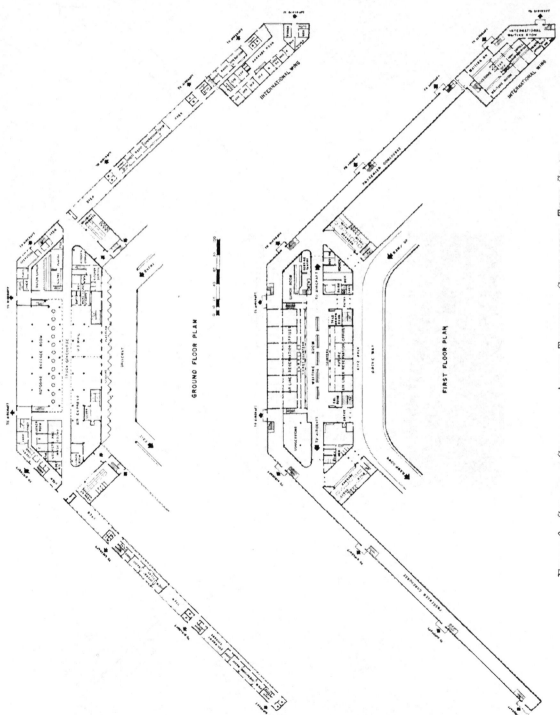

FIGURE 6. SCHEDULED COMMERCIAL AIRPORT TERMINAL—CENTRALIZED—THIRD STAGE

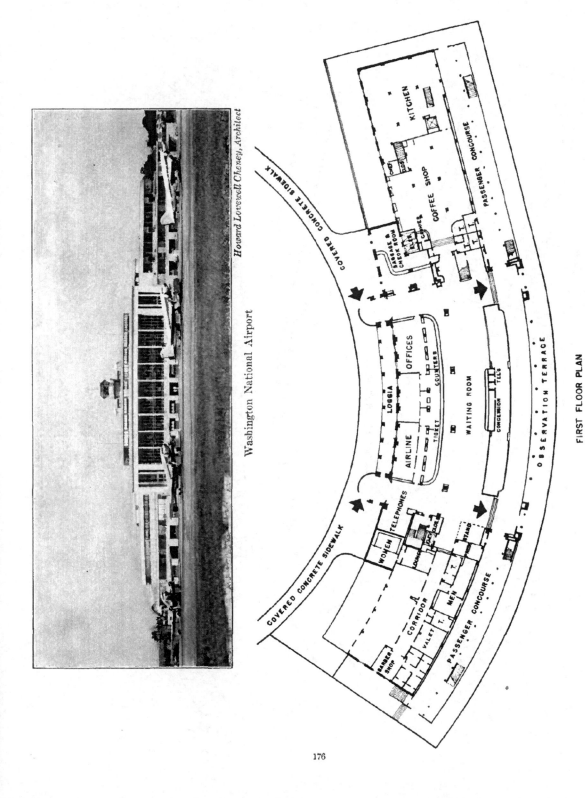

Howard Lovewell Cheney, Architect

Washington National Airport

FIRST FLOOR PLAN

FIGURE 7. SCHEDULED COMMERCIAL AIRPORT TERMINAL—CENTRALIZED—FOURTH STAGE

176

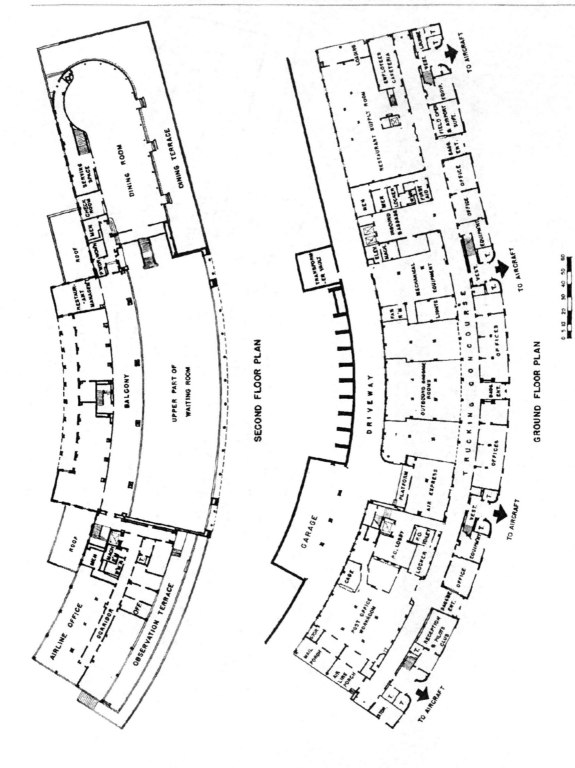

FIGURE 7. SCHEDULED COMMERCIAL AIRPORT TERMINAL—CENTRALIZED—FOURTH STAGE

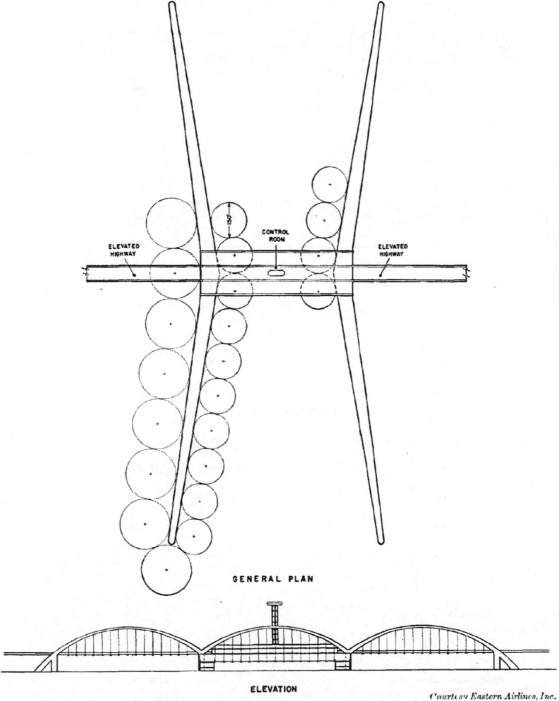

GENERAL PLAN

ELEVATION

Courtesy Eastern Airlines, Inc.

FIGURE 8.   CENTRALIZED TERMINAL DESIGN FOR MAJOR AIRPORT

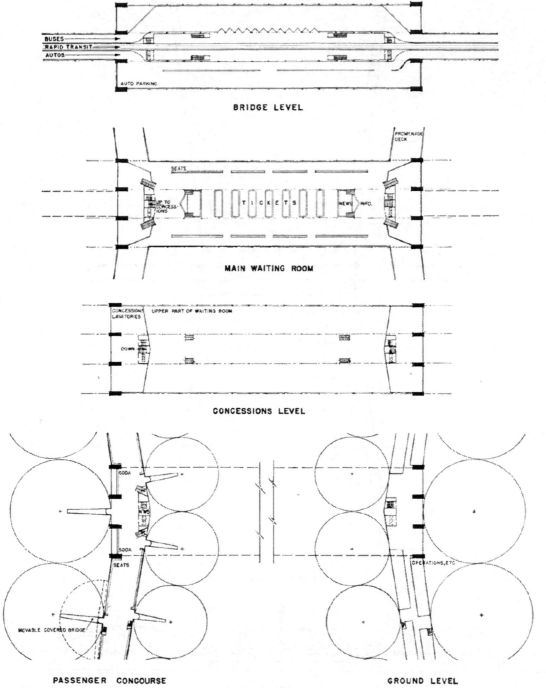

FIGURE 8. CENTRALIZED TERMINAL DESIGN FOR MAJOR AIRPORT

operation as that offered by the more recent San Antonio plan

A centralized terminal, designed for an airfield of 240-movement capacity, is shown in Fig 8. It will be noted that in this design the terminal is approached by an elevated roadway to permit unimpeded flow of aircraft on the ground, rather than by a tunnel which would be of economic importance in the case of airports located near sea level Furthermore, the main lobby of the terminal is suspended above ground to allow uninterrupted flow of aircraft through the terminal, resulting in an increase in efficiency of space utilization Although this design is somewhat radical both in planning and construction, it is presented here to stimulate creative thinking on the general problem of airport terminal building design

The terminal is reached by an elevated structure accommodating automobiles, buses, and rapid transit Passengers embark or debark from these vehicles under cover and descend to the floor below by escalators Into the central waiting room is discharged all the public traffic of the elevated structure Concessions and lavatories are easily accessible Information as well as tickets are dispensed here An unobstructed view of the berthing of planes is provided Additional viewing facilities are provided by promenade decks on the roofs of the passenger concourses, the decks being on the same level as the waiting room (If desired, one or more of these decks would provide an excellent location for an outdoor restaurant)

The public reaches the passenger concourses by an easy flight of stairs from the waiting room Circulation is controlled at this point by having guards at the head of the stairs who admit ticket holders together with friends or relatives only.

Additional seating space is provided on this level grouped conveniently around plane gates Soda fountains and newsstands also occur at intervals along these concourses

The floor level of the passenger concourse is approximately 12 feet above ground This height permits more or less level entry onto or exit from planes through a covered bridge (Cf Fig 11)

Operations are housed directly below the passenger concourses and at ground level, providing complete separation of passengers from operations A small stair at each plane gate is provided for vertical contact between operations and passenger control

Offices are provided for CAA, Weather Bureau, airway traffic control etc, on a floor above the bridge level They are in direct contact with any other part of the building by elevators or stairs The control

tower has been raised to the level shown to provide an unobstructed view of all runways The control tower has been split up into three separate but interconnecting rooms One handles inbound planes, another outbound planes, and the one in the center handles all movement on the ground, including the docking of the planes

Two separate systems of vertical circulation are employed The first, for the public, uses escalators and stairs and interconnects only the waiting room, concourses, concession, and elevated structure The second, for working personnel, uses elevators and stairs and interconnects speedily all floors of the building —from operations on the ground up to the control tower At floor levels where the public and working personnel intermingle, such as concourses or restaurants, lobbies have been provided to prevent the public from using such circulation

Decentralized

Central Building

Lobby
Central information desk.
Waiting room
Airlines reservation and information counters
Management offices
CAA
Weather Bureau
Control tower
Airway traffic control
Airline offices
Post office
Air express
Interairline cargo room.
Employees' cafeteria
Toilets
Locker rooms.
Building services
Concessions
  Restaurant, bar, coffee shop
  Spectators' observation deck
  Barber
  Beauty parlor
  Newsreel theatre
  Drug store
  Florist
  Haberdashery
  Telephones, Telegraph
  Nursery
  Bank
  Hotel
  Parcel-checking lockers

Airline Terminals

- Waiting room
- Ticket counters
- Baggage rooms—outbound, inbound.
- Station manager's office
- Reservations
- Operations office
- Radio and communications room
- Pilots' room
- Flight attendants' room
- Apron service personnel
- Fleet service
- Minor repairs shop
- Storage
- Toilets—public, personnel
- Concessions
  - Cigarette and candy vending machines
  - Parcel-checking lockers
  - Snack bar or restaurant.
  - Newsstand

The quality of an airport terminal plan for scheduled operation may be measured largely by the segregation provided between passenger handling on the one hand and airline operations (including cargo handling) on the other. The provision for such segregation becomes progressively more important as the size of the terminal increases, as the volume of traffic increases. And successful achievement becomes, likewise, progressively more difficult. For the largest termini which, by their very size, must be planned in some decentralized manner, the only efficient solution lies either in providing underground tunnels for cargo handling with operations and passengers at grade level or in placing operations and cargo handling at grade level and passenger handling above grade, entailing the use either of an elevated roadway or escalators at frequent intervals. The latter is the preferable solution, being simpler in function, providing more complete segregation, and eliminating the necessity of constant lighting and ventilation underground.

The functioning of a decentralized plan may be illustrated by an examination of the plans for the proposed terminal building for the Logan Airport at East Boston, Massachusetts.

The hub of the plan is a large central building which contains facilities used in common by all the operating airlines and for the general public. Surrounding the hub is a continuous apron structure housing individual airline functions. A departing passenger having a reservation for a definite flight will drive or be driven directly to the waiting room of the airline for which he is ticketed. At this point the various ticketing and baggage-checking procedures take place, and the passenger will walk a short distance to his plane. If a departing passenger does not know which airline he wishes to take, he will go to the central building first, receive his information, and proceed along a pedestrian overpass to the desired airline waiting room in the apron building. The interconnecting passenger may proceed from one airline unit to another, traveling all the while at second-floor level. The deplaning passenger may board a conveyance near his plane gate and proceed into the city without having to go through the central building. The plan provides for passenger handling at the second-floor level throughout, thus affording complete segregation of passenger from cargo and operational traffic, for the final stage.

Air cargo is handled in the following manner. Trucks from the city deliver mail and express to their respective quarters in the central building, from which they flow to the cargo room. There mail, express, and interconnecting baggage are assembled according to flight, loaded onto a truck, and dispatched directly to the departing plane. The flow is, of course, reversed for incoming cargo. Each airline will have its own smaller cargo room in its ramp structure. There smaller amounts of cargo can be held over to make up last-minute adjustments for full payloads on the plane. For lines operating routes in several different directions, this smaller room will serve as the airline's own interchange cargo room.

The roadway system contemplates a ramped entrance to the central building, depositing passengers and visitors at the second-floor level. Truck traffic remains at grade. Traffic destined for the apron terminals remains at grade. Numerous traffic circles are planned so that a complete circuit does not have to be made in getting to or from any airline terminal. Traffic from the central cargo room is so laid out that trucks never cross but always merge with other traffic in traveling from point to point.

Provision has been made in the plans for the eventual extension to the airport of Boston's Rapid Transit System, with a station in the basement of the central building. The inclusion of this service is unique among airport terminals in the United States. It reveals progressive planning the real value of which will become increasingly apparent as the years go by. It will benefit not only the air passenger but also those thousands who will be employed at a transportation center of such size.

The overall plan has been carefully studied for future expansion. Space is provided for expanding the

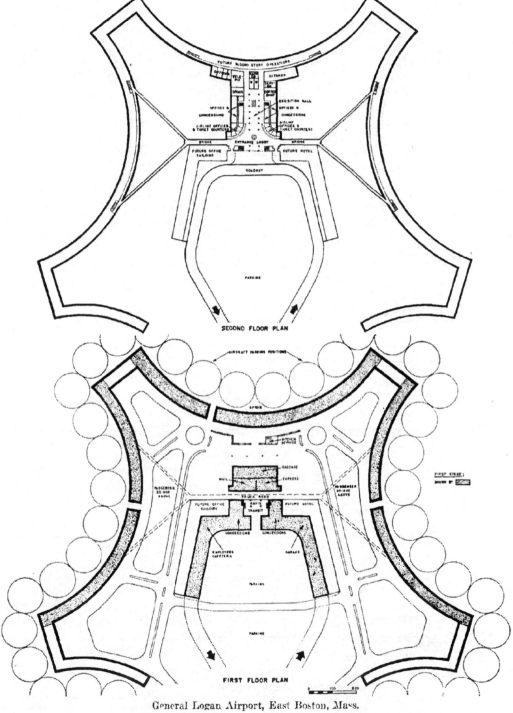

General Logan Airport, East Boston, Mass.
FIGURE 9. SCHEDULED COMMERCIAL AIRPORT TERMINAL—DECENTRALIZED

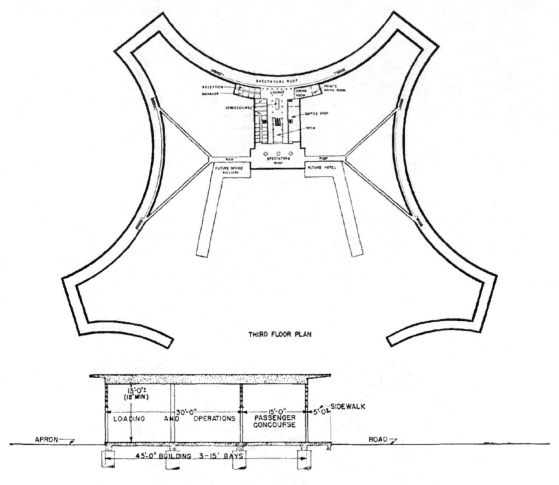

THIRD FLOOR PLAN

FIRST STAGE · SECTION

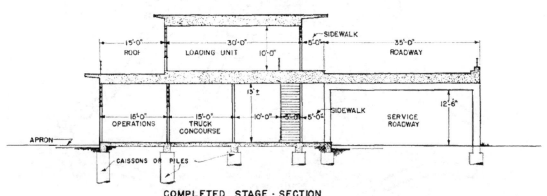

COMPLETED STAGE · SECTION

*Courtesy Massachusetts Emergency Public Works Commission,
Thompson and Lichtner Co., Engineers. Coolidge, Shepley, Bulfinch and Abbott, Architects*

FIGURE 9. SCHEDULED COMMERCIAL AIRPORT TERMINAL. DECENTRALIZED

central building and all its functions as required. Expansion of apron facilities can be taken care of by second-floor addition to the apron structure. There is room for an "airplane row" for aircraft sales offices, a hotel, and 30 large hangars. Ample space for all types of car parking will be provided at all stages, as well as a garage where a passenger's car may be serviced while he is out of town. It should be noted that the provision of expansion in number of airplane gates by the means shown permits orderly expansion of the facilities of any or all airlines with a minimum reshuffling of original plant layout.

Combination Scheduled and Non-Scheduled

A large number of airports exist which do not have sufficient traffic of a purely scheduled or non-scheduled type to warrant the erection of a building to house each, or which have insufficient volume of scheduled traffic to meet financial obligations and, therefore, promote the inclusion of non-scheduled operation. The program of a building for such an airport would be a compounding of the facilities outlined under programs for *special services* and *centralized, second stage*. Since the requirements to meet such a program would be of an endless variety, it may be profitable to examine the

Alexander D. Crosett, Associated Architects and Engineers

Westchester County Airport

FIRST FLOOR

FIGURE 10. COMBINATION SCHEDULED AND NON-SCHEDULED COMMERCIAL AIRPORT

plans of a practical, good example—the Westchester County Airport.

This plan provides for both scheduled airline and feeder line operation. It has, in addition, space for a flying club, offices of a flight-testing laboratory, and various other activities. The intention is to make the airport a center of interest for the surrounding population, and, therefore, a restaurant, larger than the average for such a community, is included. In this building the needs of private flyer and commercial operator (both scheduled and non-scheduled) are equally well taken care of.

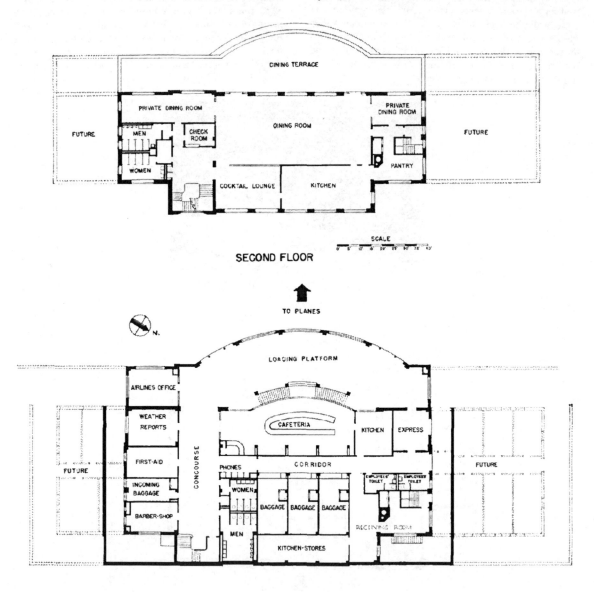

SECOND FLOOR

GROUND FLOOR

FIGURE 10. COMBINATION SCHEDULED AND NON-SCHEDULED COMMERCIAL AIRPORT

Special Planning Problems

Technological advances are occurring so rapidly in the fields of air traffic control and weather observation that it would be impracticable to lay down definite specifications for the housing of these facilities at this time. These advances, coupled with the fact that each airfield will present local problems, make it appear that the best course in each case will be to consult with the authorities in question and obtain their latest ideas and requirements directly. Accordingly, only basic considerations, as they may affect the planning of the rest of the building, are discussed herein.

Civil Aeronautics Authority

Space requirements for the CAA will vary with each airport program according to the type of activity and the volume of air traffic at each particular field. Quarters are usually established on a floor above that occupied by the general public, since the activities of this agency require less continuous contact with the public or with operations. In each case, the regional office of the CAA should be consulted and their individual program requirements ascertained.

Control Tower

The control tower is an essential function of every airport that has sufficient traffic to warrant its installation. Generally speaking, only those fields having some type of commercial operation require a control tower. Most personal planes are not radio equipped and, therefore, are not capable of being directed to the field by the control tower. This condition may eventually change and may be dictated by denser traffic later on.

The actual equipment of the control tower has been discussed in Part 3. Its location must be such that it will have an unobstructed view of the entire field and approaches. The most common, and in most cases the best, location is atop the central terminal building. This location will usually fulfill the aforementioned requirement, and will allow close integration with the CAA offices, Weather Bureau, and airway traffic control.

Details of arrangement should be discussed with regional CAA officers. As to construction, the glass enclosure should be designed so as to withstand heavy gusts of wind and avoid reflections of ground lights, plane lights, and astral bodies. The glass should be of a heat-absorbing, "actinic" variety to prevent sunburn of the occupants, and tinted green to reduce glare. It should be of double thickness with a sealed air space between lights. Each light should be equipped with a window wiper. The room should be air conditioned the year around.

Airway Traffic Control

Offices for airway traffic control are required only at points designated by the CAA. They are equipped and manned by the CAA and, therefore, that agency should again be consulted for space requirements and details of arrangement. The favored location is on an upper floor adjacent to the other CAA offices.

U. S. Weather Bureau

Requirements and locations for Weather Bureau offices are, again, a matter of local arrangement and consultation with proper authorities. Locations will differ according to the equipment available for "measuring" the weather. At smaller stations where the installation of remote-reading electrical instruments is not warranted, the office may be located on the ground floor for accessibility to instruments. For the more expensive installations, it will be located on an upper floor. If located here, it may be equipped with a revolving turret, housing forecasting equipment and facilitating the work of the Bureau.

An important consideration for both Weather Bureau and control tower is the location of the chimney for the heating plant of the building proper. It should be placed so that there will be no interference from the exhaust gases in the reading of meteorological instruments, or impairment of the control tower operator's view.

The offices will require space for the preparation of weather charts, and their arrangement for examination by pilots. Helium storage must be provided in the basement (at a location having easy truck access for delivery of tanks). With a suitable manifold arrangement in the tank room and piping to the offices, observation balloons may be easily filled in the offices and sent aloft through a roof hatch.

The offices should be located with views in the directions of "weather"—that is, the prevailing direction of approaching storms—and, preferably, in all directions.

Special Buildings

In addition to the central terminal buildings and hangars, some airports will require additional facilities to house special equipment. Rather than attempt to incorporate everything in one central structure it may be operationally more expedient to house fire-fighting and snow-removal equipment in a separate building with the most direct access possible to the field. The same building may also contain a repair shop for keeping the mobile equipment in good order. Storage space for sand, bituminous pavement patching mixtures, and other roadway and runway maintenance

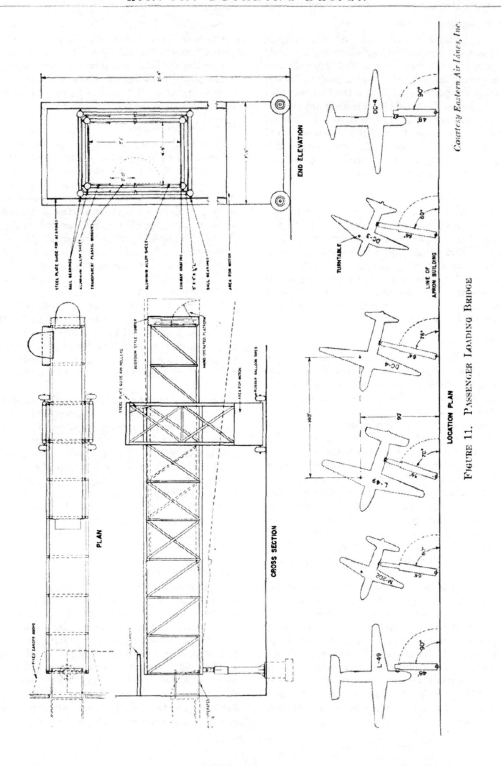

END ELEVATION

PLAN

CROSS SECTION

LOCATION PLAN

Courtesy Eastern Air Lines, Inc.

FIGURE 11. PASSENGER LOADING BRIDGE

equipment should be provided   It may happen that a pumping station or stations will be needed to provide the required amounts of water at the proper pressure for both building use and fire-fighting   Another special building that may be included in many airport programs is the familiar gasoline service station, serving public, passengers, and personnel

It is beyond the scope of this book to discuss special buildings in detail   They cannot be considered typical of airport planning   Wherever provisions for their inclusion must be made, the customary practices followed in sound planning and building will achieve the desired results

Loading Bridge

The illustration on page 187 shows a design for a loading bridge which permits passengers to embark and debark from a plane under cover and directly from the upper level of a terminal   Protection from the elements is not the only consideration which renders such a device a necessity   The newer planes have floor heights as much as 11 feet above the ground   Since the passenger should proceed to the proximity of his plane on an upper level to provide segregation of passengers and operations, it is illogical to make him descend a flight of stairs at the plane gate, walk across the apron to the plane, and climb another stair to emplane   Further advantages of a loading bridge are that it permits operations concerned with servicing and loading a plane to proceed uninterrupted by passenger movements   It also reduces the number of pieces of accessory apron equipment which customarily clutter the areas surrounding a plane-parking position

The design illustrated may be installed at relatively low cost   Its basic design premise is flexibility; it may be used with any type of commercial plane now in use or planned for the next five to ten years   The bridge may be used for either nose or side loading

Bibliography

"Plan That Terminal Now," by A F Heino, *Air Transport*, January, 1945

"Designing the Large Terminal," by A F Heino, *Architectural Record*, April, 1945

"Airport Terminal Design," by A F Heino *S A E*, December, 1945

"Architecture and Air Transportation," by F R Meisch *New Pencil Points*, November, 1943

"Air Terminals for Mass Air Travel," by F R Meisch, *New Pencil Points*, November, 1944

"What's Wrong With Our Air Terminals?", by Marc Thompson, *Architectural Forum*, January, 1946

10

HANGAR DESIGN

Hangar Types

The type of hangar to be erected on any airfield is determined by the type of aircraft using the airfield and the kind of operation being carried on

Hangars serve two primary functions to provide aircraft storage and aircraft servicing and overhauling. Storage is required for lighter, smaller aircraft to protect them from the elements. As aircraft become larger, they are built more ruggedly and of materials better able to resist the effects of adverse weather. Also, as aircraft increase in size, providing shelter for them becomes a progressively more serious economic problem, since the required increase in clear span and height causes a rapid rise in construction costs. Thus, in much the manner that the fleet of a truck operator is stored outdoors, the larger commercial transports (both cargo and passenger) will not be provided with enclosed shelter for storage alone. Some form of enclosed space, however, must be provided for all types of aircraft for maintenance, service, and overhaul. The smaller craft will be serviced in conventional type hangars as will medium-sized transports. The larger craft will be serviced by some type of "nose hangar" in which only the forward section of the plane, including the engines, is enclosed, with the major portion of the fuselage and tail surfaces left exposed

Personal Flying

For the personal-flying field the storage requirements of a wide variety of users will have to be met. Hangar area must be provided for transient aircraft with facilities for overnight maintenance and service of aircraft. The personal flyer will house his aircraft either in a private "garage" of the semi-attached variety or in a conventional type of hangar. The "fly-yourself" agency or local aircraft taxi service will require shelter for its fleet. If a flying school is located at the field, it will need shelter for its flying equipment

Aircraft sales will have adequate storage space for stocking unsold equipment and service parts in addition to showrooms

Provisions for servicing aircraft will accompany most of the above hangar storage areas, either as a portion of the entire hangar area or in adjacent quarters if the volume of business is sufficient to justify segregation of storage from service. The itinerant flyer, traveling for business or pleasure, will wish to have his aircraft serviced while making an overnight stop or while transacting business in town. If personal flyers base their aircraft in separate garages, they will require a service station where the maintenance and overhaul of the aircraft may be done. Often such servicing will be combined with that for transients. Taxi service and flying schools will maintain their own overhaul shops in their own hangars, as will also aircraft sales and service agencies

Non-Scheduled Commercial

An analysis of the hangar requirements for non-scheduled commercial flying will disclose two basic patterns of operation. The first follows closely that encountered at the personal flying field. The second parallels scheduled airline operation. In either case, the type of aircraft being used will determine the necessity of providing hangar space for storage, and, again, all types will have to have sheltered space for overhaul and maintenance

State and local police, National Guard, and other similar groups will usually operate radially from a fixed base. Therefore this base will include hangars for both storage and servicing. This will also apply to special services, such as crop-dusting, relief work (Red Cross), aerial photography, sky advertising, and aerial survey

If a company has a national network of plant facilities which it desires to bring closer together by means of its own air fleet, it will probably find that the most economical operation will call for one central base for major overhaul located, probably, at its main plant At this point will occur the largest investment in hangar facilities At other strategic points throughout its system it may own or rent lesser facilities for servicing and routine check-up At the majority of the points along its system no aircraft storage and servicing will be provided except for fuel and oil The entire framework of maintenance organization will parallel closely that for an airline, and, therefore, facilities required for its operation will be similar in concept In some instances the company may contract with an airline for all services, in which event the requirements of the scheduled and non-scheduled operators must be added together to obtain total requirements

Scheduled Commercial

Hangar requirements for airline operation will be governed largely by the type of equipment being operated, the climatic conditions prevailing over the route or portions thereof, and the extent of the route If operations are carried on in temperate regions, no extensive storage space will be required A terminal point in a cold region will require storage areas to protect flying equipment from storms and extreme cold. No general statements can be made regarding servicing requirements for airlines, since the operation of each route system poses individual problems However, every airline will require one or more major overhaul bases, a radial or "X" route system may be more economically served from one point, a long, transcontinental or transoceanic route may be more economically served by several major bases In addition to these bases, which will contain extensive shops and offices, provision will be made at terminal points for "turn-around" maintenance and periodic checks

Location of Hangars on Airport

The disposition of hangars must be determined individually for each airport plan The factors governing the choice of a site for terminal building development have been discussed in Part 9 If the terminal site is sufficiently large to accommodate hangars with no possibility of interfering with future expansion of the terminal, this location will possess many advantages However, such a choice should be made with extreme caution, and only after a most complete analysis One of the major defects in many existing airport developments has been the tendency to crowd airport buildings too close together As a result, needed expansion of either terminal or hangar facilities could not be undertaken without costly building operations, and therefore, the functional efficiency of the entire

airport has been impaired If the slightest doubt exists as to complete freedom of future plant expansion, it will be far better to allow the hangars to occupy a site or sites separate from the terminal building

A good hangar site will conform to the following requirements

1 Convenient road access to site from a main highway serving the airport, and from site to terminal area
2 Proximity to, and ease of installation of, utilities—gas, water, electric power, sewage, telephone
3 Reasonable proximity to terminal area
4 Favorable situation with respect to topography, prevailing winds, direction of frequent storms to allow placement of hangar doors on protected side of building and prevent drifting of snow
5 Subsoil of sufficient bearing power to take concentrated column loads
6 Sufficient area to provide ample car-parking facilities for working personnel
7 Good natural drainage

Good planning suggests that, even though first-stage hangar requirements may be moderate, additional hangar sites should be earmarked from the start This foresight will allow airfield construction work—grading, drainage—to be planned and executed with future building needs in mind, and will save much costly site preparation when the area is finally required

General Planning Considerations

Hangars intended to accommodate more than a single airplane should be either square or greater in width than in depth Hangars with excessive depth cause a loss of maneuverability in aircraft since too many aircraft near the front of the hangar must be moved to get out one in the rear

A method of increasing accessibility is to plan the hangar with two doors—one at either end This design has particular merit for service or overhaul hangars, since it allows the installation of an "assembly line" technique for fleets of similar type aircraft Such hangars will be more costly than the one-door type Two aprons must be provided—one in front of each door—instead of only a single one, and each apron must be connected with the general taxiway system of the field It is practicable only for isolated units At major airports, where rows of hangars are required to fulfill space requests, planning difficulties will arise in attempting to group two-door hangars Single-door units may be strung along a row with a continuous apron area along the front of the hangars and service roads and car-parking areas along the rear

SINGLE-OPENING HANGARS

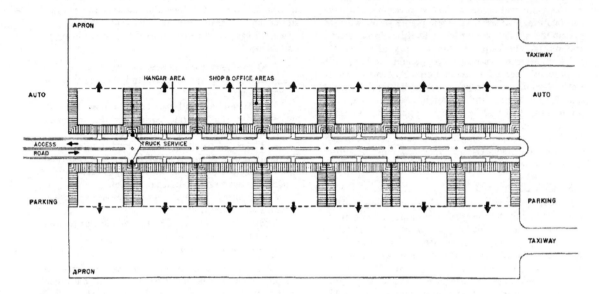

DOUBLE-OPENING HANGARS

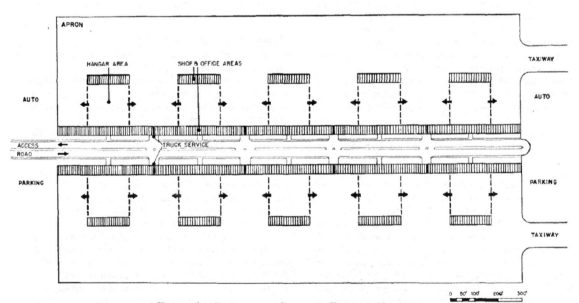

FIGURE 1. COMPARATIVE STUDY OF ROWS OF HANGARS

Shop and office areas are usually placed along the rear and/or sides of the hangar In the case of the single hangar, these facilities may be several stories in height and all of them may have natural light and ventilation If a row of hangars is built with multi-storied shop and office space between the units, considerable space will be created which must be artificially lighted and ventilated A more satisfactory solution of this problem is to confine the areas between hangars to single-story height, which will permit natural ventilation and lighting along the roof, unless the ground floor can be used for engine test cells, paint shops, or other rooms which require artificial ventilation and lighting

It should be decided fairly early in the design stage what type of hangar door will be used, since this decision will have an important effect on the structural design (This topic is covered more fully under "Hangar Doors ') Also, and for similar reasons, it should be determined whether hoisting mechanisms will be used in the hangar so that the structure may be designed to support crane rails, monorails, jib cranes, or other similar devices

Considerable discussion may be raised over whether a service hangar should have definite fixed locations for performing different types of work—one spot for oiling, another for cleaning, etc The authors' opinion is that, until plane types have become standardized to the degree which will permit standardization and systemization in servicing devices, or unless a condition exists where planes of a single type are moving through the hangar in large volume, it is safer to plan a hangar on the basis of maximum flexibility Thus portions of the hangar (or possibly the entire plant) are prevented from becoming obsolete, the making of expensive changeovers is avoided, and better protection is afforded for the investment As stressed elsewhere in this book, the air transportation industry is still in its formative stages and, therefore, premature tendencies to standardization should be avoided

The general planning of the hangar should include consideration of apron areas to accommodate engine testing and warm-up The air stream created by this necessary operation is considerable, particularly in the larger four-engine aircraft Therefore, aprons must be so laid out and must be wide enough to permit turning the aircraft so that the blast will be directed away from the hangar to prevent damage to surrounding structures or discomfort to operations This will be a fairly simple accomplishment in a single hangar, but at airfields which will have rows of hangars the problem must be studied carefully

Space should be provided in hangars at major overhaul bases for engine test cells adjacent to engine overhaul shops Test cells present special problems in ventilation and noise control which must be analyzed and solved for each particular operation The cells should be designed so as to be completely vibration-isolated from the rest of the buildings Volume of testing to be done, engine size or sizes, and other similar factors will influence the design Engine manufacturers should be consulted to obtain specific design data

General Structural Considerations
Trusses

Four main types of trusses are in general use for hangar construction

Flat or arched truss, supported on columns, of the Pratt, Warren or Bowstring variety Of these trusses, the wood bowstring type has been built to span 200 feet and the steel parallel chord type 250 feet These types possess the advantage of providing full headroom along the sides with a consequent clear area (except for the columns) for lean-tos and office or shop space They also occupy less ground area for given clearance requirements

Segmental arch rib truss The clear span which may be created by this type of truss is practically unlimited Side thrust is taken care of either by tie rods placed below the floor slab or by heavy concrete buttresses or battered piles If the arch springs from the ground, the headroom at this point is obviously zero Therefore structures of smaller span do not employ this truss For spans of 100 feet and over, this type is both economical in cost and may be satisfactorily utilized The principal objection is the loss of floor space at each truss from grade up to clear headroom height This loss may frequently be minimized by locating shop or office areas along the sides with as many partitions as possible falling at truss center lines

Lamella system This truss follows, in general outline and use, the characteristics of the segmental arch However, instead of consisting of separate trusses spaced some distance apart, the entire roof structure consists of an interwoven system of similar-sized sections, creating a series of diamonds which transmit the roof load evenly to the adjoining lower member on down to sill beams and buttresses, or down to the ground This truss, through its interwoven system, absorbs wind pressure against gables, eliminating conventional sway bracing The advantages and disadvantages are similar to those described for the segmental arch rib truss. The interior of a hangar framed by this method has a cleaner appearance than one framed either by the flat or

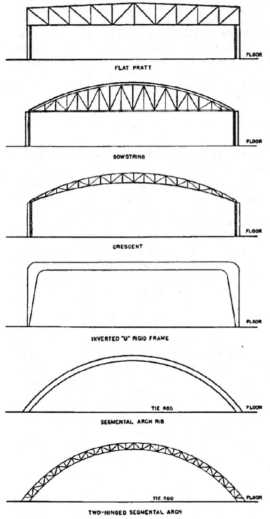

FLAT PRATT

BOWSTRING

CRESCENT

INVERTED "U" RIGID FRAME

SEGMENTAL ARCH RIB

TWO-HINGED SEGMENTAL ARCH

FIGURE 2. TRUSS TYPES COMMONLY USED FOR HANGAR CONSTRUCTION

arched truss or the segmental arch rib truss. Clear headroom is not interrupted at intervals by trusses.

This system is of particular interest where a number of hangars are to be built at the same time, since the required "tooling" costs or "form" charges may be written off at a lower unit charge.

A fourth type of hangar construction, which might be called "*truss-less*," employs dome-like roofs of either steel or concrete. They are built of curved slabs with or without stiffening ribs and employ design principles similar to the monocoque construction of aircraft.

In the stress analysis for hangar design the customary rules for wind bracing do not apply. Stresses which occur in the roof of a large-domed hangar due to strong winds are of a more aerodynamic than static nature, and the principles applying to aerodynamics should be used, in adapted form. For instance, it can be clearly demonstrated that a wind of more or less horizontal force will create downward pressure on one side of the hangar roof and suction on the other.

Three main types of materials are in general use for hangar frame construction: wood, reinforced concrete, and steel. Each type of structure described previously may be built of each of these materials. Each material possesses inherent advantages and disadvantages, which are set forth in detail.

Wood Hangar Construction

The art of building hangars of wood has been advanced tremendously during recent years, for which three factors have been largely responsible. The first factor, structural in nature, has been the development and application of metal connectors for joining wood members, which permits the establishing of more accurate and efficient design criteria for wood joints with a consequent reduction in the section of timber required, together with an increase in safety factor. Metal timber connectors also allow "prefabrication" of the main structural elements, permitting simple and rapid erection in the field. The second factor, also structural, has been the tremendous development in synthetic wood adhesives. This development has led to the wide use of laminated wood arches of great strength and permanence with relatively slight cross-sectional area. The third factor has been the rapid development of chemicals for preserving wood and rendering it fire resistant, plus methods of impregnation in quantity. Heavy timber construction has always been rated as "slow burning." The addition of a fire-resistant chemical impregnation further increases this property. It is generally acknowledged that a structure of heavy timber, properly treated, will be more fire resistant than one of unprotected steel.

For clear spans up to 200 feet wood may be used economically. Spans in excess of this figure should be of steel or reinforced concrete, since the sizes of the wood members required for these larger spans become too great. The Lamella truss finds its greatest and most economical application when built of wood.

Courtesy Timber Structures, Inc.

Bowstring

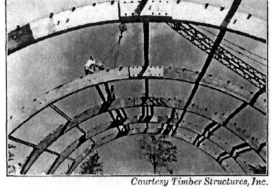

Courtesy Timber Structures, Inc.

Laminated Arch Rib

Courtesy Roof Structures, Inc.

Lamella

Courtesy Timber Structures, Inc.

Crescent

FIGURE 3. WOOD HANGARS

Wood hangars are quickly fabricated and erected. They may be moved to another location with comparative ease and safety without the danger of cracking or twisting out of shape, because of the inherent elastic properties of wood. If suitably impregnated, they will not be susceptible to decay or fungus growth over a reasonable period of time, and will be fire retardant. If metal connectors are used, they may be dismantled and re-erected in another location with comparative ease.

Their main disadvantage at this time lies in the lack of proper seasoning of wood, brought about by the tremendous increase in amounts of wood used with no attendant increase in facilities for seasoning. As a result, shrinking is excessive, cracks and shakes are likely to appear in time, and completion of a job is usually followed by a continual process of tightening all connections as shrinkage appears. This condition will be improved in time.

The Lamella truss is less affected by the disadvantage of seasoning, since the joint design prevents loosening of nuts or separation in the joint. The only effect appears in the shortening of the arch, through slight joint rotation, and results in a slight uniform settlement of the roof between the supporting sill beams. If tie rods are used, the settlement requires the shortening of the tie rod hangers, by means of turnbuckles, to restore the slight camber usually given the tie rods.

Wood should not be used for hangar construction in the tropics unless treated with a fungus-resisting chemical impregnation.

Wood technology has made such great strides in recent years that this material need no longer be thought of as "inferior" or "temporary" for hangar construction, particularly small hangars for personal aircraft.

Reinforced Concrete Hangar Construction

The technique of both design and construction of reinforced concrete structures has developed considerably during the past few decades. It is now possible to

Courtesy Charles S. Whitney

Whitney Design

Courtesy Portland Cement Association

Rigid Frame

Courtesy Roberts and Schaefer Company

Exterior Rib

Courtesy Roof Structures, Inc.

Lamella

FIGURE 4. CONCRETE HANGARS

Flat Truss

Courtesy American Institute of Steel Construction, Inc.

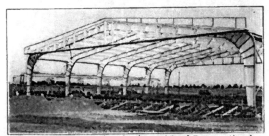

Courtesy American Institute of Steel Construction, Inc.

Rigid Frame

Courtesy American Institute of Steel Construction, Inc.

Arch Rib

FIGURE 5. STEEL HANGARS

Courtesy American Institute of Steel Construction, Inc.

Arch Truss-Girder

Courtesy Roof Structures, Inc.

Lamella

FIGURE 5. STEEL HANGARS

use this material for structures which are subjected to extremes of temperature and are of great size.

For spans up to 150 feet concrete rigid frames, solid or hollow, may be economically used. Segmental arch ribs and Lamella structures may be built of almost unlimited span length in concrete, although the form costs for the latter type will be high unless the repetition of similar ribs is considerable.

A fourth type of structure may be built of reinforced concrete (but not of wood or steel). Both the Z D system and the Whitney design are based on the shell type of construction.

In the Z–D design for small spans no ribs are employed. The roof area consists of a reinforced concrete shell of a thicker section at the spring line of the arch tapering to a thickness of a few inches at the top. For large spans this design utilizes ribs 25 to 30 feet on centers with a thin slab flush at the bottom of the ribs spanning between. The slab design is based on the theory of plate and shell action which results in a very thin section.

The Charles S. Whitney design employs many of the same principles as the Z–D except that the roof slab is placed at the approximate neutral axis of the rib. A lighter and more flexible rib is used in the Whitney design which reduces the thrust at the ends of the arch. This slab design is also based on the theory of plates and shells, but a constant thickness is employed. To utilize this design to maximum efficiency requires a lean-to on both sides. The thrust from the arch can be taken into the lean-to rigid frame and dissipated into the ground by spread footings or battered piles. If the foundation conditions are very poor, tie rods under the floor slab must be used to take the thrust. The entire area of the roof slab is reinforced with steel mesh.

Reinforced concrete is the most fireproof of all building materials. If properly designed and placed, it will perform satisfactorily under almost all climatic conditions. It is not affected by moisture and requires practically no maintenance. The cost of concrete hangars will approach the cost of wood or steel hangars when a large hangar or a number of similar hangars are built allowing the reuse of concrete form work.

The principal disadvantage is the greater weight, which, in subsoils of poor bearing capacity, calls for more foundation work. The inherent rigidity and the weight of such structures make moving impossible. Columns or arch ribs are of greater cross-sectional area than in other types of construction, reducing the area of clear floor space.

Steel Hangar Construction

The widest use of steel for hangars is found in flat or arched trusses supported on columns. The nature of the material lends itself very well to girder construction. Lamella structures have been built of steel, but not widely in the United States because of very high tooling costs. Arched rib trusses have also been built of steel but (with the exception of the Armco prefabricated hangar discussed later) have not been widely used. The flat or arched truss is economical for spans up to 250 feet.

The principal advantages of steel for hangars are comparatively slight column sizes, affording clear working areas; easy attachment of appurtenances, such as tracks for hangar doors and crane rails; relatively light weight; rigidity of frame; reasonable cost. The principal objections to steel are necessity of maintenance to afford rust protection; little resistance to buckling and collapse under flash fire conditions.

Prefabricated Hangars

Several interesting developments have been made in demountable prefabricated steel hangars. In the larger

Courtesy the American Rolling Mill Company

FIGURE 6. PREFABRICATED HANGAR

category, the structure offered by the American Rolling Mill Company appears to be very thoroughly worked out and successful. The framing consists of arch ribs spaced 17 feet, 4½ inches on centers. Each rib consists of a number of straight segments of equal length and cross section which are bolted together to form the complete arch. Roof purlins consist of interlocking formed sections of sheet steel known as Steelox panels, which run from rib to rib, and form a continuous surface upon which insulation board and roofing may be placed. Vertically placed panels form sidewalls for lean-to areas and hangar doors. All the components are designed to such dimensions that the entire hangar may be shipped on railroad flat cars.

Two sizes of extreme overall width are offered—160

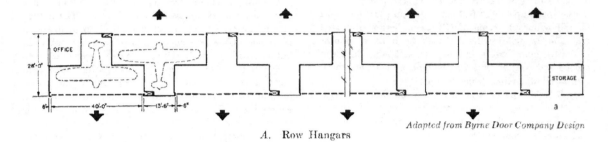

A. Row Hangars   *Adapted from Byrne Door Company Design*

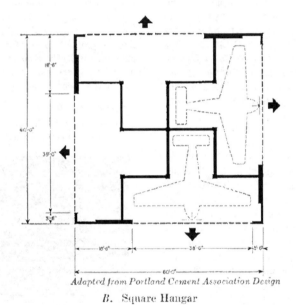

Adapted from Portland Cement Association Design

B. Square Hangar

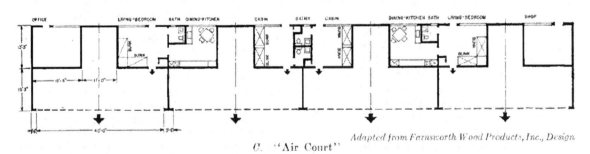

C. "Air Court"   *Adapted from Farnsworth Wood Products, Inc., Design*

FIGURE 7. HANGARS FOR PERSONAL AIRCRAFT

feet and 202 feet, 8 inches Any length in multiples of 17 feet, 4½ inches may be attained Monitors may be placed continuously along the roof ridge to afford natural light and ventilation

Another type of prefabricated hangar for small private plane storage is offered by Byrne Doors, Inc As the plan in Fig 7A shows, planes are alternately tailed in and nosed in, resulting in maximum use of space. The depth is determined by the plane size, and the length of the structure, by the number of units to be stored Additional units may be added as required The entire structure is steel, framing as well as side walls and roof

A variation of this plan is shown in Fig 7C which provides living quarters adjacent to each of the aircraft storage spaces A structure such as this would be the counterpart of the Motel which has proved its value to the traveler by motor vehicle

Nose Hangars

As mentioned before, the larger planes are rugged enough not to require protected areas for storage Wing spans and height of rudders are so great that it becomes uneconomical to enclose them completely for servicing Therefore, the early "emergency" nose hangars are being revived and have been developed to provide shelter for the forward section of the aircraft including engines, thus allowing maintenance work and engine overhaul to proceed under comfortable working conditions

The customary structural arrangement of a nose hangar is a cantilevered roof which overhangs the nose and wings of the aircraft with either a canvas flap (fitted around the fuselage), which lets down from the face of the cantilever and provides protection against the elements, or a canopy type door fitted with cut-outs to accommodate the fuselage Shop and office space may be conveniently arranged along the rear of the structure

Air-Supported Structures

A radical departure from conventional structure has been made to provide large, unobstructed, enclosed areas It is known as "air-supported" construction It utilizes a series of thin sheets of steel, welded together and sealed at all joints to the foundation. These sheets are then inflated to become a vaulted structure By means of continuous air pressure in excess of atmospheric pressure, the structure is maintained in that condition

Since this method is still in the design and experimental stage, it is too early to predict eventual success or failure Its use has been advocated for hangars

However, several complications present themselves which indicate doubts of such a use The entrance must, of necessity, contain an air lock to prevent too rapid an escape of compressed air This lock will prevent free and rapid movement of planes into and out of the enclosure A circular shape presents planning problems which are more difficult to solve than for a rectangular shape, notably the provision of shop space Such a structure would, of necessity, have to be entirely air-conditioned and artificially lighted, increasing maintenance costs

Hangar Doors

Four general types of doors are commonly used for hangars canopy, vertical lift, jack-knife, and side-sliding The first three must be mechanically operated, the fourth may be either manually or mechanically operated

Canopy Door

The canopy door is counterbalanced by means of a series of cables attached to weights In planning the hangar space must be allotted to these weights They may be placed anywhere along an unobstructed interior wall, but in common practice they are placed on a side wall near the doors in order to reduce the length of cable required Advantages of this type follow In opening, the door has an initial vertical travel before it begins to swing outward, of great value in regions of ice and snow, since it permits the door to be used without preliminary snow shoveling The door may be raised to any desired height and allowed to remain there An aircraft of low height, therefore, may enter the hangar without having to open the doors completely, a real saving of heat in cold climates When the door is entirely open, a portion of it projects beyond the face of the building, affording protection against rain or intense sunlight

The main disadvantage of this door is cost, this being the most expensive hangar door The provision of space for counterweights may possibly prove a hardship by using valuable wall space A canopy door cannot be used for hangars framed with Lamella roofs and will necessitate costly bracing in connection with arch rib roofs.

The installation of a sprinkling system is complicated by a canopy door since the ceiling area occupied by the door in its open position must be protected, requiring the installation of special sprinkler heads to cover this floor area below the door A similar complication arises in lighting when canopy doors are used

An advantage claimed for the canopy door alone is that it is a one-piece unit Consequently, there exists

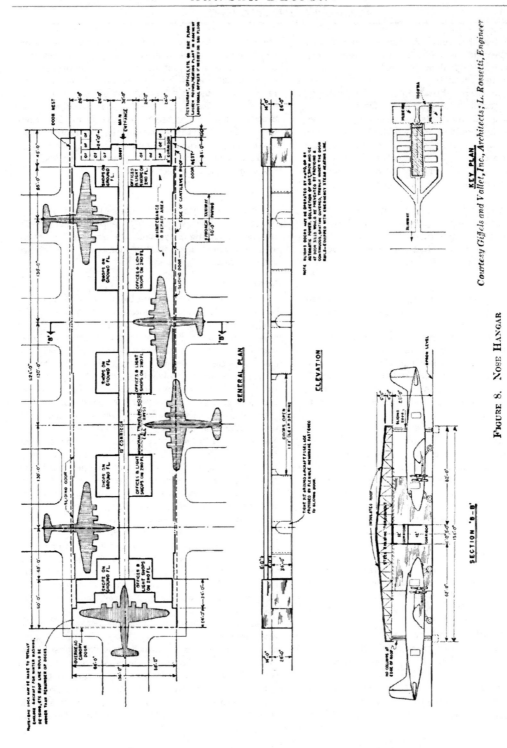

GENERAL PLAN

ELEVATION

SECTION 'B-B'

KEY PLAN

FIGURE 8. NOSE HANGAR

Courtesy Gifels and Vallet, Inc., Architects; L. Rossetti, Engineer

a minimum of joints which may be easily sealed, reducing heat losses and resulting in savings of fuel costs

Vertical Lift Door

Vertical lift doors are composed of several horizontal panels, each of which is offset from the adjacent one Each panel travels at a different rate of speed, so that all panels arrive at their destination simultaneously In climates where snow and ice occur this type has the same advantage as the canopy door of eliminating the necessity of snow shoveling before the door may be opened Operation again depends on cables and counterweights, and space must, therefore, be provided for them. The door may be raised to any desired height, according to the plane which is seeking entry

The main disadvantage of a vertical lift door lies in the fact that two trusses must be provided in place of the one required for other types the first outside the door, and the second immediately inside They are needed to support the vertical tracks upon which the leaves of the doors will slide Thus the increase in cost of steel framing must be taken into consideration when deciding upon the door type The cost of this door is a sum midway between the cost of a canopy and the cost of a side-sliding door

Jack-Knife Door

Jack-knife doors are less frequently used than any of the other types Their operation is somewhat more complicated than the other types Advantages and disadvantages follow closely those of the vertical lift door, with the exception that additional heavy framing is not required

Side-Sliding Door

Side-sliding doors are the least costly There are two types. One type operates on an accordion principle employing leaves about 4 feet wide which fold into door pockets The other has each leaf offset from the adjacent one, each one travels in its own track and at a different speed from its neighbor so that all arrive at the open or closed position simultaneously When mechanically operated, they use cables or winches The floor track must, of course, be kept clear of ice, dirt, sand, or snow, which presents a maintenance problem In cold climates a heating pipe is frequently run under the floor track to keep it clear of ice Door pockets in snow areas must be provided at each side of the opening to house the doors when in open position, calling for additional construction expense

If cost is a prime consideration, side-sliding doors of considerable size may be hand-operated The leaves may be supported either on a floor track or an over-

head track If the overhead track is used, it becomes a consideration in the design of the structure The side-sliding door is almost universally used with arch rib and Lamella structures

General Comments

In some cases a combination of side-sliding and center, roll-up "tail door" is used Airplanes of lower clearance may then enter the hangar by only the side-sliding door, for planes with higher vertical surfaces both doors are needed This combination permits an economical operation tailored for individual plane heights

The smallest, individual hangars for small aircraft may use overhead doors, hand-operated, of the general type used for garages This door is thoroughly proven, economical, easily installed, and easily operated

Mr. E H Sittner of Trans World Airlines has suggested that large hangar doors, particularly of the canopy type, may be operated more satisfactorily hydraulically than by means of cables, winches, and counterweights There may be considerable merit in this suggestion The action would be more positive, a door held in a partially open position would be thoroughly braced against wind pressure, the entire installation would be simpler and would free the wall section of the hangar ordinarily occupied by the counterweights. At least one door manufacturer is working on the development of an operation of this type

The most important single statement which may be made concerning hangar doors is that the type to be used should be decided upon at a fairly early stage in the design of the hangar Provisions can then be made for supporting all the appurtenances which hangar door operation requires in the most integrated and economical manner.

Mechanical Services

Electric Power

In general, the layout of electrical work for a hangar follows closely that of conventional building design The total connected load should first be estimated in kilowatts Estimated operating loads for various peak conditions should then be plotted, from which a determination may be made of the current required from the local utility and the sizes of main feeder lines and transformers

The main feed and distribution should be alternating current, with direct current confined to certain specialized applications Storage batteries may be used in larger plants for fire alarms, paging and intercommunicating telephone systems, and emergency lighting The charging of these batteries, as well as of

Canopy

Vertical Lift

Side-Sliding

FIGURE 9. HANGAR DOORS

those of the aircraft, call for motor generator sets or vacuum tube rectifiers. Twelve- and 24-volt direct-current outlets are required in the hangar area to allow plug-in for aircraft electrical systems, thereby relieving their storage batteries. Twenty-four-volt direct-current outlets are also required in engine test cells to energize aircraft engines on test stands and in the radio repair rooms for testing radio equipment.

Convenience outlets should be located throughout hangar and shop areas furnishing 110-volt and 220-volt alternating current. They will serve many purposes, providing power for portable tools, special lighting, and other equipment. The machine tool layout in the shop areas should be carefully studied, so that power for these tools may be brought to the proper locations in such a manner as underfloor ducts, which

Courtesy Byrne Doors, Inc.

Counterweights

Courtesy Lee Engineering Company

Floor Slot for Heating

Courtesy Byrne Doors, Inc.

Tail Door

Courtesy Lee Engineering Company

Heating Slot—Exterior Effect

FIGURE 10. HANGAR DOOR DETAILS

will not interfere with the efficient functioning of the shops

If portions of the shop layout contain working benches at which portable power tools are required, an overhead electric power supply is recommended This supply will eliminate the confusion resulting from a maze of electric cables mingled with the work, and will provide increased flexibility in the use of the tools.

Should hangar or shop areas be serviced with overhead cranes or monorails, the motors for this handling equipment may require direct current

Hangar Lighting

The lighting requirements of the main area of the hangar will vary from an average of 35 foot-candles on the horizontal working plane at 3 feet above the floor for service or overhaul hangars to 15 foot-candles for storage hangars The technique of high bay lighting with fluorescent fixtures has been proved effective with fixture mounting heights up to 60 feet Advantages claimed for this type of lighting are the elimination of harsh shadows and reduction of glare, with resulting lessening of eye fatigue Another type of lighting combines the use of fluorescent and mercury vapor lamps arranged alternately in a diamond pattern A third type uses high-intensity mercury vapor lamps exclusively A fourth, and recent, development is a combination unit which utilizes a high-intensity mercury and an incandescent lamp in the same fixture This type is reasonable in first and operating cost, and improves the color mix of illumination

White cement floors for hangar areas increase the level of illumination by causing considerable reflection of light, which is of particular benefit in working on the under surfaces of various portions of a plane

Certain hangar shop areas pose problems which must be solved by the use of specially designed lighting units The lighting for engine test cells must withstand extremes of vibration, high wind velocities, and oil vapor in the air The units should be arranged so as to light the sides, top, bottom, front, and back of the engine The preferred mounting is on the walls, utilizing recessed flush fixtures designed for this particular application Engine test cell lighting must, of necessity, be explosion-proof

Paint spray booth lighting must be composed of units which will not allow explosive gases to enter the fixture and at the same time provide an even, high level of illumination from fixed, built-in locations Local, portable lights may not be used A unit has recently been developed which provides an efficient output of light Gases are prevented from entering by maintaining a greater interior than exterior pressure by the use of compressed air connections to each fixture

Rooms designated for the storage of inflammable materials, such as paints and oil, should have explosion-proof wiring and fixtures

The level of illumination for shop and office areas should range from 35 to 40 foot-candles on the horizontal plane at working level The type of fixture selected (incandescent or fluorescent—direct, indirect, or semi-indirect) can best be determined by an analysis of individual requirements

The periodic maintenance of lighting fixtures—cleaning and relamping—should be considered in the preliminary design stages If the fixtures are relatively few, as in mercury vapor lamps, they can be maintained by the use of hangars, which permit lowering each individual fixture to the floor by cables and cranks where it may be easily serviced If the number of fixtures is considerable, monorails, catwalks, or cranes should be provided for economical maintenance.

Sprinkling System

Wood and steel hangars should be sprinklered throughout for the protection of the structure Reinforced concrete hangars do not require sprinkler protection, since they are of fireproof construction Analysis will determine whether the additional cost of a sprinkling system will be offset by reductions in insurance rates, and whether the protection afforded the stored aircraft is worth the additional cost of sprinkler installation plus possible water damage

The structural design of the hangar areas will have an important bearing on the layout of the sprinkling system Where deep trusses occur, the areas between trusses must be compartmented by means of curtain walls of incombustible materials extending from the ceiling down to the low point of the trusses Structures with shallow ribs do not require such compartmentation

The special arrangement of sprinkler heads which must be provided when canopy type hangar doors are used has been discussed on page 200 Storage rooms for inflammable materials and engine test cells should be protected with sprinkler heads of the "water-fog" type

Since heat is customarily provided for hangars, a "wet" system is advocated in preference to a "dry" system It provides more immediate protection

Careful study should be given to the benefits obtained by designing a central sprinkling system for all the structures on an airport versus individual systems for each building Since it may reasonably be assumed that fires will not occur simultaneously over the entire

High Bay Lighting

High Bay Lighting Unit for Incandescent or Mercury
Vapor Lamps

FIGURE 11.   HANGAR LIGHTING

area of a development which is as dispersed as an airport, great economies may be effected in the capacity of pumping equipment required and related items.

The water volume and pressure required by the sprinkling system should be determined, at least roughly, at an early stage so that provisions for an adequate water supply may be made.

Heating

In developing a layout for the heating system cognizance should be taken early of all the air, vacuum and pressure pumps, air-conditioning equipment, and related equipment required as well as of the heating plant proper. By grouping all these elements within close proximity to each other, economies in piping and electrical work will be effected. Furthermore, such a grouping will, in most cases, lead to more efficient supervision and maintenance of the plant, permitting reduction in engineering personnel.

In designing the heating plant it is good practice, wherever possible, to provide two boilers rather than a single unit. One boiler can be used as a stand-by in shutdowns, and will operate more economically during seasons requiring low heat.

For small and moderate-sized hangars a circulating hot water system, utilizing floor or ceiling mounted unit heaters, is an economical installation for the hangar proper, with direct radiation used for smaller shops and offices. A layout consisting of a large number of hangars will probably be served more economically with a central heating plant, generating high-pressure steam. The steam is piped at high pressure to a service room in each hangar, where it is converted to low pressure and distributed to individual unit heaters and radiators. If the plan calls for a cafeteria or plane food preparation kitchens, the high-pressure steam may be used directly to generate hot water for dishwashing. Domestic hot water may, of course, be generated from either type of heating plant for use in washrooms and showers.

A by-product of the high-pressure system is the generation of electricity for the plant from wasted steam in the winter months, with a stand-by agreement with the local utility for power during the off-heat season. The possibility should not be overlooked, in the high-pressure system, of having the plant operated as a concession with the steam metered to individual tenants.

"Radiant" floor heating has been used in a number of recently built hangars. This type of heating undoubtedly produces the most comfortable form of heat, since the working surface—the concrete floor—attains a uniform, pleasant temperature. No drafts are set

Catwalks for Servicing Lights

Thompson Hangar, Showing Chains for Lowering to
Floor

Fixture Being Serviced from Floor

FIGURE 11. HANGAR LIGHTING

Courtesy Pennsylvania Central Airlines Corporation

FIGURE 12.   HANGARS—WASHINGTON NATIONAL AIRPORT

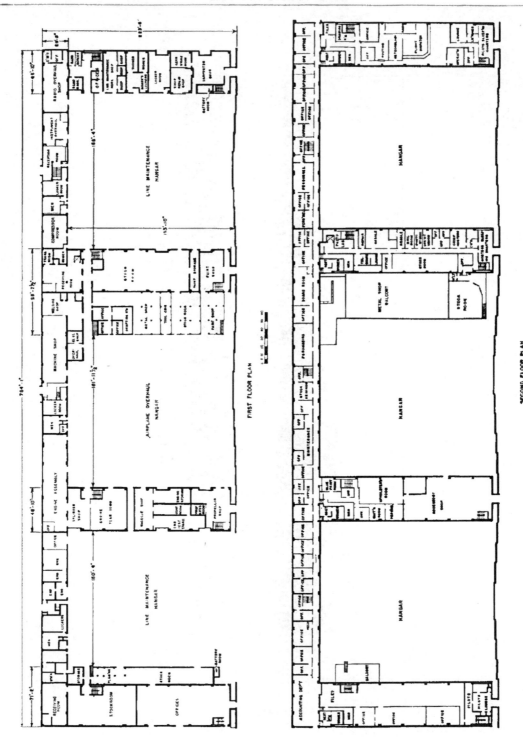

FIGURE 12.   HANGARS—WASHINGTON NATIONAL AIRPORT

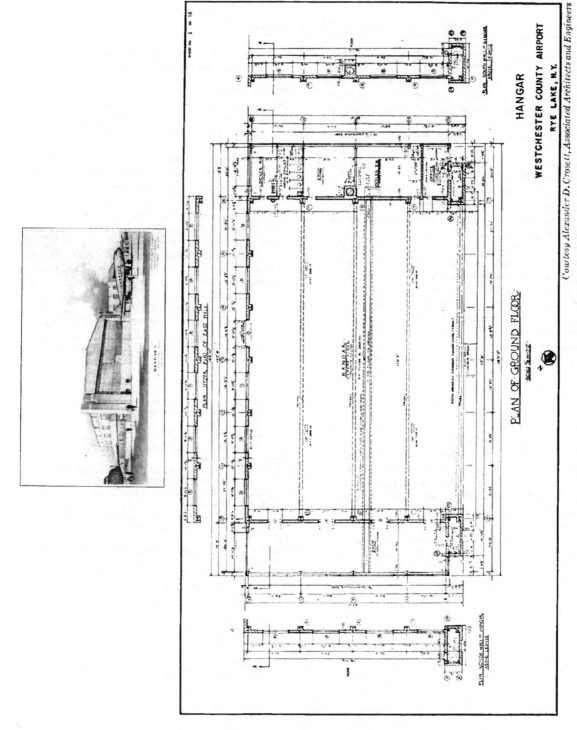

PLAN OF GROUND FLOOR

HANGAR

WESTCHESTER COUNTY AIRPORT
RYE LAKE, N.Y.

Courtesy Alexander D. Crosett, Associated Architects and Engineers

FIGURE 13. HANGAR—WESTCHESTER COUNTY AIRPORT

up by this method in contrast with the blower method Stratification of the air, which may occur with unit heaters because of the large horizontal surfaces of the planes' wings, is overcome. Two methods of radiant floor heating are in general use. The first utilizes a series of ducts constructed of hollow tile over which the concrete floor slab is poured. Warm air is forced through the ducts and during its passage warms the slab above. The second utilizes hot water coils embedded in the floor slab.

The primary disadvantage of floor heating is the higher installation cost as compared with the other types. This higher initial cost, it is claimed, is offset by lowered operating costs.

For hangars located in areas of cold climate, the opening of hangar doors creates discomfort and results in an appreciable loss of heat. To overcome this, slots may be placed in the floor immediately inside the hangar door. Hot air at high velocity is forced upward through these slots, forming a barrier and preventing cold air from entering the building. The blower for this installation is cross-connected with the motors operating the doors by suitable relays, so that the hot air jets function only while the door is in the open position.

Plumbing

Floor drains should be installed in the main hangar area spaced approximately 40 feet on centers both ways. They should be equipped with sand and dirt traps. The main sewage drain should be equipped with a grease and oil interceptor. The type of activity carried on in the various shops will determine whether or not floor drains and grease traps are required in these areas.

The rest of the plumbing installation of a hangar follows conventional practice. Wash fountains are more satisfactory than individual lavatories for the toilets accommodating personnel working in the shop and hangar areas. Showers, conveniently arranged between locker and toilet rooms, should be provided.

Special Services

Although, in a general discussion of this type, a definite program cannot be set up for incidental services the possibility of their requirement should be kept in mind.

Gas, compressed air and vacuum, may be required in shop and/or hangar areas. Their inclusion should be determined at an early design stage so that the required piping may be accommodated without the later necessity of cutting and patching. Also space allocation and power distribution should be planned for pressure and vacuum pumps and tanks.

The requirements of communication should receive careful study, so that telephones, teletype machines, pneumatic tube systems, and other similar devices may be easily installed.

Rooms for the storage of inflammable materials, such as paints and oil, must be built of incombustible materials throughout. They must have self-closing fireproof doors, and be provided with direct access to the exterior.

Bibliography

Aircraft Hangars and Terminal Buildings of Reinforced Concrete, by Charles S Whitney Privately published

Publications issued by the Portland Cement Association, Chicago, Ill

"Types of Hangar Buildings, Hangar Doors," *New Pencil Points*, November, 1943

"Wide-span Hangars for the U S Navy," by Anton Tedesko, *Civil Engineering*, December, 1941

"Navy Builds Concrete Hangars at San Diego," *Engineering News-Record*, December 4, 1941

"Monolithic Concrete Construction for Hangars," by John Ernst Kalinka, *The Military Engineer*, January–February, 1940

"Monolithic Concrete Seaplane Hangars," by Robert Zaborowski and Otto Gruenwald, *Civil Engineering*, August, 1944

"Roofs Supported by Air Pressure," by J A Wise, *Engineering News-Record*, November 30, 1944

11

SPECIAL SERVICES

Fueling of Aircraft

When hundreds of thousands of personal aircraft fly the airways and the airlines extend their service to every corner of our country, as well as every country in the world, the supplying of adequate quantities of the right kind of fuel and lubricating oil and their proper dispensing will become a problem of major importance

Extensive personal flying will demand speedy and efficient distribution of a large number of small quantities of fuel at airparks and small airports Transport aircraft will require much larger amounts of fuel to be dispensed with equal speed as, in scheduled operation, every moment must be saved to maintain the highest possible overall or system speed Even if multiple-tank filling is adopted, delivery must be much more rapid than heretofore, particularly for aircraft having fuel tank capacity of several thousand gallons

It is a far cry from refueling directly from 50-gallon gasoline drums with a hand pump to the 200-gallon tank mounted on a Model T Ford truck chassis of the early 1920's and the present Army Air Forces' fuel service train, consisting of a tractor and two tank trailers (capacity 8,000 gallons), which can service either four airplanes or four separate tanks of any of the larger aircraft simultaneously Mobile equipment of this size may be satisfactory for the military services, which must often operate from newly conquered bases or fields hastily constructed It has no place on modern landing facilities except where conditions do not permit the installation of permanent accommodations. The size of truck and tank must then depend on expected requirements, which will necessitate the truck tank's being refilled not more than once or twice daily

The sale of aviation gasoline and oil as well as lubrication service can be a very important source of revenue for the airport operator and should be better merchandized than it has been in the past This applies particularly to airpark, air harbor, fixed base, and non-scheduled commercial airport management Airlines generally have their own plane-refueling facilities, often by contract direct with fuel refiners and oil companies The automotive practice of furnishing niceties to the personal flyer, such as windshield cleaning and checking tires, should go a long way to boost service sales which invariably include gasoline and oil The habits of the motorist will undoubtedly be reflected in the aviation business Soliciting wash jobs, battery recharging, and other service work will pay dividends, especially when conducted in clean and appealing surroundings

Refueling facilities should be designed to provide

1 A minimum of labor for each operation
2 Easy aircraft tank fueling
3 Use of unskilled labor

Speed of refueling, of any quantity, with absolute safety is an essential criterion Thus, whatever the equipment, it must be properly protected for safe usage at any time The small aircraft may need but 5 to 50 gallons, the medium-sized airplane, 50 to 200, and the transport airplanes, 200 gallons up to several thousands per fueling operation Thus it can be deduced that three types of refueling systems should satisfy the needs of all types of aircraft For the sake of discussion, they can be classified as follows

1 Twenty-five gallons per minute capacity for airparks
2 Fifty to 75 gallons per minute for small personal and Classes I, II, and III airports
3 Seventy-five gallons per minute and up for all larger airports

Cost of furnishing service, availability of bulk fuel supply, and apron arrangement will determine whether mobile or stationary dispensing units should be used for the first two classifications By mobile unit is meant fueling trucks refilled from a large storage tank. Stationary dispensing units can be standard automotive pump stands or the newer cabinet types.

Fueling pits or modifications thereof appear to be the most practical and expedient method to date to service aircraft at the larger airports. In this system each plane position has a group of conveniently placed pits, each performing its portion of the service routine and each protected with steel plate covers. One pit should house flexible hose connections for aircraft air

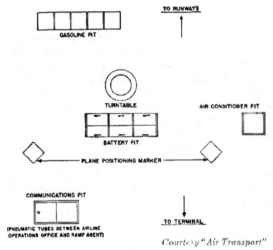

FIGURE 1. PIT ARRANGEMENT AT WASHINGTON NATIONAL AIRPORT

conditioning in the summer and heating in the winter. Another pit should house 12- and 24-volt direct current for plug-in for the plane's electrical system and booster for plane engine starting; 110-volt alternating current for trouble lamps and electric appliances; compressed air and telephone. At least two pits should house gasoline lines for filling plane fuel tanks with two different grades of fuel. They will require special safety features to prevent accumulation of gasoline vapors, as well as non-sparking fittings. All pits will have to be properly drained and designed to prevent the entrance of sand, dirt, ice, and snow. The typical pit details for the Washington National Airport, shown in Fig. 1, are an example of successful pit design.

The main benefits derived from apron service pits are twofold. They speed up the servicing of a plane at the ramp and thereby promote greater utilization of this customary "bottleneck" at airport terminals. They also eliminate many of the vehicles of all sizes and types which customarily swarm about a docked plane,

thereby cleaning up the entire area and reducing accident hazards both to personnel and aircraft.

Superairports will require a more radical solution because of the fuel quantities involved and the rate of delivery. For instance, it is estimated that when Idlewild, New York City's superairport, is fully developed, a fuel storage capacity of 6 million gallons will be needed, with an hourly delivery rate of 50,000 gallons during the evening peak traffic hours, dispensing through ninety or more fueling pits. These requirements present a major engineering problem involving refinery and pipe line practice combined with ramified distribution.

Small Airport Fueling Systems

Fueling at the smallest airports, servicing a limited amount of traffic, can be accomplished by a 500- or 1,000-gallon tank truck if bulk storage is relatively near by, thus eliminating the necessity of underground tank, piping, and refueling pits or pump stands. Although this method involves the upkeep of a motor vehicle, it has the advantage of flexibility, which is important when a row of airplanes needs to be fueled. As a matter of interest, perhaps the smallest installation of this type ever made is shown in Fig. 2, which illustrates a Bantam Chassis with a 50-gallon tank

FIGURE 2. AUTOGIRO REFUELING TRUCK

used by Eastern Air Lines in 1938 to refuel its autogiro on the Philadelphia Post Office roof.

Small airports having a greater rate of traffic and located away from bulk storage warrant the installation of a storage tank of 1,000 to 2,000 gallons or more capacity, with refueling pits or dispensing units.

Figure 3 shows a typical dispensing system for small airports, consisting of an underground tank, a dispensing pump near the hangar door from which small aircraft can be refueled as they are wheeled out of the hangar, and a submerged refueling pit for fueling at the apron.

A typical fueling pit unit is illustrated in Fig. 4, designed to deliver at the rate of 25 to 40 gallons per minute. It consists of a circular pit box with hose and nozzle, with their support, shut-off valve, strainer, and meter.

In an effort to improve the sales appeal at airports frequented only by the personal flyer, fueling has been

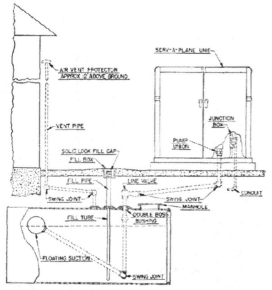

FIGURE 3.   TYPICAL FUEL-DISPENSING SYSTEM FOR SMALL AIRPORTS

designed to present a pleasing appearance without sacrificing efficiency and utility. Figure 5 shows the Bowser Serv-a-Plane with its cabinet doors open showing the refueling hose and reel, meter pump, and strainer. The two extra shelves can be used to store the more commonly used service tools.

Another version of a similar type of equipment is the Erie Flight Fueler shown in Fig. 6. It is a self-contained unit capable of being located at the most convenient place on the apron, piping to the underground tank fuel line being made through one of its supporting legs.

Medium-Sized Airport Fueling Systems

Non-scheduled commercial airports and airline trunk stops today use for the most part large tank trucks as typified in Fig. 7 showing a Shell Oil Company tank truck of 1,500 gallon capacity, used by American Air-

lines. It delivers fuel at the rate of 80 gallons per minute.

As flying activities at these airports increase and the daily requirements of fuel rise, it will be found that fairly large bulk storage connected to a series of refueling pits is a desirable facility to be added to such air-

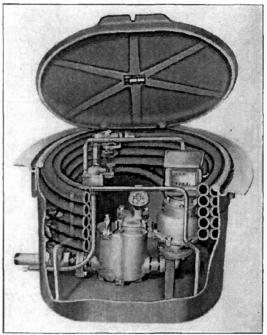

Courtesy Erie Meter Systems, Inc.

FIGURE 4.   FUELING PIT OF 25-GALLON CAPACITY

Courtesy S. F. Bowser and Company, Inc.

FIGURE 5.   SERV-A-PLANE FUEL-DISPENSING UNIT

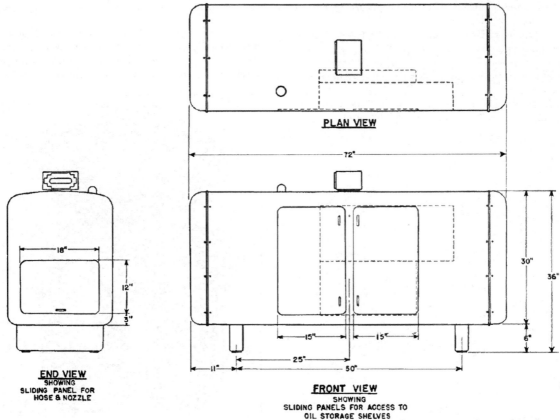

PLAN VIEW

END VIEW
SHOWING
SLIDING PANEL FOR
HOSE & NOZZLE

FRONT VIEW
SHOWING
SLIDING PANELS FOR ACCESS TO
OIL STORAGE SHELVES

Courtesy Erie Meter Systems, Inc.

FIGURE 6. FLIGHT FUELER

ports. Figure 8 illustrates a typical installation of underground fuel storage tanks with tank car connection and railroad spur. Dispensing can be accomplished by a 50- to 100-gallon per minute fueling pit as shown in Fig. 9.

Large-Airport Fueling Systems

At the larger airports today, both tank trucks and fuel-dispensing pits are used. With larger aircraft requiring greater amounts of fuel and higher rates of delivery to speed up refueling operations, it is obvious that tank trucks will be displaced by fueling pits exclusively.

The conventional type of pit and pumping equipment, however, must be considerably improved as fueling hoses larger than $1\frac{1}{2}$ or 2 inches are too heavy to handle when full of fuel. Furthermore, the shock of closing the nozzle of a high-pressure hose 2 inches in diameter while pumping fuel presents a definite personnel hazard.

An interesting development to overcome this objection has been advanced by the Wayne Pump Company of Fort Wayne, Indiana. It consists of using an improved centrifugal pump in conjunction with a low-pressure, large-diameter, and deflatable hose. One scheme devised by F. A. Page, superintendent of maintenance for United Air Lines, includes a light truck with a double reel. One reel consists of a 100-foot length of standard wet hose connecting with a fuel "hydrant" or pit; the other reel has a 30-foot length of dry deflated hose for refueling the aircraft. A booster pump is located between the two hose reels. The sequence of operation is as follows: The wet hose is connected to the "hydrant" or pit; the truck is driven to the airplane, unreeling the hose as it proceeds to the airplane. When in front of the airplane, the truck stops, the dry hose is unreeled, and the mechanic places the hose nozzle in the tank. The booster pump is then started and fueling proceeds. When the tank is full, the hose is deflated and put back on the reel.

Courtesy Shell Oil Company, Inc.

FIGURE 7.   FUEL-DISPENSING TRUCK OF 1,500-GALLON CAPACITY

The truck is backed and the wet hose automatically re-reeled, thus completing the fueling cycle.

This method combines the advantage of the multiple-fueling pit arrangement with the flexibility of the tank truck, besides permitting a high rate of fuel delivery. However, it means an additional motor vehicle to service and maintain; and, in simultaneous airplane refuel-

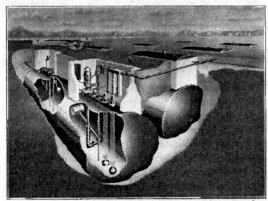

Courtesy S. F. Bowser and Company, Inc.

FIGURE 8.   UNDERGROUND STORAGE TANKS INSTALLATION

ing, the loading apron is covered with refueling hoses which hamper the movements of other service vehicles, besides involving a personnel hazard. It is, obviously, not the final answer but it is a step toward the expedi-

tious refueling of large-capacity aircraft at the passenger and cargo loading station.

Some thought is also being given to providing refueling docks away from loading apron and closer to bulk storage in order to eliminate large-capacity fueling pits and extensive underground piping.

Another possibility is the building within large and small transport aircraft of a tank-filling manifold system with only one outlet connection. This manifold could be suitably valved to allow filling of any one tank or any combination of tanks. By properly positioning the airplane at the ramp with respect to the fueling pit, only a short refueling hose would be needed. A scheme of this sort would greatly simplify the airport refueling problem, but would involve an increase in airplane empty weight. It is certain that many schemes will be tried before a satisfactory compromise is reached to solve this knotty problem.

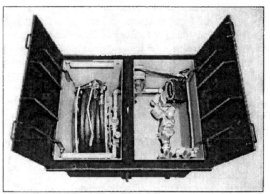

Courtesy Erie Meter Systems, Inc.

FIGURE 9.   FUELING PIT OF 50-GALLON CAPACITY

Storage of gasoline and delivery to the pits can be done in two ways, by the conventional pump-operated storage tank or by the flotation system as represented by the Flotrol System, formerly known as the Aqua System. In the former system, fuel pumped out of the tank is displaced with air by means of a tank vent; in the latter, fuel is displaced by water pressure when the fueling hose nozzle is open. In other words, there is never any air in the tank.

Figure 10 shows diagrammatically the Flotrol flotation fueling system for airports. It consists of storage tank (or tanks), water control pit, underground water trap (on the fuel delivery line), and fueling pit boxes (flush with ground surface). The main operating element is a three-way plunger-type valve in the water control pit. This valve permits water to enter or discharge from the tank. It has three ports: one con-

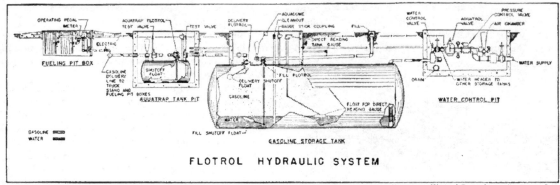

Courtesy Flotrol Petroleum Systems, Inc.

FIGURE 10. AIRPORT FLOTATION FUELING SYSTEM

nected to the drain outlet, one to the tank, and one to the water supply line. In fueling operations, the valve is controlled by an electrical valve switch from any fueling pit or loading stand. Water power to propel the fuel is consumed only during dispensing, the operating head of water then being maintained by pressure-reducing and safety relief valves. The flow of gasoline and water within the storage tank is controlled automatically by a double-unit mechanism of floats, levers, and valves. Automatic shut-offs maintain the fluid between predetermined maximum and minimum volumes.

The advantages of flotation fueling systems include:

    1. Elimination of evaporation losses.
    2. Elimination of explosion hazards.
    3. Greater stability of tank emplacement position.
    4. Supply of cleaner fuel.

To offset these advantages, however, the following are requirements for their satisfactory use:

    1. Inexpensive and adequate water supply.
    2. They must be installed so as to prevent freezing of water and can, therefore, be applied only to underground tank installations in cold climates.

Airport Fuel-Dispensing Equipment Maintenance

In order to reduce fuel-dispensing delays due to any possible mechanical failure of airport fueling systems, Gulf Oil Corporation has devised, and operates at the Washington National Airport, a service truck to cope with any emergency, illustrated in Fig. 11. This piece of equipment consists of a half-ton panel truck outfitted with a chain hoist of half-ton capacity and derrick frame mounted at the rear end, a 5-ton hydraulic jack, fire extinguisher, tow chain, shown by Fig. 12, mine safety fresh air mask with 25-foot hose, and miscel-

laneous tools and spare parts stored in the cabinets on the side walls of the truck. Mounted on the bumper is a gasoline-engine-driven water pump of 100-gallon-per-minute capacity. On the roof of the truck are mounted two searchlights and flashing red light, together with three amber lights and four red obstruction lights. Figure 11 also shows a small test tank in tow for checking the accuracy of the dispensing meters.

Courtesy Gulf Oil Corporation

FIGURE 11. AIRPORT FUEL-DISPENSING SERVICE TRUCK

Fire Protection and Control

With air traffic undergoing a tremendous expansion, airport managements are faced with an increased incidence of fires. It is not solely a problem of protecting ground facilities and their investment, because as long as highly inflammable materials, such as gasoline and lubricating oil, are used in the operation of aircraft, there is always the danger of a sudden fire, which unless quickly extinguished can be serious.

Any program for airport fire protection and control must, therefore, take into account the possibilities of aircraft fire during engine warm-up, taking off and landing, as well as special hazards found in hangars, engine test cells, maintenance and overhaul shops, and storage spaces. Airport fires are of two kinds: those relating to aircraft and those relating to airport buildings.

A fire aboard a flying aircraft can start from many sources, but the most common causes for such fire can be traced to failure of the engine proper, its fuel, oil, or hydraulic system, a short circuit in its electrical system, or for other reasons, to the cargo compartments and cabin. Many aircraft fires start instantaneously

Courtesy Gulf Oil Corporation

FIGURE 12. HOIST AND DERRICK, AIRPORT MAINTENANCE TRUCK

and without warning, and with large quantities of fuel and oil aboard can spread rapidly and be both large and very hot. Most airplane ground fires are caused by engine backfire during starting or while the engine is being tested prior to take-off. Perhaps the next most common causes of fire are defective fuel and oil line connections on the back of the engine. In such instances, vibration loosens the joints, permitting leakage onto hot engine parts such as the exhaust manifolds. The third main cause can be laid to defective electrical wiring.

In spite of excellent protection and alertness, in addition to fireproof construction, fires still occur in engine test cells. These fires are generally caused by the combination of the first two items mentioned above. Fire protection for this contingency was discussed in Part 9.

Airline transports and military aircraft carry oxygen tanks for altitude operation and emergencies. Although no fires on scheduled airliners have yet been traced to this source, it should receive serious consideration because of its potential hazard.

Any means considered for airport fire protection must meet three fundamental requirements:

1. It must possess maximum mobility. It must be highly and quickly maneuverable. Airport fire-fighting equipment must be capable of traveling at high speed on the airport runways, as well as on the soft shoulders, mud, and sand without getting stuck.

2. It must be designed functionally so as to go into action immediately when arriving at the scene of the fire. Eventual control of the fire or preventing its spread to other areas is not sufficient. It should carry sufficient crash equipment to effect immediately the rescue of personnel aboard the aircraft at the same instant that its fire-fighting equipment goes into action.

3. It must have sufficient extinguishing capacity to deal effectively with large fires. This will depend in a large measure on the efficiency of the apparatus and the kind of extinguishing medium used.

Extinguishing Agents

There is no single extinguishing agent which can cope successfully with all types of fires. Each commonly used agent has its advantages and drawbacks, and often the best solution is obtained by using several extinguishing agents, either separately or in combination. The best-known fire-extinguishing agents are water, water fog, methyl bromide, mechanical foam, and carbon dioxide (CO_2).

Of these agents, methyl bromide is used only for aircraft power plant fire protection in flight. It is light but possesses toxic characteristics. It has not been used extensively on American aircraft although it is very popular in Europe. It is not used to fight airport fires.

Water is very effective on combustible materials such as wood, sawdust, and textiles where a tendency to form glowing embers requires a prolonged cooling action. High-pressure streams have been used in rescue operations by cutting a path through a fire curtain. Being a liquid, however, water tends to serve as a spreading agent for gasoline and oil.

To overcome this undesirable feature, water is used as a fog by atomizing it. As a fog, it has been successfully used to combat oil and electrical fires as well as to give excellent protection to rescue crews because of its cooling effect. It has good penetrating power. Because of a limited water supply on airfields, water fog must be used in combination with other agents. In this manner it can be used as primary fire control agent supplemented by foam for final extinguishing.

Mechanically formed foam is another agent satisfactorily used on fires. It smothers fire, clings to the surface, and prevents re-ignition.

Carbon dioxide (CO_2) has long been recognized as the fastest and one of the most effective extinguishing agents for fires involving gasoline and oil, providing its rate of discharge and quantity applied are sufficient to smother the fire completely. That is the secret of its success. Carbon dioxide is a gas heavier than air, possesses high penetration characteristics, has no corrosive or toxic effect, and is quickly controlled. In combination with foam, it has speed and effectiveness without harmful results.

Types of Airport Fire-Fighting Equipment

The kind of fire-fighting equipment which best fits the need of any given landing facilities depends on the types of airplanes which use the facility and the ground accommodations in the way of buildings and services provided.

Irrespective of the size of the airport, however, the person charged with the responsibility of selecting the equipment should err on the large side rather than recommend equipment of inadequate capacity. He should consult freely with the National Board of Fire Underwriters, the Safety Division of the Civil Aeronautics Administration, as well as qualified manufacturers, such as Walter Kidde and Company, Cardox Corporation, and American-La France-Foamite Corporation, before formulating his equipment recommendations.

For the airpark or Class II airport, used exclusively by personal aircraft, it would seem that a compact two-wheel trailer unit, shown in Fig. 13, should cope with the average aircraft fire. Quickly coupled to the back of a motorcar or light truck, it can be driven rapidly to the scene of a crash fire. This particular unit is equipped with a battery of six tank units having a combined capacity of 300 pounds of carbon dioxide and manifolded to a hose reel with a heavy-duty nozzle. In addition, four portable CO_2 extinguishers are mounted at the front end of the trailer to increase its capacity and fire-smothering power. It is a low-cost unit which either singly or in multiple should fit the budget of any small landing facility.

An interesting piece of fire-fighting equipment for the handling of small fires is the motorcycle illustrated in Fig. 14. Altered to make it a tricycle, it carries

two 50-pound cylinders with hose and reel besides two 10-pound portable CO_2 cylinders.

An example of the equipment used at larger airports is shown in Fig. 15. This is a six-wheel truck equipped

Courtesy Walter Kidde and Company

FIGURE 13. AIRCRAFT FIRE-FIGHTING TRAILER

with safety and rescue gear. Fire-fighting equipment consists of ten 100-pound CO_2 cylinders arranged in two batteries of five, with each battery connected to a 200-foot hose reel; six 15-pound portable CO_2 cylinders; two 2½-gallon water type extinguishers; two extension ladders, two gas masks, a first-aid kit, two

Courtesy Walter Kidde and Company

FIGURE 14. SMALL MOBILE FIRE-FIGHTING UNIT

asbestos suits, and a power-operated winch with two chains.

Another piece of fire-fighting equipment of this type equipped with the most modern facilities is the six-wheel American-La France fire truck illustrated in Fig. 16.

Large long-range aircraft carry several thousand gallons of gasoline and a few hundred gallons of oil. To extinguish fires successfully which may develop from crashing with such loads of fuel and oil, it is essential that fire-fighting equipment of much greater

Courtesy Walter Kidde and Company

FIGURE 15. LARGE AIRPORT FIRE TRUCK

capacity be immediately available to prevent catastrophic results.

This problem has been forcefully brought to the attention of the military services during the war in the handling of flights of long-range bombers. One of the solutions is the fire truck illustrated in Fig. 17. It permits a mass discharge of 3 tons of carbon dioxide supplemented by 300 to 500 gallons of foam solution. Across the front of the truck, immediately below the

Courtesy American-LaFrance-Foamite Corporation

FIGURE 16. AMERICAN-LA FRANCE SIX-WHEEL UNIT

bumper, is a linear nozzle with a discharge capacity of 1,250 pounds of carbon dioxide per minute. Mounted on this nozzle are four fixed foam guns, each of which discharges at the rate of approximately 24 gallons per minute. (The foam is under pressure supplied by the carbon dioxide itself.) The function of this nozzle is to direct the application onto the base of the flames and

at the same time prevent the spread of the fire beneath the truck, which is driven within a very few feet of the blaze. From the boom nozzle, which is mounted on the top of the truck and projects forward out and over its front, carbon dioxide is discharged at approximately 2,500 pounds per minute directly down into the fire. This nozzle also has a foam gun of 20 gallons per minute capacity. Controlled from within the cab, the boom itself can be swung left or right, raised or lowered, while the nozzle proper is maneuverable in a vertical plane. In this way powerful concentrations can be directed as necessary to any part of the fire.

Mounted in front of the truck radiator is a CO_2 nozzle with a capacity of 1,250 pounds of carbon dioxide per minute. Affixed to this is a 40-gallon-per-minute foam gun. This front nozzle is also maneuverable from the cab, and is of particular value in backing up the action of the hose line operators.

The truck has two CO_2 hose lines, each of which releases approximately 750 pounds of carbon dioxide per

Courtesy Cardox Corporation

FIGURE 17. HIGH-CAPACITY AIRCRAFT FIRE-FIGHTING UNIT

minute. These hose lines are mounted on reels, one on each side, immediately behind the truck cab. When the nozzles are removed from their resting place on running boards, the release mechanism automatically opens a master valve, supplying CO_2 under pressure to the nozzle. Actual discharge is controlled by a squeeze type valve. Each of these reels is equipped with 100 feet of hose, $1\frac{1}{2}$ inches in diameter.

There are also two 100-foot by 1-inch foam hose lines equipped with guns which discharge both foam and a straight stream. A two-valve body allows the operator to discharge this foam or straight stream, either separately or together. These guns have an approximate capacity of 30 gallons each.

In addition to all this discharge equipment, there are two CO_2 bayonet type nozzles which are used to pierce and flood plane compartments with CO_2. They are particularly effective in engine nacelle fires or in the inerting of other closed sections of the plane.

Intense gasoline and oil fires can also be fought successfully by the use of Dugas, a chemical having sodium bicarbonate as a basic element. Its effectiveness is illustrated in Figs. 18 and 19, which show, respec-

Courtesy Dugas Engineering Corporation

FIGURE 18.   LARGE GASOLINE FIRE BEFORE EXTINGUISH-
MENT

tively, a simulated aircraft fire before the use of Dugas and less than 30 seconds afterward. The burning area covered 1,000 square feet and the fuel used was 100-octane gasoline. A path to the metal in the center was cut within 15 seconds by using two streams of Dugas dry chemical from two 350-pound mobile units. This

Courtesy Dugas Engineering Corporation

FIGURE 19.   SAME FIRE, LESS THAN 30 SECONDS LATER

test was made with standard nozzles. A new type of nozzle with a quick outlet size adjustment has been developed to permit the use of a solid stream at the beginning of extinguishment, changing to a fanned fog pattern for blanketing the fire, or to provide a protective curtain of extinguishing agent.

Protection of Buildings and Shops

The practices followed by industrial organizations and in office buildings apply to airport shops and buildings. In this respect airport fires are the same as those experienced elsewhere.

However, the best and most adequate fire-fighting equipment will fail to fulfill its duty if it is improperly manned, irregularly inspected, and not kept in perfect operating condition.

The danger from ground fires at any airport can be lessened by good housekeeping. By good housekeeping is meant cleanliness of shops and airfield, seeing that proper precautions are used in the handling and storing of inflammable material, keeping all facilities in repair and good working order, and seeing that all fire laws are strictly enforced.

Air Conditioning

The term "air conditioning" covers the treatment of the air to render it more comfortable and healthful,

Courtesy Eastern Air Lines, Inc.

FIGURE 20.   MOBILE AIRCRAFT AIR CONDITIONER

and is often used loosely. To condition completely the ambient air means to control its motion and distribution, temperature and humidity, odor and toxic gases, and its content of dust and bacteria. As commonly used, air conditioning means artificial cooling and dehumidifying or heating of the air, as well as the control of ventilation.

It is not within the scope of this book to discuss the equipment used commercially to condition the air but rather to point out the specific requirements of modern airports which affect the capacity of the equipment to provide satisfactory and reliable conditioning service under any operating conditions. With the exception of a few fixed installations, aircraft air conditioning has been provided in the past by means of mobile units consisting of a combination heating and refrigerating unit mounted on a standard truck chassis. Heating is obtained by passing air over large-capacity electric heaters and forcing it through the aircraft ducts.

Cooling is provided by using standard refrigeration units, generally with "Freon 12" and a cold water tank. A separate gasoline engine is used to drive the electric generator for the heating cycle and the compressor for the cooling cycle, also the blower to circulate the air being conditioned.

The high cost of these units and the fact that several must often be used simultaneously at terminal stations

F. L. Ankers Photograph

FIGURE 21.   AIR-CONDITIONING HOSE CONNECTION

and connecting points to service properly all departing and arriving aircraft during peak traffic hours of the day combine to make this air-conditioning solution far from the best answer to the problem. The problem is further complicated by the varying sizes of flying equipment, sizes from the 14-passenger aircraft for local schedule operation to the 100-passenger (or more) transport for transcontinental or transoceanic service. It also means additional vehicles on the apron to impede the flow of other traffic necessary to service or load parked aircraft.

Where the passenger station is air-conditioned or conditioning is contemplated in the design, serious consideration should be given to the provision of sufficient excess capacity to air-condition the parked aircraft at the apron. An excellent example of such installation is the Washington National Airport. A pit is provided

at the apron with a retractable hose extension to connect with the aircraft ventilating system ducts. This pit is connected by underground duct to the main building air-conditioning system.

A possible improvement in new installations would be to pipe the refrigerant to stations in the building closest to each pit in order to reduce duct losses to a minimum. The duct from that point to the pit should be properly insulated and sufficiently pitched to drain any moisture condensation.

The capacity of the conduits and excess capacity of the central plant to accommodate the requirements of aircraft conditioning vary according to the sizes of aircraft to be serviced. Let us assume an airport apron having ten aircraft positions which, during peak hour operation, might be occupied by four 15-passenger airplanes, four 20- to 25-passenger airplanes, and two 50-passenger airplanes. This might well represent the peak hour scheduled air traffic of a city of 100,000 population within 10 to 15 years. Assuming 30 minutes at the apron for loading and unloading, it means 20 departures and arrivals per hour and a total possible traffic of 1,040 passengers, which is not beyond the realm of probability.

The cabin volume of these three types of aircraft to be conditioned would be approximately as follows:

15 passenger aircraft—800 cubic feet.
20 to 25 passenger aircraft—1,300 cubic feet.
50 passenger aircraft—2,400 cubic feet.

Assuming that it is desirable to displace the air volume of each airplane cabin once every minute, the capacity of the central conditioning plant for this requirement would have to be 13,200 cubic feet of air per minute for the ten occupied positions. This capacity may seem high, but it will provide, in this example, enough reserve for expansion at a later date either owing to an increase in the number of plane positions or in the size of airplane cabins.

In the summer, it should be possible to cool air from 95° F dry bulb and 75° F wet bulb to 55° F and 90 per cent relative humidity at the pit hose outlet. For winter operation, it should be possible to heat air from 0° F to 120° F at the pit hose outlet. Allowing for heating and cooling losses, 13,200 cubic feet of air per minute through ten outlets would require approximately 40 boiler horsepower for winter heating and 60 tons of refrigeration for summer cooling. This is in addition to airport building air-conditioning needs.

The ventilating fan and duct installation should be designed so that the noise level in the cabin with the heating or cooling system does not exceed 30 to 35 decibels.

The portable hose extension from the apron pit to the connecting outlet of the airplane duct system should be not less than 6 inches inside diameter nor longer than 20 feet, as each foot of flexible hose, even if insulated, has a loss of, roughly, ½° F when heating, and a similar gain when cooling. This flexible hose length should retract into the pit when not in use.

A great deal of thought is being given to the study of air-conditioning equipment built in aircraft to make it independent of external sources of comfortization, but the prospects for integral summer conditioning are not very bright for small aircraft owing to the heavy weight of such equipment, unless a far more efficient material than the now standard "Freon 12" dichloro-difluoromethane used for small installations is found.

Integral heating by means of separate combustion heaters is now standard on many new transport aircraft, but the electrical power required to provide the necessary circulation of the heated air while the aircraft is at the apron is such as to indicate that heating and ventilating from a central heating plant are more desirable. Constant volume and close temperature control are assured as in aircraft in flight.

Snow Handling

Airport snow handling is a problem of primary importance in northern regions, where snowfall occurs for several months of the year.

There are two methods of solving the snow problem. In the heavy snow belt where snow is likely to stay all winter, compaction by rolling has been found satisfactory. In regions where snow falls and melts intermittently during the winter, complete removal after each storm is recommended.

The purpose of compacting snow by rolling is to provide a paving of snow which eventually changes to an icy surface. The success of this method depends on properly packing the first snowfall so as to cement it to the runway surface and form a bond for successive snowfalls, which are rolled immediately after each storm. In compacting the first snow, rolling should start after the first 2 or 3 inches of snow have fallen, and be continued until the storm stops. From then on, the surface should be rolled only once after each storm. Excessive rolling would have a tendency to break up the snow layer and the first bonding layer as well. Uneven surfaces can be leveled off with a drag and the low spots filled if necessary. In early spring, when the temperature rise softens the surface during the day, it becomes necessary to roll it in the evening before it hardens again. This precaution will prevent honeycombing during the late spring thawing period.

When the snow and ice coating disintegrates, it should be completely removed, preferably by blowing it as far away as possible on each side of the runway to prevent water from draining back to it and forming ice, which would create a serious hazard. If the ice surface is still hard, it can be scraped by using equipment similar to that shown in Fig. 22, which illustrates a Willett truck grader and center plow cutting ice approximately 2 inches thick.

Contrasted to packing and rolling, complete snow clearance is generally accomplished by mechanized equipment, which either throws or blows the snow

Courtesy Willett Manufacturing Company

FIGURE 22. WILLETT TRUCK GRADER AND CENTER PLOW

away from the landing surface or runway. Snow plows of the single angular blade type or V-type can push snow aside a few feet to 15 or 20 feet, depending on the size of the blades and the power which drives them. Rotary auger type snow plows can blow the entire width of the runway and up to 150 to 200 feet if strong winds help the process. Either type is best used with heavy type four- or six-wheel drive trucks to provide the necessary traction in heavy snows.

The principal advantage of the rotary snow plow is that it immediately disperses the snow away from the runway over a wide area, thus eliminating windrows. Also, it does the job in one operation whereas single-blade or V-type plows require echeloning to clear the runway completely. On the other side of the ledger, V-type plows are fast and positive. Best results are obtained by combining equipment, using the blade type snow plows for clearing the area and the rotary and auger plows for removing windrows and dispersing the snow.

Small airports, such as airparks and CAA Class I and II airports, can be satisfactorily and inexpensively serviced by single-blade plows as shown in Fig. 23. This type of snow plow is used by small municipalities, and, in many instances, arrangement can be made by the airport management to contract with the local authorities for runway snow removal.

Larger airports require speedy snow removal and, therefore, the use of high-capacity equipment. Figure 24 illustrates the Walter snow fighter team specially designed for airport snow clearing. The front truck is equipped with a one-way plow and speed wing permitting clearance of a 16-foot width of snow. The

FIGURE 23. SINGLE-BLADE SNOW PLOW

following truck is equipped with a V plow and a wing with a widening width of 13 feet. This unit is also equipped with a demountable Roto Wing. This combination is capable of dissipating and spreading deep accumulations of snow at high rates of speed. These two trucks, working as a team, can clear on a single trip a snowfall width of 28 feet.

Courtesy Walter Motor Truck Company

FIGURE 24. WALTER SNOW FIGHTER TEAM

Figure 25 shows a Snogo auger type snow blower manufactured by the Klauer Manufacturing Company of Dubuque, Iowa. It is available in several sizes to meet the requirements of the various airport sizes and operating budgets. Figure 26 shows the Snogo in operation.

At the apron, snow cannot be removed completely by mechanical means and some must be shoveled off manually. After removal is completed, apron and working areas should be sprinkled with sand or cinders to reduce to a minimum personnel hazard of slipping on wet snow or ice.

Chemicals and salts should be used sparingly because these solutions may splash on the surface of parked aircraft, causing corrosive action.

Airfield Turf Maintenance

Airfield turf, wherever used, must be cut regularly to keep it in good condition.

It is also important that the field be mowed as quickly as possible in order to permit its continuous use. This schedule calls for large-capacity mowers.

Courtesy Klauer Manufacturing Company

FIGURE 25. AUGER TYPE SNOW BLOWER

Figure 27 illustrates the Worthington airfield "Grass blitzer" 9-unit gang which can mow up to 46 acres per hour at 20 miles per hour. It can be dismantled and transported in the trailer, shown in the background, to another airfield in order to obtain the highest possible utilization by serving several fields in any given region. It can cut a swath 21 feet wide. Each

Courtesy Klauer Manufacturing Company

FIGURE 26. SNOGO IN OPERATION

of its 9 units is interchangeable. Units can be joined together to form gangs of 3, 6, or 9 units, depending on the cut width desired.

The tractor used as motive power can be equipped with a rotary broom to sweep the paved runways when

Courtesy Worthington Mower Company

FIGURE 27. AIRFIELD GRASS MOWER

Courtesy Willett Manufacturing Company

FIGURE 28. TRUCK GRADER

Courtesy Willett Manufacturing Company

FIGURE 29. TRUCK GRADER WITH SCRAPER BLADE RE-
TRACTED

not used with the mower or with a light 6-foot blade plow to clear snowed areas, as an auxiliary snow plow, where the snowfall is light. In addition, it can also be employed as a regular tractor for towing light planes.

Properly established and maintained turf airfields on well-drained soil can withstand extensive use by most types of personal aircraft up to light transport aircraft, such as may be used for feeder operation.

Characteristically, turf fields are more resilient than pavements. However, to maintain this quality, care must be taken to prevent weeds from growing or spreading. Weeds have a short life, leaving bare spots which quickly develop into holes.

In order to provide a good grass foundation, the soil should be free from stones and properly graded. A typical grader to prepare the soil is shown in Figs. 28 and 29. It is a flexible piece of equipment which can be used for any other purpose after retracting the scraping blade. In extremely sandy soil, it has been found that clay can be successfully used to fix the sand.

The rule which applies to lawn watering is also good

for turf fields, that is, occasional watering is not so satisfactory as a good soaking which penetrates to a depth of 3 or 4 inches to promote grass root depth and strength.

Miscellaneous Airport Equipment

Aircraft Turntables

Apron space is expensive space as its pavement must be designed and built to withstand the heaviest air-

F. L. Ankers Photograph

FIGURE 30. AIRCRAFT TURNTABLE AT WASHINGTON NATIONAL AIRPORT

craft to be used at a particular airport and the static loads they impose on the apron pavement. Furthermore, where a large number of airplanes are to be parked at the apron at the same time, it is highly desirable that the walking distance from the administration building lobby or passenger waiting room be as short as possible for the convenience of the air traveler and in the interest of saving time.

In order to utilize apron area efficiently, parked aircraft should be spaced as close as possible, consistent with freedom of movement and ample maneuvering clearances. This problem was solved at the Washington National Airport by permanently located turntables to fix the radius of turn of loading and unloading aircraft (Fig. 30). These turntables are bolted to the apron pavement, which must be reinforced at that point, with provisions for draining the turntable pit. The rotating portion consists of a cup-shaped plate mounted on a large diameter ball bearing and is turned by the airplane itself when maneuvering into position by speeding the propeller or propellers on the opposite side of the pivot wheel.

Figure 31 shows the Ideco portable aircraft turntable designed for flexibility of parking. The ring

Courtesy International-Stacey Corporation

FIGURE 31. IDECO PORTABLE AIRCRAFT TURNTABLE

plate is tapered so as to have its periphery practically flush with the apron surface. It is made in two sizes, one capable of supporting 20 tons, the other 40 tons.

The primary advantages of turntables are increased speed of docking operations, ease of docking, and maximum accuracy in aircraft positioning at the apron.

Bibliography

Comfortization of Aircraft, by Albert A. Arnhym, Pittman Publishing Corporation, New York, 1944.

"Driving the Driven Snow," by George Herrick, *Air Transport*, December, 1943.

Snow Removal. Geng Tells How He Does It," by Francis J. Geng, *Air Transport*, August, 1944.

"Snow Doesn't Ground R.C.A.F.," *Aviation*, November, 1944.

"Let Your Airport Go to Grass," by Joan David, *Flying*, February, 1945.

12

SPECIAL PROBLEMS
AND MISCELLANEOUS FACILITIES

It has been pointed out repeatedly in previous chapters that the airplane and the airport cannot be treated separately. The design of one affects the other.

The planning of any landing facility must be based on the fundamental fact that such landing facility will of necessity outlive any type of aircraft for which it is designed today. Liberal thinking must guide the conception of new projects as well as modernization of existing facilities. Modernization of existing facilities deserves careful consideration and presents a problem which taxes the resourcefulness of the engineer and architect to find the best possible solution.

Modernization of Existing Facilities

A great number of airports in this country—particularly those serving large cities—are rapidly becoming obsolete for scheduled air transportation because of inadequate size or capacity. It is unfortunate that many of these airports were conceived and constructed to preclude any possibility of satisfactory modernization at reasonable cost.

Generally, they suffer from three fundamental planning deficiencies: (1) They prevent further expansion except at prohibitive property acquisition cost, (2) their buildings are erected as civic monuments with little regard to function and airport economies, and (3) they are located without due consideration of regional growth and possible traffic-generating centers. These airports may be, however, quite suitable as landing facilities for industry and, as such, can be operated satisfactorily to meet the requirements of non-scheduled commercial services.

Another large group of present-day airports, although not obsolete, have certain deficiencies which render them less dependable or less economical for scheduled air transport operation. In many cases, such defects can be remedied fairly simply with rela-

tively moderate expenditures. It is the purpose of this section to point out the more prevalent of these defects and to suggest ways and means of overcoming them so that these airports may be brought up to par by present-day standards. Whenever possible, plans should be made in the light of what can be expected years hence.

Any modernization program must be planned in the same manner as a new airport project and carried through within the framework of the master air traffic plan outlined in Part 5. In other words, every community should start off its airport program by the initiation of a comprehensive air traffic survey. And all work, whether new or modernization, should have its orderly place within the master plan, derived from such a survey. This is absolutely essential as every modernization involves a series of compromises in order to salvage intelligently as much of the existing facilities as may be possible.

Where the additional land acreage required is a large portion of the cost of modernization, care must be exercised to design a plan which will provide a balanced and efficient use of space for both airfield and buildings. The mere extension of runways is meaningless if the entire pattern is not correctly related to the wind rose, the taxiway layout, and the apron capacity.

The revised building plan should realistically appraise the needs of the community, or region, for its air transportation requirements now and in the future, as well as recreational activities conforming with local habits and the wealth of the area. It must be kept in mind that concessions can be used to pay for a large share of the entire development if properly balanced and made sufficiently attractive to secure the patronage of a large number of people. Modernization must be considered in the light of a utility for the benefit of the community. Proper design must make it pay

Among the frequent deficiencies of conventional airport designs, the following can be cited:

1. *Excessive taxiing distance between the passenger loading apron and the end of the landing and/or take-off runway.* This is not only an economic waste, but also means increased schedule time from point to point. In many cases excessive taxiing may be cut down by the addition of taxi strips. For instance, in the simple taxi pattern shown in Fig. 1, the taxi distance has been cut substantially by the addition of taxiways as shown.

2. *A single runway for both take-off and landing limits the capacity of the airport,* as under present operating conditions it does not appear safe to land or take off at closer intervals than 1½ minutes, in good weather, so that, for an equal number of take-offs and landings, the maximum capacity of the single runway

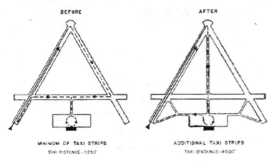

FIGURE 1. REDUCTION OF TAXI DISTANCES BY ADDITION OF TAXIWAYS

is but 20 take-offs and 20 landings, or 40 operations per hour. It is, of course, much less in instrument weather.

First, the layout of the taxi strips should be investigated to ascertain whether the flow of incoming and outgoing airplanes is not interrupted by having taxiing airplanes cross the path of other airplanes which are about to land or take off. If this situation is found to be satisfactory, one may be sure that the runways are capable of being utilized to their maximum, that is, 40 operations per hour.

If greater capacity is required, the entire runway pattern should be restudied. This study may show that a dual parallel runway system should be installed. In order to utilize such an arrangement to its maximum, a system of taxiways should be developed concurrently with the runways which will allow airplanes to taxi from the ends of either landing or take-off runways directly to the terminal without crossing in front of an arriving or departing plane. Thus a continuous flow of traffic will be obtained. If this is not done, the additional investment of dual runways will be only fractionally utilized.

3. *With the conventional location of the traffic control tower facing the airport runways, runway length is limited by the visibility from the tower, in hazy weather.* This distance seldom exceeds ¾ to 1 mile, which is inadequate for major airports. The possibility of relocating the control tower should be studied concurrently with the runway pattern. A modification of runway pattern will often permit a more favorable

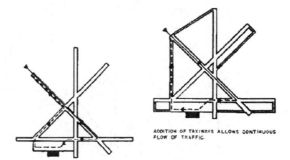

FIGURE 2. ADDITION OF TAXIWAYS TO INSURE CONTINUOUS TRAFFIC FLOW

placing of the control tower, as shown by Fig. 3. Although it is customary to have the tower built as part of the administration building, this is by no means a necessary requirement. The tower should be located where it will perform best, not where it will look best.

4. *Inability to segregate properly passengers from airport administration, aircraft servicing, and visitors, as well as incoming from outgoing passengers.* This inability has been the cause of many delays and must

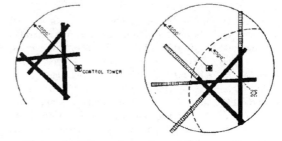

FIGURE 3. PROPER LOCATION OF CONTROL TOWER

be avoided if mass transportation by air is to become a reality.

In many of the smaller airports passengers, spectators, and cargo may be segregated inexpensively by erecting fences and barriers at strategic points, thus channeling traffic flow. At the larger airports the problem becomes more difficult of solution as it becomes more acute. For such cases it is impossible to

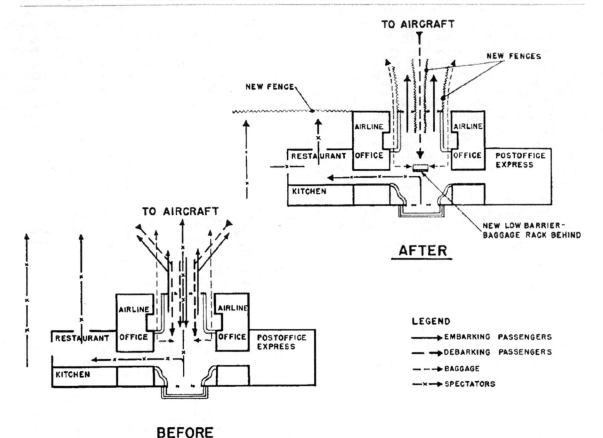

FIGURE 4. SEGREGATION OF PASSENGERS, CARGO, AND SPECTATORS AT SMALL AIRPORTS

make suggestions since each problem has to be studied by itself and its own solution found. Where traffic within the administration building is poorly arranged, a relocation of concessions and ticket booths—using them as traffic islands—may solve the problem.

An example is the passenger station modernization shown in Fig. 5. There the improvement is apparent. Incoming passengers are channeled on one side of the building and departing passengers on the other. This channeling was accomplished by extending the building on one side, achieving a more functional waiting room shape, and at the same time providing a more efficient ticketing and counter location.

5. *Excessive walking distance from passenger loading apron to administration building concessions at some of our larger airports; also excessive handling distance for air cargo.* This problem is receiving the most serious consideration by airline operators and airport engineers. Where new facilities are being

built, much apron space may be saved by the mechanical docking of planes, thus permitting loading stations to be closer together and cutting down on walking distance.

Studies should be made of mechanical means of handling cargo to determine whether such an installation will be justified by saving in time and manpower. Generally speaking, manual handling of cargo is cheapest except for conditions of steady flow and large volume.

6. *Inability of the present arrangement of many airport facilities to accommodate a substantial increase in traffic and schedules without delays and confusion.* This deficiency and its solution are closely tied up with deficiency 2 if study has disclosed that the trouble arises from the runway layout. If the trouble is in loading and unloading aircraft, additional passenger apron facilities will be the solution. If the integration of loading apron with administration building is at

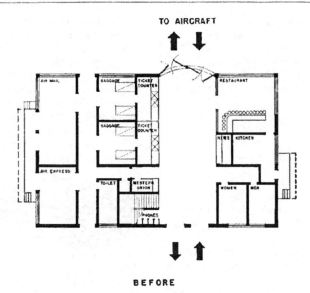

BEFORE

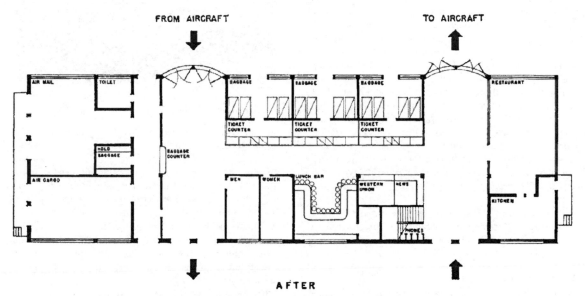

AFTER

FIGURE 5. SKETCH OF POSSIBLE STATION MODIFICATION FOR SEGREGATION

fault, this may be corrected by the installation of additional means of access from one to the other to permit rechanneling of passenger movement. Or, finally, it may be a combination of all these faults, the correction of all of which will be required.

7. *Inability of many intermediate point airports to handle the larger equipment now contemplated.* This problem may be met only by extending the runways and increasing their load-bearing power. The cost of doing this together with the cost of the additional land required, and removal of man-made obstructions due to more stringent zoning, should be carefully weighed against building a new transport airport elsewhere, embodying all the most advanced design features, and then using the existing airport for personal flying and instruction.

8. *Inefficient layout of airport administration building lobby and traffic counters to handle both passengers and baggage, thus impeding flow by lost motion.* The solution to this deficiency will be found only in the study of each actual case involved. However, the answer to deficiency 4 will often be the answer to this problem.

These are but a few typical deficiencies found at many of our airports today. They can be corrected in many cases.

The most important point to be made regarding modernization is that the need for it exists always. The airport management on the alert for improvements will be rendering the citizens of the community a real service and thus will enable the airline operator to do likewise. These benefits will also accrue to the personal flyer.

Although modernization programs are highly recommended whenever feasible, the thinking of the municipal planner must not be distorted by the belief that military airports—having served their national defense purpose—can be suitable in every case for commercial operation. Such airports have, as a rule, only one point in their favor and that is size. They are generally too large for the needs of the average city and are invariably located too far away. So that although their acquisition costs may be low, their upkeep and unpopularity will make them "white elephants." It must be borne in mind that military airports, including training fields, are designed for the landing and take-off of mass formation flying involving fifty or more aircraft almost simultaneously, and, as such, have an overcapacity airfield in relation to their administration building. Furthermore, their general layout does not usually conform to commercial airport requirements.

As a concluding remark, it may be stated that modernization and remodeling programs will tax the ingenuity of the best airport planner in conceiving a sound plan.

Airline Terminals

The purpose of this book is to advance the functional planning of airports and discuss the more important details of airport design, but the interrelationship of the airport proper and the complementary facilities in the city to consolidate air traffic and dispatch it to the airport is so vital that one cannot be planned independently of the other if maximum service to the air traveler is to be achieved. "Airlines terminal" is the designation adopted by the air transport industry to define a joint or consolidated city ticketing and checking office from which air passengers

can be dispatched to the airport and board departing flights without any further formalities at the airport.

New York City was the first to have such a building for the convenience of airline passengers. Formerly, each airline had its own ticket office and limousine or bus pick-up service, involving considerable duplication of service with attendant confusion and high cost. These offices were located within a few blocks of each other, yet their individual location caused a great deal of inconvenience and delay to the passenger who, if unable to book for a given flight on a particular airline, for

International News Photograph

FIGURE 6. NEW YORK AIRLINES TERMINAL

lack of available space, could obtain passage on the flight of another airline departing at approximately the same time, but had to take a taxi to get to that airline. The grouping of all airline city ticket offices under one roof has the further advantage of providing additional accommodations for the passenger in the way of personal services, such as restaurant, newsstand, telegraph and telephone, and a newsreel theatre to pass waiting time away. It also furnishes a convenient meeting place for those desiring to see passengers off or to meet them on arrival without going to the airport.

Figure 6 shows the exterior appearance of the New York City Airlines Terminal, which measures 104½ feet by 194 feet. The entrance at street level, which leads to the city ticket office and lobby on the second floor by an escalator and steps, is flanked by a newsreel theatre and shoestore on one side, and a restaurant on the other. Figure 7 is a view of the lobby showing the ticketing and baggage-checking counters of the airlines, waiting room seats, a newsstand, and an information booth in the center. This lobby is 133 feet long and 70½ feet at its widest point. There are 34 ticket counters with room for many more. The indirect lighting and ceiling décor are appropriate for this room. Here the air passenger purchases his ticket, either in advance or just before departure, his baggage is weighed and checked, and both passenger and baggage are loaded on limousines leaving on schedule to arrive at the airport a few minutes before plane departure time. There are three office floors above the lobby for the use of the airlines' managerial staffs. This is a convenience which seldom could be combined with individual ticket offices, ordinarily consisting of a rented store or hotel space.

FIGURE 7.   LOBBY, NEW YORK AIRLINES TERMINAL

Every large community served by several airlines will eventually have an airlines terminal. It should be centrally located, preferably in the business district which is, as a rule, the largest traffic-generating area. Metropolitan centers, such as New York and Chicago, are even debating the advisability of considering satellite terminals in place of one large central terminal. There are several excellent reasons why satellite terminals serving very large regions may be more logical than one large building. The final decision must be based on the airport pattern for the region, that is, the anticipated number of airline airports and their location with respect to the densely populated areas served.

The most important factor to be considered in selecting the site for an airlines terminal is the availability of adequate, rapid, and inexpensive ground transportation to and from the airport, together with its accessibility from any point within the area it is to serve. The vehicular traffic which the terminal will discharge on city streets should not place an excessive burden on the street vehicular traffic during peak hours because of resulting street traffic saturation as well as time

loss. Furthermore, local authorities would soon request that the airline traffic be staggered with disturbing effects on schedule time and passenger volume handled. With airports widely separated within the same region, a single centrally located airlines terminal may increase the ground time to each airport to a point where much of the time saved by flying is lost when compared to rail, bus, or even private car travel. In this case, satellite terminals may prove to be a better solution.

The next factor of importance is to determine the percentage of air passengers who will avail themselves of the facilities offered by an airlines terminal. This percentage may vary from 50 to 75 per cent of the total number of air travelers, depending on the density of population of the area served, the distance to the airport, and local travel habits. The necessity for providing direct rapid transit facilities and most direct arterial highways to save time and permit lower fares should be considered. For instance, a study of air fares between cities approximately 200 miles apart in relation to ground transportation costs at the rate of $1.00 at each city shows the ground transportation costs to average 22 per cent of the air fares. Obviously, as the mileage between cities becomes less, the ratio of ground transportation costs increases proportionally, and vice versa.

For economic considerations, an airlines terminal may be planned in conjunction with an office building in order to reduce the rental cost of the terminal proper to the participating airlines.

Prefabricated Airport Equipment

The prefabrication of airport equipment and shipment as complete packages, technically known as basic airport units, was originally planned and developed to meet the requirements of the Amazon Rubber Procurement Project of the Rubber Development Corporation after the large rubber plantations of the Dutch East Indies fell to the Japanese in 1942. The units were designed for export and use in places where no manufactured item required for their construction could be available locally for their erection, and thus were complete in every detail. Also, they were of simple design so that only ordinary engineering skill would be needed to assemble them and prepare them for operation.

In 1944, Westinghouse Electric International Company announced a plan to supply the export market with "Packaged Airports" in several sizes to meet the functional requirements of three types of airports, including knocked-down buildings for temperate, tropical, and arctic climates.

Every commercial airport, to operate efficiently, must have a minimum of equipment including control tower and accessories, electrical power, meteorology station, radio communication equipment, an administration building and passenger station, field lighting, gasoline storage facilities, and refueling units. In many locations, particularly in relatively undeveloped countries, facilities for water purification and storage, sewage disposal, hangars and warehouses, repair shops, and living quarters must also be provided.

Starting with these basic essentials, Westinghouse engineers designed standard assemblies for each airport component to meet the requirements of the smallest airport, in order to use them in multiples for each successively larger airport. This conception provides standardization of units, flexibility of combination, and compact shipments. Thus economies result from standardized production and low shipping costs if delivery is to be made at very distant points. The facilities, once erected, can readily be expanded by adding units, ordered by mail, with the complete assurance that they will fit without involving expensive construction changes.

Among the advantages of packaged airports, the following merit serious consideration:

1. The time saving due to the elimination of building design, study of all airport requirements to balance all facilities, and construction follow-up.

2. Easy purchase.

3. Standardization of materials and equipment.

4. Simplified and systematized erection of equipment.

5. Low cost.

These advantages loom large to the foreign pioneering airline or the small community desiring to create landing facilities at the lowest possible cost. Although prefabricated airport equipment cannot reflect the individual aesthetic characteristics of particular regions or countries, they possess functionalism to a far greater extent than many airport buildings and their facilities offer today.

For the small airport station, Westinghouse Electric International proposes a prefabricated building, shown in Fig. 8, which includes living quarters if required. If not, the bedrooms can be eliminated and the living room furnished as a restaurant. Figure 9 illustrates an administration and passenger building suitable for a terminal station or major trunk line stop. Power is packaged in units of 50- and 75-kilowatt assemblies, each composed of two identical Diesel engine-generator units, one acting as auxiliary. Figure 10 shows a typical installation. Airport lighting assemblies consisting

of range lights, beacon tower assembly, floodlights, lighting control units, and other miscellaneous lighting materials can be supplied for any number of runways and lengths. Figure 13 shows a schematic layout of a runway flush marker light assembly for a three-runway system airfield.

Much thought has been given to fuel storage and refueling facilities. Their capacity can be varied by increasing or decreasing the number of storage tanks and refueling pits as may be required.

The availability of standardized prefabricated airport equipment, including everything to outfit an airfield, should accelerate the development of many airports and the growth of aviation, particularly in those

Courtesy Westinghouse Electric International

FIGURE 8.   PREFABRICATED TERMINAL BUILDING FOR SMALL AIRPORT

parts of the world which are lacking in local building materials and skilled labor. Availability of equipment will also permit modernizing good existing airfields having inadequate building and servicing facilities with up-to-date structures and equipment at reasonable cost. This is an important factor in most foreign countries, where the rate of currency exchange is invariably unfavorable to them.

Airport Field Rules

In the interest of safety, the authors feel that the set of simple field rules * prepared by Sanford L. Wartell, chief pilot, and Wilfred M. Post, Jr., airport manager of the Allentown-Bethlehem Airport, for governing air traffic at that airport should be recorded as an example for other airport managements to follow. These rules apply primarily to fields where there is no control tower to direct air traffic.

1. Taxi slowly and zigzag to see clearly ahead.

2. Takeoff and climb straight ahead to at least 200 ft. and at least 1,000 ft. horizontally from the edge of the airport. Make a climbing turn to the left. LOOK AROUND BEFORE ALL TURNS.

3. To stay in traffic for landings and takeoffs continue in a climbing turn to an altitude of 800 ft. At a point downwind

* See "Progressive Airport Service at the Allentown-Bethlehem Airport," by Robert C. Blatt, *Aviation Maintenance Magazine*.

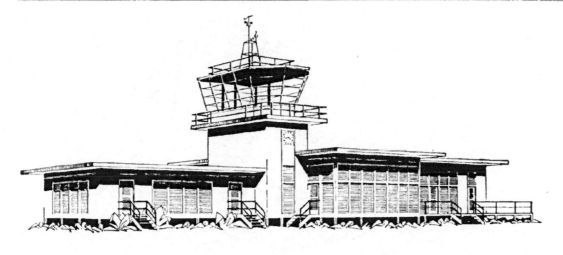

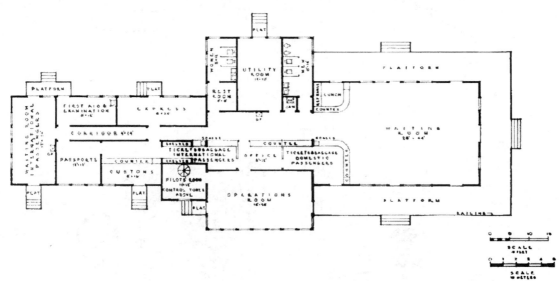

FIGURE 9. PREFABRICATED TERMINAL BUILDING FOR LARGE AIRPORT

and parallel to the wind line opposite the spot, the throttle is closed and a 180 degree circular approach is initiated.

4. To break away from traffic, start a climbing turn to the left after the 200 ft. vertical and 1,000 ft. horizontal minimums are attained. When 180 degrees from line of takeoff and at 500 ft., a 45 degree turn to the right is made. LOOK AROUND BEFORE ALL TURNS.

5. BE ALERT. WATCH ALL TRAFFIC. DO NOT TAKE CHANCES. RIGHT OR WRONG, IN THE AIR OR ON THE GROUND, ALWAYS GIVE WAY. THE OTHER PILOTS MAY NOT SEE YOU.

6. Familiarize yourself with local area boundaries and restricted zones.

7. Reenter traffic through point x-ray on the north side of the field at a 45 degree angle. Traffic altitude will be 800 feet.

8. After landing, turn sufficiently to the LEFT so that all incoming traffic may be observed.

9. DO NOT taxi on landing paths.

In order to avoid any possibility of collision or disruption of schedule by a Commercial Air Carrier on the Allentown-Bethlehem Airport, the following regulations have been adopted:

1. The airport beacon will be turned on at least five minutes before airline time. All aircraft will discontinue all un-

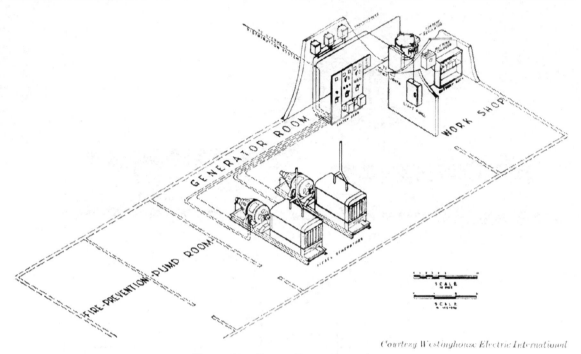

Courtesy Westinghouse Electric International

FIGURE 10.   POWER HOUSE EQUIPMENT

Courtesy Westinghouse Electric International

FIGURE 11.   MOBILE ROTATING BEACON

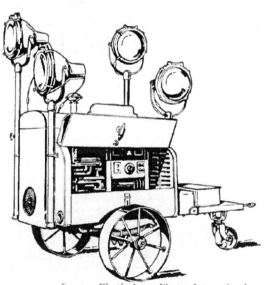

Courtesy Westinghouse Electric International

FIGURE 12.   MOBILE SEARCHLIGHTS

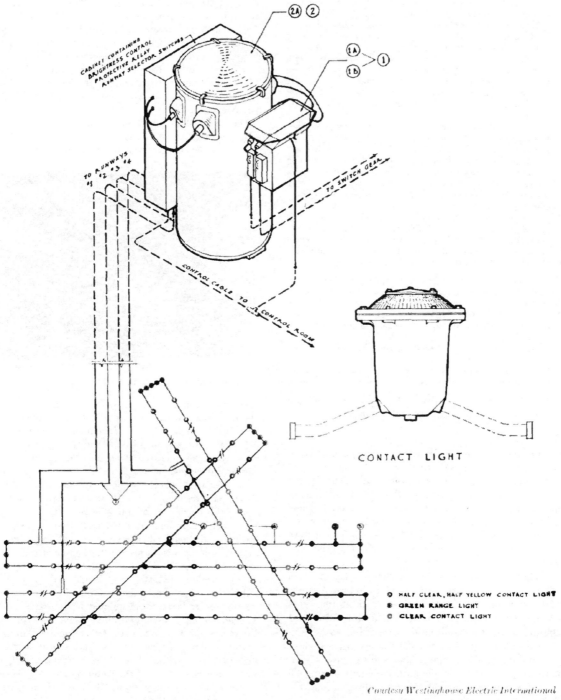

CONTACT LIGHT

○ HALF CLEAR, HALF YELLOW CONTACT LIGHT
◉ GREEN RANGE LIGHT
○ CLEAR CONTACT LIGHT

Courtesy Westinghouse Electric International

FIGURE 13. FIELD LIGHTING FOR PACKAGED AIRPORT

necessary landings and takeoffs to eliminate the possibility of forcing the airliner to go around.

2. Commercial Air Carriers are requested to have their aircraft circle the airport so that all other aircraft can more easily see the airliner and give way.

3. It is requested that Commercial Air Carriers land with traffic at all times. Traffic is set by use of a tetrahedron on the east end of the field. Should the wind velocity be less than 5 miles per hour, traffic will land west or east on the EW runway, depending on whether the wind is more easterly or more westerly.

4. The pilots of Commercial Air Carriers are requested not to turn their aircraft around on the taxi strip in such a manner as to blow dust, rocks and sundry material in the faces of potential customers standing in front of the administration building. All inconveniences suffered by spectators in this respect could be eliminated if the airliner were taxied away from parking area and turned around further up or down the taxi strip.

5. It is requested that Commercial Air Carriers have their aircraft takeoff with the traffic unless load limitations prevent. In such cases it is requested that Air Carrier personnel inform our tower operations so that he can hold traffic until Commercial Air Carriers are off the ground.

(The tower at Allentown-Bethlehem Airport is a Corliss lamp used only on aircraft engaged in the training program. Because no CAA approval is requested for our tower, we cannot govern the actions of itinerant aircraft.)

In case of an air raid, approaching thunderstorm, approaching nightfall or should the weather fall below minimums, both the airport beacon light and the boundary lights will be turned on. LAND IMMEDIATELY.

We urge your cooperation. Please be alert and observant.

Any violation of the above rules will be dealt with severely.

Strict adherence to rules of this sort will eliminate congestion and minimize accident hazards.

Seaplane Bases

The operation of commercial seaplanes and flying boats has not been so extensive as the operation of landplanes, though no less spectacular. The United States, Great Britain, France, Holland, and Germany had many overwater routes before the war. These routes were flown mainly with flying boats. The two outstanding airlines using this type of equipment were the Pan American Airways System and Imperial Airways.

Today there are two United States Flag Airlines which use flying boats, Pan American World Airways and American Airlines Overseas. To the former goes much credit for having developed landing facilities and equipment for the handling of large flying boats.

Although the present tendency is toward a greater use of land-based airplanes and a lesser use of seaplanes and flying boats, the authors believe that as the size of commercial aircraft increases for transoceanic flying, the flying boat will return to popularity because of two specific advantages. They are, first, that it requires no expensive landing and take-off facility from which to operate and, second, that engineering studies have indicated that it is more efficient in the larger sizes (over 250,000 pounds gross weight).

The two outstanding commercial seaplane bases in this country are located at Dinner Key, Miami, Florida, and at LaGuardia Field, New York City's Municipal Airport.

Once a small island, Dinner Key was joined with the mainland during World War I, when the U. S. Navy dredged Biscayne Bay and filled in around the isle to

Courtesy Pan American World Airways

FIGURE 14.   DINNER KEY SEAPLANE BASE

provide a training field. It was used in the late 1920's by the New York, Rio, and Buenos Aires Line (NYRBA) for its Miami Terminal. In 1930, Pan American Airways acquired NYRBA and moved its inter-American operation from its Thirty-sixth Street Airport to Dinner Key. It constructed a steel bulkhead, raised the whole section 3 feet to make it 8 feet above sea level, and added 13 acres to bring the total area of this marine air base to 43 acres. It also dredged a channel 1 mile long and 700 feet wide for use as a sea lane. A modern passenger terminal and administration building was located in the center of the extension. (See Fig. 14.) Four loading ramps and float stations are provided, two on each side. In the spacious lobby, there is a steel globe 10 feet in diameter, revolving on an axis tilted to match the earth itself. Accommodations include dining room, cocktail bar, rest rooms, information booth, ticket counters, and immigration and customs office. Flying equipment is serviced and overhauled in three hangars, the flying boats being hauled out of the water by means of beaching gears up the ramp shown on the left, or up the marine railway on the opposite side.

At LaGuardia Field, the seaplane base has been built adjacent to the airfield, thus permitting combined land and sea operation. Figure 18 is an airview of this base showing the Marine Traffic Building, a Boeing 314 moored at the float, the seaplane loading ramp, and

Courtesy Pan American World Airways

FIGURE 15. SEAPLANE SERVICING STAND

the bifurcating canopy connecting to the airfield, also the maintenance hangar and general offices.

The Marine Traffic Building is circular, 144 feet in diameter. In the center of the circle is a large public area, 74 feet in diameter, and around the rim are offices for the airline and for the various government agencies

Courtesy Pan American World Airways

FIGURE 16. LA GUARDIA MARINE AIR TERMINAL

which have functions to perform in connection with international air transport. On the second floor of this building are various offices. On top and facing the loading float is a small control tower.

The hangar is of a "semi-hexagon" shape. Four

of the sides consist entirely of large doors; the fifth flat side is occupied by shops and offices. Its greatest length is 352 feet. Two of the doors are 180 feet long, the other two are 148 feet, and all have a 40-foot clearance. As now constructed, the hangar is large enough to accommodate four large flying boats at the same time. The aircraft move up the ramp from the water and into the hangar on a railway complete with beaching gear and so arranged that any aircraft can move in or out of the hangar even if three others are already parked inside.

At the rear of the hangar on the ground level are complete shops for every maintenance operation. Additional shops and stockrooms are located on the second floor of this rear section. On the third floor are offices for supervisory personnel, locker and rest rooms for flight crews, and a classroom for instruction of pilots, flight engineers, mechanics, and radio operators.

One feature of the servicing facilities is the fuel storage and distribution system which can be seen at the upper right of Fig. 18. The fuel tanks provide

Courtesy Pan American World Airways

FIGURE 17. SEAPLANE FLOATING DOCK

storage space for 120,000 gallons of fuel, which can be of several grades, necessary because aircraft from foreign countries may require other grades of gasoline than that used for U. S. Flag aircraft, and the fuel requirements may even include fuel oil for Diesel engines.

Figure 17 is a close-up of a Boeing 314 flying boat moored to the loading float.

An idea of the size of the service hangar can be obtained from Fig. 15, which illustrates one of the "Clippers" being checked by means of a special servicing stand designed by engineers of the Pan American Airways system. This stand is virtually a self-contained service shop, having compressed air and electrical outlets, all the necessary tools and parts to complete all maintenance operations. Even engine changes can be made. After completion of maintenance and service, the bridge is removed and the two

Courtesy Pan American World Airways

FIGURE 18. LA GUARDIA SEAPLANE BASE

halves of the stand are wheeled away to be prepared for the next job.

In anticipation of increasing commercial flying boat operating activities and because of the interest of the U. S. Navy in this type of equipment, as well as the remarkable operating record of the large Martin "Mars" flying boat, the Glenn L. Martin Company of Baltimore, Maryland, has studied seaplane docking problems and has advanced designs for high-traffic marine air terminals applicable to medium-sized seashore communities and large port cities. The principal element from which the various plans are evolved is a U-shaped dock pontoon with a platform on each side. This pontoon is connected to the fixed dock by means of a swiveled ramp as shown. Cleats and other equipment are conveniently located on the surface of the dock. It is also equipped with compressed air lines, electrical connections, refueling lines, and water lines

connected to the pier and shore by means of rubber hoses and flexible connections. Docking is accomplished by cables running to fixed electrically operated winches anchored on the pier.

The experimental installation from which this design was conceived is illustrated in Fig. 20, which shows a floating dock built from three large flat floats, two of them being separated to provide a berth for the seaplane.

Another suggested possibility is to use the U pontoon assembly with narrow sides as a tug to permit a large degree of maneuverability for the towing of seaplanes through congested harbor waters to the dock of a marine air terminal of the type shown in Fig. 21. After having docked the flying boat, the tug could be detached to repeat the operation with another flying boat.

The Marine Air Terminal illustrated in Fig. 21 includes two floating docks connected to a double deck

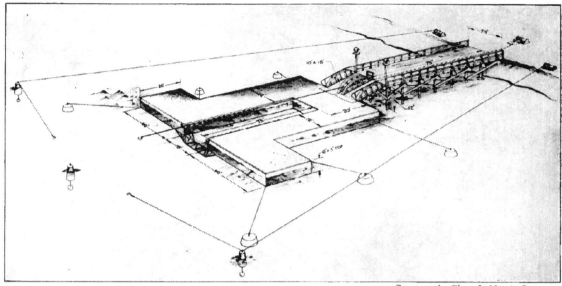

Courtesy the Glenn L. Martin Company

FIGURE 19.   SEAPLANE PONTOON DOCK

Courtesy the Glenn L. Martin Company

FIGURE 20.   U. S. NAVY "MARS" FLOATING DOCK

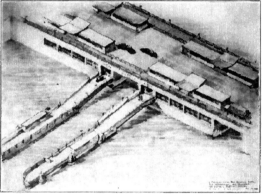

Courtesy the Glenn L. Martin Company

FIGURE 21.   MARINE AIR TERMINAL

pier housing aircraft servicing and maintenance facilities as well as accommodations for the handling of mail and cargo.

Seaplane Lanes

Lanes for the landing and taking off of seaplanes must be provided. Their pattern corresponds to that of land airports. They are outlined on the surface of the water by anchored buoys for daytime use, generally spaced 500 feet apart. At night these buoys are distinctively lighted, thus combining two markers in one. Figure 22 illustrates a typical sea lane layout and electrical circuits. Figure 23 shows buoy-mounted marker light details as developed by the U. S. Navy.

In shallow water, marker lights can be mounted on piles to save cost of installation and maintenance.

One of the problems attendant upon the safe operation of seaplanes and flying boats in regularly scheduled commerce is the establishment of restricted sea and harbor areas for their protection as well as the protection of any other watercraft maneuvering in navigable waters. This problem is the natural result of rapid development in overseas air commerce and the fact that flying boats cannot readily comply with the International Rules of the Road as applying to watercraft be-

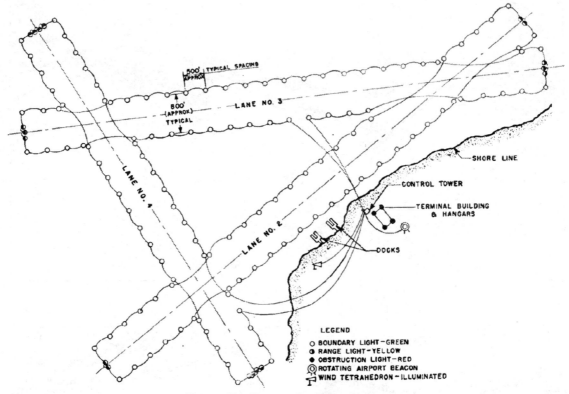

FIGURE 22. TYPICAL SEA LANE LAYOUT

cause of their operating characteristics. Because of the design characteristics of engines used in large seaplanes, they cannot be run at the idling speeds often required while waiting for surface watercraft to clear the operating areas, although this condition can be greatly improved by the use of integrally built cooling fans.

Approximately 15 minutes' time is generally required to patrol and clear the area prior to the time a large seaplane taxies to its position for take-off. As with landplanes, a speed of approximately 90 miles or more per hour must be obtained before large seaplanes leave the water. Furthermore, during the take-off run, which can be as much as 1½ to 2 miles, and while still on the water, a large seaplane cannot be maneuvered to avoid any object on the water. After it leaves the water, as with any land aircraft when it becomes airborne, its climb is gradual and it must continue in a straight line to a safe height before it can be maneuvered to avoid obstacles. In this connection, it should also be realized that because of the noise from the engines and propellers the pilots cannot hear surface

craft warning signals, and they cannot gauge the movements or location of surface craft at a distance of approximately 4 miles, especially in times of limited visibility.

In addition to take-off requirements, landing procedure for large seaplanes requires that the approach for a landing be started while several miles away. It is therefore considered unsafe to require such craft to change the plan of landing procedure in order to avoid surface craft moving in a landing area not properly restricted. While completing orientation procedures, under instrument flying conditions, it would be difficult if not dangerous for a large seaplane to alter the approach and landing procedure as it cannot be maneuvered with safety to avoid moving objects during the final approach for a landing. In connection with maneuvering on water, after landing and prior to take-off, it should be realized that a seaplane cannot go astern unless equipped with reversible pitch propellers.

Taking cognisance of these possible conditions, the CAA in its *Technical Development Note 32*, dated January, 1944, entitled, "The Establishment of a Re-

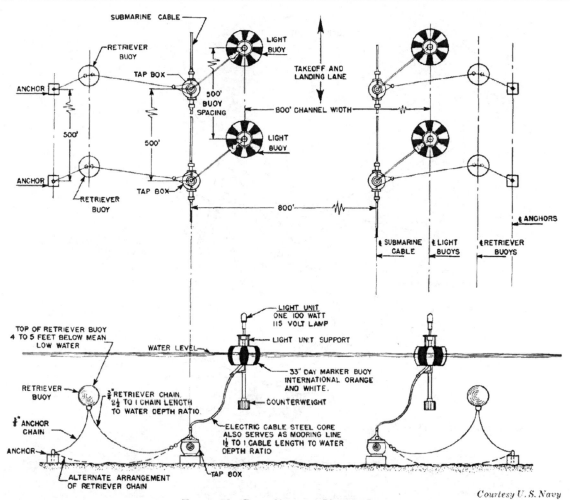

Courtesy U. S. Navy

FIGURE 23. BUOY-MOUNTED MARKER LIGHT

stricted Area for Seaplane Operation," outlined recommendations for the provisions of suitable seaplane operating areas, as follows:

In considering the problem of the adequate size of water area required for seaplane operating bases, it is convenient to divide the discussion as follows:

1. Major seaplane terminals.
(*a*) For large seaplanes in current use or under construction.
(*b*) For larger seaplanes as anticipated for future operations.
2. Intermediate bases for so-called medium-sized aircraft and emergency landing bases.
3. Small bases suitable for private-owner and smaller type aircraft.

1(*a*) A major seaplane terminal (to adequately accommodate seaplanes of 40,000 to 100,000 lbs. gross weight, which are the major sizes now in use) should have a sheltered water area large enough to permit the layout of landing courses or operating lanes at least 2½ miles in length. The actual takeoff run on the water of the current major seaplanes may range from 3,000 to 7,000 feet, depending upon such variable conditions as load, temperature, wind, water, or sea conditions, etc. The additional length of water area provided constitutes a necessary factor of safety in that it enables the seaplane to gain sufficient altitude and speed while still over a usable landing area without the necessity of dangerous maneuvering at low altitudes at relatively slow speed. The main operating lane should be at least 600 feet wide with a water depth of 10 feet at mean low tide. Turning basins of the same depth and at least 2,000 feet in diameter should be provided at each end of the operating lane. This channel should be in alignment with the general direction of the prevailing wind in the given locality and should be supplemented by at least one auxiliary lane 2½ miles in length with the same depth and diameter of turning basins.

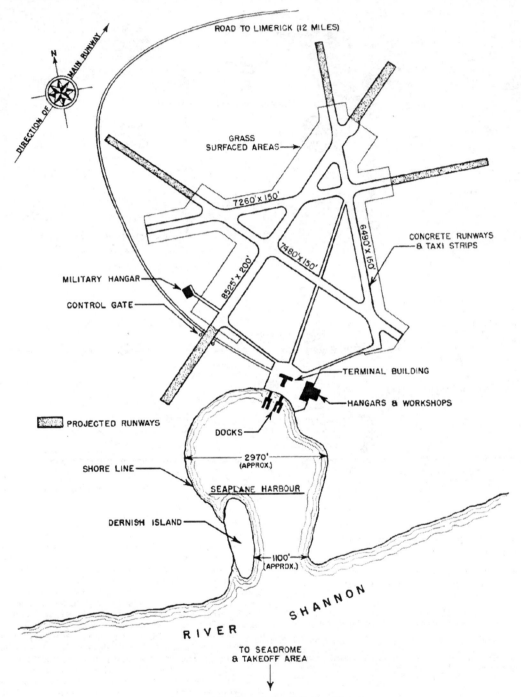

FIGURE 24. SHANNON AIRPORT, EIRE

The auxiliary landing lane should be so aligned that the two lanes together, or supplemented by still other operating lanes, permit landings to be made directly into the wind at least 90 per cent of the time

1(b) In considering future anticipated developments in large flying boats, it would be advisable to provide for unobstructed sheltered water areas of such extent as to permit the layout of operating channels approximately 5 miles in length The channel depth should be increased to an estimated minimum of 15 feet with lane widths and turning basins enlarged to a lesser proportion In fact, the above operating channel width may be expected to remain somewhat constant, with the lane (or channel) depth being the variable factor as flying boat sizes increase. The ultimate required diameter of turning basins should not exceed 3,000 feet

Seadromes with clear approaches, and having dimensions as described above, should be entirely adequate for the different sizes of flying boats as outlined in paragraphs 1(a) and 1(b)

2 The intermediate seaplane base may be expected to accommodate seaplanes or amphibians of gross weights from approximately 10,000 to 40,000 lbs For such aircraft the water area should provide the possibility of laying out landing lanes approximately 350 feet wide, not less than 1½ miles in length, with clear approaches, and having a minimum depth of 6 feet One main landing course should be provided in the direction of the prevailing wind, and sufficient auxiliary landing courses should be provided so that landings can be made into the wind at least 80 per cent of the time

3 Small seaplane bases suitable for the operation of light privately-owned planes can be established on numerous lakes and rivers scattered rather generally throughout the country Since private owners do not operate their planes on schedules which require flights under unfavorable wind, weather, and water conditions, it is difficult to establish minimum standards for light seaplane operations In many cases, seaplanes can be operated from small water areas with reasonable safety if flights are not attempted under conditions when the wind is not aligned with the long dimension of the landing area, as, for example, where a narrow river is being used Consideration should be given to the probable number and types of seaplanes which may be expected to use the seaplane base when it is established and the water areas then developed which will best be adequate for such use

A landing area having a minimum of 3,500 feet effective length in all directions, with clear approaches, and a depth of at least 4½ feet, is large enough for most light seaplanes Similarly, a river having a minimum width of 500 feet and a straight unobstructed course of 3,500 to 4,000 feet may be used under favorable wind conditions

NOTE Any of the aforementioned classes of seaplane bases may be located at elevations above sea level on lakes or rivers It is, therefore, essential that the effect of both altitude above sea level and expected minimum temperatures be taken into consideration in determining the dimensions of the landing area It should be understood that these standards are tentative and subject to change as seaplane operating experience increases

These recommendations for water airport standards are extremely liberal as it is not expected that increases in flying boat size will require greater clearance areas than found necessary now with the largest type in operation For instance, operating experience indicates that a channel length of 2 to 2½ miles should be ample The width of such a channel should be 800 feet and its depth at mean low water level not less than 12 feet. A turning basin diameter of 1,500 feet should be ample, considering that all very large flying boats will be equipped with quickly reversible pitch propellers.

Furthermore, since these recommendations were published, major seaplane terminals 1(a) might well be reclassified according to size as follows

1(a) Seaplanes of 40,000 to 100,000 pounds gross weight

(b) Seaplanes of 100,000 to 250,000 pounds gross weight

(c) Seaplanes of 250,000 or more pounds gross weight

Large coastal cities or cities adjacent to large bodies of water can gain the distinct advantage of combining transport aircraft operation from either land or water by locating a land airport adjacent to a seaplane base if the desirable location characteristics discussed in Part 5 are not sacrificed or compromised seriously.

The large flying boat can fill the need for long-range, high-capacity international traffic at low cost and feed such traffic to land aircraft for continental distribution Vice versa, the landplane can collect traffic from domestic points, widely separated, and feed it to the flying boat for long-distance oversea destinations An excellent example of such an arrangement is the Shannon Airport near Foynes, Eire (Fig 24) Idlewild, New York City's new superairport located on Jamaica Bay, is ideally situated to provide similar facilities

Bibliography

Packaged Airports, Westinghouse Electric International Company, New York, N Y

"The Establishment of a Restricted Area for Seaplane Operation," by F H Greene, *Technical Development Note 32*, January, 1941, Civil Aeronautics Administration, U S Department of Commerce, Washington, D C

Airport Seadrome Lighting, September, 1945, Bureau of Aeronautics, U S Navy Department, Washington, D C

GLOSSARY

air harbor A landing facility for seaplanes and amphibious aircraft on a quiet body of water adjacent to a community

aircraft Any weight-carrying device designed to be supported by the air either by buoyancy, as an airship, or by dynamic action, as an airplane, autogiro, or helicopter

airfield The area of an airport designated for the landing and take off of aircraft as distinguished from the area occupied by buildings

airpark A community landing facility for personal aircraft providing a convenient landing area built within the confines of residential areas or business districts

airplane A mechanically driven fixed wing aircraft, heavier than air, which is supported by the dynamic reaction of the air against its wings.

airport A tract of land or water which is adapted for the landing and take off of aircraft and provides facilities for their shelter, supply, and repair, a place used regularly for receiving or discharging passengers or cargo by air

airship An aerostat provided with a propelling system and with means of controlling the direction of motion

airway An air route along which aids to air navigation, such as radio beams, radio ranges, beacon lights, and intermediate airfields, are maintained

amphibian. An airplane designed to take off and land either on water or on land

approach light One of several lights to indicate a favorable direction of approach for aircraft landing on a runway

approach pattern A prescribed course over which an airplane maneuvers preparatory to landing at an airfield

approach zone The area surrounding an airfield within which landing aircraft must fly a prescribed course

apron The hard surface adjacent to buildings or hangars used for loading, unloading, and servicing airplanes

autogiro A type of rotor plane whose support in the air is chiefly derived from airfoils rotated about an approximately vertical axis by aerodynamic forces, and in which the lift on opposite sides of the plane of symmetry is equalized by the vertical oscillation of the blades.

beam component. A force or component in the beam direction, that is, parallel to the transverse axis and the plane of symmetry of an airplane

boundary light Any one of the lights designed to indicate the limits of the landing area of an airport or landing field

capacity, airfield The number of movements per hour which can be safely accomplished

ceiling The height of the lower level of a bank of clouds above the ground

contact light A light used to outline runways on an airfield

fixed-base operation Non scheduled flying and ground servicing activities performed for profit, and radiating from one airport

flight path. The path of the center of gravity of a flying aircraft with reference to the earth

flightstop An airstrip located adjacent to highways with service station accommodations, used as an intermediate stop for refueling or located where community landing facilities would not be available

flightstrip A one directional landing area, generally used for emergency landings

floodlight, landing area. A device designed to illuminate the surface of a landing area

flying boat. A form of seaplane whose main body or hull provides flotation

gate position The space allotted to one airplane for parking at a terminal building

glide path ratio The ratio of any horizontal flight distance to the altitude loss for such distance ·

helicopter A type of rotor plane whose support in the air is normally derived from airfoils mechanically rotated about an approximately vertical axis

instrument runway The runway of an airport designated for and equipped with devices permitting the landing of an airplane under conditions of minimum visibility

landing field Any area of land designed for the take off and landing of aircraft It may or may not be part of an airport

landing strip A narrow and comparatively long area forming part of a landplane airport or of an intermediate or auxiliary field, which is suitable for the landing and take off of airplanes under ordinary weather conditions

marker, boundary A painted cone, solid circle, or dish denoting the boundary of the available area for landing on an airfield

movement The landing or take-off of one airplane at an airport

obstruction light A red light used to indicate the position and height of an object hazardous to flying aircraft

personal aircraft Aircraft privately owned for pleasure or business, but not used for hire

power loading The gross weight of an airplane divided by the rated horsepower of the engine (or engines) computed for air of standard density

pressurization The maintenance of atmospheric pressure in the cabin of an airplane which approximates lower altitudes while flying at higher altitudes

ramp A sloping way used sometimes for the beaching of sea planes

range light One or more lights placed at the ends of a runway to indicate the end and relative length of the runway

runway An artificial landing strip designed for the landing and take off of airplanes

sea lane A marked channel in the water indicating a strip available for the landing or take-off of seaplanes

seaplane An airplane designed to take off and land on water

stalling speed The speed of an airplane in steady flight at its maximum coefficient of lift

taxiway A prepared strip to enable an aircraft to taxi to and from the end of a runway

tetrahedron A polyhedron of four faces with weathercock characteristics located on a landing field to indicate the direction of the wind

tire footprint The area of the tire of an aircraft wheel in contact with the landing surface when the aircraft is at rest

visibility The greatest distance at which conspicuous objects can be seen and identified

wind rose A diagram of the points of the compass with lines indicating the relative velocity and direction of winds

wing loading The gross weight of an airplane divided by the wing area

zoning ratio Obstacle clearance requirements expressed as the ratio of horizontal distance from the end of the runway to the obstacle height above the elevation of the runway

Reference

"Nomenclature for Aeronautics," *Report* 474, National Advisory Committee for Aeronautics, U S Government Printing Office, 1937

INDEX

247